basic
Tagalog

Learn to Speak Modern Filipino/Tagalog
The National Language of the Philippines

"Books to Span the East and West"

Tuttle Publishing was founded in 1832 in the small New England town of Rutland, Vermont [USA]. Our core values remain as strong today as they were then—to publish best-in-class books which bring people together one page at a time. In 1948, we established a publishing office in Japan—and Tuttle is now a leader in publishing English-language books about the arts, languages and cultures of Asia. The world has become a much smaller place today and Asia's economic and cultural influence has grown. Yet the need for meaningful dialogue and information about this diverse region has never been greater. Over the past seven decades, Tuttle has published thousands of books on subjects ranging from martial arts and paper crafts to language learning and literature—and our talented authors, illustrators, designers and photographers have won many prestigious awards. We welcome you to explore the wealth of information available on Asia at **www.tuttlepublishing.com**.

Publisher's note:
While the national language of the Philippines has come to be known as Filipino within the Philippines, we refer to it in this book as TAGALOG, as this remains the basis for the language and the name by which it is known internationally.

basic
Tagalog

Learn to Speak Modern Filipino/Tagalog
The National Language of the Philippines

REVISED THIRD EDITION

By Paraluman S. Apillera & Yolanda Canseco Hernandez

Revised with a new Foreword by **Karen Llagas**

TUTTLE Publishing

Tokyo | Rutland, Vermont | Singapore

In memory of my father, Lope K. Santos

Acknowledgments

We are grateful to the following persons who have helped in the publication of this revised edition of **Basic Tagalog**: Dr. Monita Manalo, University of Wisconsin-Madison for reviewing the updated manuscript; Dr. Isagani R. Cruz and Dr. Luis P. Gatmaitan for granting us permission to include their materials in this book.

Published by Tuttle Publishing, an imprint of Periplus Editions (HK) Ltd.

www.tuttlepublishing.com

Copyright © 2007, 2020 by Jazmin A. Jocson
All rights reserved.

No part of this book may be reproduced or utilized in any form or by any means, electronic or mechanical, including photocopying, recording, or by any information storage or retrieval system, without permission in writing from the publisher.

First Tuttle edition, 1969
First Tuttle paperback edition, 1993
Second edition, 2007
Revised third edition, 2020

LCC Card No. 2007933898
ISBN 978-0-8048-5195-4

Distributed by:

North America, Latin America & Europe
Tuttle Publishing
364 Innovation Drive
North Clarendon, VT 05759-9436 U.S.A.
Tel: 1 (802) 773 8930; Fax: 1 (802) 773 6993
info@tuttlepublishing.com
www.tuttlepublishing.com

Japan
Tuttle Publishing
Yaekari Building, 3F
5-4-12 Osaki, Shinagawa-ku
Tokyo 141-0032, Japan
Tel: (81) 3 5437-0171; Fax: (81) 3 5437-0755
sales@tuttle.co.jp
www.tuttle.co.jp

Asia Pacific
Berkeley Books Ptc Ltd
3 Kallang Sector #04-01
Singapore 349278
Tel: (65) 6741 2178
Fax: (65) 6741 2179
inquiries@periplus.com.sg
www.tuttlepublishing.com

26 25 24 23 22   7 6 5 4 3 2   2205VP

Printed in Malaysia

TUTTLE PUBLISHING® is a registered trademark of Tuttle Publishing, a division of Periplus Editions (HK) Ltd.

Table of Contents

To Download or Stream Audio Recordings:

1. You must have an internet connection.
2. Type the URL below into your web browser.
   https://www.tuttlepublishing.com/basic-tagalog-revised-3

For support email us at info@tuttlepublishing.com.

Foreword to the Revised and Expanded Edition

This revised and expanded edition still has all the grammar lessons and the tried-and-tested teaching methodology developed by the author, **Paraluman S. Aspillera**, for the original version. It also retains the vocabulary and expressions added in the previous revision by Yolanda Canesco Hernandez. The main strengths of Aspillera's method are its simplicity and clarity in explaining grammar rules. This has been extremely effective for tens of thousands of foreigners and non-Tagalogs who have used this book to learn Tagalog, including many who have successfully learned to speak and write Tagalog through self-study. As with the previous revised edition, the audio files of each chapter's vocabulary can be accessed online on the Tuttle website (www.tuttlepublishing.com). Audio for this new edition now also includes the dialogues for each chapter, meant to be read aloud, ideally with a study partner or teacher.

What's new in this revised and expanded edition are the dialogues that students will find at the beginning of each lesson, that utilize the vocabulary and grammar points presented in each lesson. Much care and attention has been given to these situational dialogues, so that students can learn Tagalog grammar in a contemporary, accessible and conversational context.

Another significant revision to this edition are the sample sentences contained in each lesson and their corresponding exercises. As much as possible, they have been revised to reflect how contemporary native Tagalog speakers will use the language in their daily lives. Students can find more in-depth discussion of this on Lesson 5, which is about Sentence Formation.

The appendices, as with previous editions, offer rich supplementary materials to those who want to go deeper into their language learning by doing more grammar exercises, reading more sample dialogues and even honing their reading skills with more literary and historical texts. More context and explanation on the skill level required for these conversations and the reading materials in the appendices are provided in this edition.

Finally, the section in the introduction about understanding the Filipino character has been updated to reflect a more modern and empowering approach with which Tagalog learners can relate to Filipinos. I have no doubt that Tagalog students have been drawn into the complexities, humor and contradictions found in the Philippines and her people, whether they are in the homeland or in the diaspora. A more nuanced approach to the Filipino character, as seen from the point of view of Filipinos, hopefully results in celebrating these differences and complexities, and thus lead into more enriched daily interactions and communications between native Tagalog speakers and learners—whether in business, educational, social or civic endeavors.

Karen Llagas

Tagalog—A Living Language

What is a living language? It is defined as a language that is "currently in use or valid." Thus, it is alive, it is dynamic, it is vibrant.

Language is a system through which people express their thoughts, feelings and sentiments, either orally or in writing. It mirrors the kind of society they live in, their customs and traditions, and their aspirations as a nation.

Tagalog is a living language. It is the basis of the national language of the Philippines as mandated by the 1987 Constitution of the Republic of the Philippines under Article XIV, Section 6, on "Language." The provision states: "The national language of the Philippines is Filipino. As it evolves, it shall be further developed and enriched on the basis of existing Philippine and other languages. Subject to provisions of law and as the Congress may deem appropriate, the Government shall take steps to initiate and sustain the use of Filipino as a medium of official communication and as a language of instruction in the education system."

While still considered a young but nonetheless maturing national language, Filipino is constantly being developed through its usage in various fields of endeavor. As the nation develops and progresses, Filipino also grows linguistically and lexically with the assimilation of new words, concepts and ideas into the language brought about by technological advances, changes in lifestyles, globalization trends and contacts with foreign cultures, political and religious upheavals, and media developments, among others.

Historical Influences and Contacts

Tagalog as a language has very ancient roots going back thousands of years, and even had its own writing system in ancient times, borrowed from the Sanskritic writing systems of the region. According to Filipino anthropologist F. Landa Jocano, "Writing as a system of communication was fairly well-developed in many parts of the archipelago when the Spaniards came during the early part of the 16th century."

Documents unearthed by Spanish chroniclers Pedro Chirino and Francisco Colin show different types of alphabets or syllabary writing. The writing had vowel and consonant syllable signs which, according to anthropologist Robert Fox, conform "to a common phonemic pattern of Philippine (contemporary languages)."

Comparisons with other Asian language groups indicate that the Tagalog language along with other Philippine languages belong to the Malayan branch of the great Malayo-Polynesian or Austronesian linguistic family, which includes hundreds of languages now spread across almost half the globe from Taiwan through the Philippine Islands to Hawaii, Fiji and New Zealand in the Pacific, across the islands of Indonesia and the Malay peninsula to Madagascar.

Filipino linguist Juan Francisco cited many Indian influences on Philippine language and literature. He found about 336 terms derived from Sanskrit, out of which

a	ba	ka	da	ga	ha	la	ma	na	nga	pa	sa	ta	wa	ya
e, i	be/bi	ke/ki	de/di	ge/gi	he/hi	le/li	me/mi	ne/ni	nge/ngi	pe/pi	se/si	te/ti	we/wi	y/yi
o, u	bo/bu	ko/ku	do/du	go/gu	ho/hu	lo/lu	mo/mu	no/nu	ngo/ngu	po/pu	so/su	to/tu	wo/wu	yo/yu

Baybayin, the Sanskritic alphabet that was in use in the Philippines in earlier times.

150 were identified and used in the Philippine languages, specifically in the names of plants and animals. Many of these appear to have been borrowed from Malay.

Loan words from China have also crept into the Philippine vocabulary, particularly standard Tagalog. Linguist Arsenio E. Manuel, in his study *Chinese Elements in the Tagalog Language* (1948), compiled a "list of 381 Tagalog words of Chinese origins, excluding variants, derivatives and compounds." These words pertain to food, abstract ideas or terms, metal smithing, kinship, and words concerning agriculture, business, tools, industries and games.

The few Arabic words in Tagalog came in with the arrival of Islam from the southern Philippine islands where the religion has had a foothold since 1380. However, the defeat of a sultan in Manila in 1571 meant the subsequent extinction of the faith in Tagalog-speaking areas and many Arabic words fell into disuse.

The Spanish has contributed a great deal to the Philippine languages, and many Spanish loan words have now been thoroughly naturalized. These include religious, governmental, social, legal and abstract terms, including many terms for foreign articles and luxuries. Contacts with traders during the Spanish period also led to a few Mexican words, mainly Nahuatl or Aztec, creeping into the Tagalog lexicon. Other parts of the country, specifically in the Zamboanga provinces in the Mindanao region, the dominant language of the Zamboangueño people has evolved from the marriage of Spanish and Cebuano into what is now known as Chavacano or Philippine Creole Spanish.

In his 1,027-page *Diksyunaryo Tesauro Pilipino Ingles* posthumously published in 1973, Dr. Jose Villa Panganiban—who was a professor, linguist, and former director of the Institute of National Language in Manila—included 27,069 main word entries, containing almost 217,500 lexical items. He listed 12,000 loan words derived from Spanish, English, Chinese and Indo-European languages. He also included synonyms, antonyms, and homonyms with other languages along with identities and cognacies between Tagalog and 12 other Philippine languages.

While the colonization of the Philippines by the Spaniards for more than 300 years had a profound impact on the lifestyles of the Filipinos, other colonizers especially the Americans left their marks on Philippine culture and society by introducing their own brand of education and government. English words which had no exact equivalent have been adapted into the Philippine languages and given a regional treatment for suitability in the language. Although most are still quoted, some are used and spelled as they are especially with the recent modification of the Filipino alphabet. The Japanese also occupied the islands in the 1940s but seemed to have furnished no words to the Tagalog lexicon. After all these occupations, however, the construction of Tagalog does not seem to have been influenced by any of the colonizers' languages. It has retained its essentially Malayo-Polynesian structure.

A National Language Is Born

The adoption of a national language for Filipinos came during the Commonwealth years (1935 to 1946) under the American regime. It was not easy for proponents of a national language to push Tagalog as the basis for a language that was to be used from Luzon to the Visayas and all the way down to Mindanao. The three main island groupings in the Philippines each has its own distinct identity as the archipelagic nature of the country gave rise to a wide variety of cultures and languages separated by seas and strengthened by history.

Populated then by an estimated 16 million inhabitants, the Philippines had a diverse collection of 172 languages of which three are already extinct. Eight major languages (Tagalog, Cebuano, Ilocano, Hiligaynon, Bicolano, Waray, Kapampangan and Pangasinan) all belong to the Malayo-Polynesian linguistic family but no two are mutually comprehensible. In the 1980s, these eight languages and their dialects were spoken by 90% of the population (see Language Map of the Philippines on page 11). Even though they are separate languages, they are closely related (like French, Italian and Spanish), and some languages are much closer than others—for example, Ilocano and Pangasinan speakers might find little difficulty in learning each other's languages in contrast to learning any of the Visayan languages. The same can be said for Visayan speakers of Cebuano, Hiligaynon and Waray with regards to learning each other's languages and the opposite for learning the Northern Luzon languages.

It is thus understandable that fierce opposition from certain non-Tagalog legislators and rabid advocates of the English language delayed somewhat the entire process of adopting a national language. In the end, however, Tagalog prevailed when President Manuel L. Quezon proclaimed the creation of a national language based on Tagalog on December 31, 1937. The body which was responsible for the adoption of the national language was the National Language Institute created by President Quezon. It was composed of non-Tagalogs and Tagalog representatives from different regions in the country. The Chairman was Jaime C. de Veyra from Samar, Leyte, with the following as members: Santiago A. Fonacier (Ilocano); Filomeno Sotto (Cebu, Visayas); Casimiro T. Perfecto (Bicol); Felix Sales Rodriguez (Panay, Visayas); Madji Butin (Mindanao) and Dr. Cecilio Lopez (Tagalog).

Tagalog was chosen as the basis for the Philippines' national language for the following reasons:

1. **Tagalog is the most widely spoken** and the most widely understood language in all regions of the Philippines. By 1989, 25% of the Philippine

KEY

- Bikol
- Cebuano
- Hiligaynon
- Ilocano (Iloko)
- Kapampangan
- Pangasinan
- Tagalog
- Waray

Language Map of the Philippines showing the distribution of the eight major languages

population spoke Tagalog as their mother tongue. They are scattered across the Tagalog regions, or **Katagalugan**, stretching from the central to the southern parts of Luzon island and covering 10 major provinces—Nueva Ecija, Aurora, Bataan, Batangas, Bulacan, Cavite, Laguna, Metro Manila (or the National Capital Region), Quezon and Rizal—as well as parts of the islands of Marinduque and Mindoro. Further away from these regions, there has been less exposure to Tagalog and one finds a lower competency level in the language.

Compared to Tagalog, the second most widely-spoken Philippine language—Cebuano—was spoken by 24% of the population in 1989 but is mostly understood only by its own speakers. Other major languages including Ilocano, Hiligaynon, Bicol and Waray are spoken by 5% to 9% of the total population. Many other languages or dialects are spoken by the remaining 22% of the population. Recent 2015 census figures reveal that around 29% of the total population speak Tagalog as their first language and 65% speak or understand the language with varying degrees of proficiency.

2. **It is not divided into dialects** unlike the Visayan languages. There are three major Visayan languages: Cebuano, Hiligaynon and Waray. Cebuano is spoken in many parts of the Visayan and Mindanao regions but residents from various provinces have their own distinct Cebuano sub-languages or dialects. There may be variations in the Tagalog language but these are still comprehensible to all native Tagalog speakers.

3. **Tagalog has the richest literature**. More books are written and published in Tagalog than in any other native language.

4. **Tagalog has always been the language of Manila**, the country's capital city, even long before the Spanish came. As the capital city, Manila houses all the major government offices from Malacanang Palace down to the administration's smallest bureaus. At present, economic and political decisions are decided in Manila and its surrounding provinces and cities, which also speak Tagalog. Historically, though, Cebu is the first and oldest city in the Philippines. It is also an alternate gateway to the nation from abroad.

5. **Tagalog was the language of the Revolution and the Katipunan**, two major events in Philippine history.

On June 18, 1938, the Philippine National Assembly created the Institute of National Language (this institute was different from the National Language Institute which was eventually dissolved). Two years after the institute was established, two monumental language books in Tagalog were presented to President Quezon: the *Tagalog-English Dictionary* authored by Dr. Cecilio Lopez and the *Balarila ng Wikang Pambansa*, a grammar book written by Lope K. Santos, then acknowledged as the Dean of Tagalog Writers and Father of the National Language. The publication of these books paved the way for the introduction of the national language beginning with the school year 1940–41 during the fourth year of all high schools and in the second year of both public and private normal schools in the whole country.

"Pilipino" Emerges

On July 4, 1946 under Commonwealth Act No. 570, independence was granted to the Philippines by the United States of America. It provided for the use of the national language as one of the official languages of the Philippines (the others being Spanish and English) in government offices. Soon, adherents of the Tagalog-based national language increased rapidly all over the islands.

In 1954, the national language was given a further boost by President Ramon Magsaysay when he proclaimed the celebration of a **Linggo ng Wika** (National Language Week) and the national observance annually of the birthday of Francisco Balagtas, a great Tagalog poet.

In 1961, the Office of the Secretary of Education introduced the term "Pilipino" when referring to the national language. It gained wide acceptance in schools and among the general public, thus the Tagalog-based national language was soon called Pilipino. By 1974, the Pilipino movement stirred the public to "think Pilipino." School teachers were encouraged to attend seminars in Pilipino, the Department of Education started issuing memos, circulars and bulletins enjoining school organs to include sections in Pilipino in their publications, translate English and other foreign materials into Pilipino, use Pilipino on school diplomas and certificates, and sing the national anthem only in Pilipino. In schools, Pilipino was introduced at the tertiary level and in the teaching of civics and culture at lower levels. In 1990, then Philippine President Corazon Aquino ordered government offices to use Pilipino as a medium of communication. The government was encouraged to use Pilipino in naming their departments and buildings, and to print Pilipino text on their letterheads, seals and signages. Government employees were also enjoined to attend seminars on Pilipino to broaden their knowledge and skill in the use of the national language.

The Medium of Instruction and Communication

The Department of Education and the schools have continuously promoted Pilipino, now called Filipino, as a medium of instruction and communication. Other supportive forces have joined them in the propagation and enrichment of the language. Radio and television, for instance, use Filipino in a majority of their programs to reach out to the masses. Of late, more dubbing and subtitling of foreign-produced programs has been done in Filipino and has contributed much to the promotion of the language.

In the print media, the number of publishers who produce and circulate books, magazines, comics, broadsheets and tabloids in Filipino is increasing. Songs in Filipino are also "in" and played over the airwaves, sung in concerts and in theatrical performances. Composers in Filipino are now enjoying recognition and patronage from a growing audience.

Masses and services in Catholic and Christian churches are now said in Filipino. There are Filipino versions of the bible and other religious books. And when it comes to campaigning during elections, Filipino has become the language to attract voters and certainly the language that an ordinary citizen on the street is most comfortable with. At present, Filipino as a subject is taught all over the country from pre-school (3 years) up to grade school (6 years) and high school (4 years). Considering that the basic literacy rate in 2003 is high at nearly 90% (wherein 9 out of 10 Filipinos are able to read and write), it is not a surprise that Filipino is understood and spoken by most Filipinos now.

Enriching the National Language

More positive moves are being undertaken to strengthen and enrich Filipino as a national language. National language advocates and institutions like the Commission on the Filipino Language, Sentro ng Wikang Filipino of the University of the Philippines, along with many teachers, administrators, researchers, writers, authors and linguists are working hard to improve the quality of the Filipino language. They host and sponsor seminars, workshops, forums and conferences to discuss ways of translating works, produce adequate and well-researched Filipino books for schools, enrich and infuse Filipino with more words and terms from other major Philippine languages like Cebuano, Ilocano, Hiligaynon, Waray, Kapampangan and others, that are fast becoming part of the Filipino vocabulary. With their concerted efforts, these formidable groups will certainly help enliven the use of Filipino in the daily lives of the people and keep alive a national language that fosters genuine nationalism and unity among Filipinos.

Understanding the Filipino from Within: Some Points from *Sikolohiyang Pilipino* (Filipino psychology)

Learning Tagalog becomes more enjoyable and meaningful if one has an appreciation of the culture of the Philippines as well as the character of its people. As of 2020, the Philippines is populated by more than 109 million people living on 7,101 islands, which are abundantly blessed by nature. Pristine beaches, verdant mountains and rainforests, a treasure-trove of exotic fauna and flora attract tourists and locals alike. Colorful customs and traditions in the country are brought to the forefront when people share their lively and spectacular festivals and celebrations that showcase their innate creativity, spirituality, culinary skills and their well-renowned warmth.

All over the world, Filipinos are known to be very friendly, loving and caring people. They go out of their way to help others and in times of crisis, they are often portrayed in the news to keep their sense of humor and survive despite the economic and political challenges that face them. That said, contemporary scholars of Philippine Studies and Filipino Psychology rightfully caution against codifying and interpreting Filipino values and character uncritically according to Western ideas and perceptions. Foreign visitors may complain of Filipinos' verbal indirectness (i.e. hesitation to disagree or to say no), relaxed attitude towards time and even Filipino notions such as **bahala na, hiya** and **utang na loob** (often oversimplified by foreign cultural experts as "fatalism," "shame" and "debt of gratitude reciprocity").

However, Filipino historians and social psychologists such as Virgilio Enriquez, Carmen Santiago, Zeus Salazar and others have placed these and other Filipino "values" under a broader framework of **kapwa**, i.e. what it means for Filipinos to have a "shared identity" and how this becomes differentiated when Filipinos categorize their **kapwa** as an outsider or **ibang-tao** or "one of us" or **hindi-ibang-tao**. Depending on where one is placed determines the interaction that ensues. One can appreciate how much Filipinos value their relationships by the linguistic nuance of their relational terms. As a foreigner, you may be treated with anything along the spectrum of **pakikitungo** (*transaction/civility with*), to **pakikisalamuha** (*having an interaction with*), to **pakikilahok** (*joining/participating*), to **pakikibagay** (*in-conformity with/in-accord with*), and to **pakiki-sama** (*getting along with*). If you are considered family, friend or extended kin, then you can expect **pakikipagpalagayang-loob** (*being in-rapport/understanding/acceptance with*), or **pakikisangkot** (*getting involved*), or **pakikiisa** (*being one with, in solidarity with*).

What about Filipinos' tendency for indirect communication? *Sikolohiyang Pilipino's* perspective on this includes Filipinos' sensitivity to the feelings of others, and their propensity to be truthful but <u>not</u> at the expense of causing offense or discomfort (whether real or perceived). A useful distinction is the Filipinos' intuitive practice of **pakikiramdam** (*shared inner perception*), an arguably desirable skill in many situations involving Filipino social interaction. Simply put, it is a request to be sensitive to all the verbal and bodily cues of another, to feel the other's emotive energy and act appropriately. Thus, a Filipino conversation or negotiation may involve euphemisms, body language and vocal intonations that are meant to communicate more than the words themselves. Asked to go to a party of someone they are not interested in, for example, a Filipino may respond with "I'll try to go" or "I'll let you know later." A non-follow-up is usually understood among locals as a "no."

If you find yourself becoming a bit impatient, having come from a more Westernized and thus verbally direct way of speaking and relating, remember that part of the joy and effort of language learning, in this case Tagalog, is the imaginative exercise of putting yourself in the daily world and experiences of the native speakers of that language. The Filipinos' long colonial history, current socio-economic and political struggles and more importantly, their enduring resilience, humor and spirit despite and perhaps, because of the above, must be appreciated as you learn to listen and express yourself in Tagalog.

The Tagalog Alphabet

In the 1930s, when Tagalog was chosen as the basis for the national language, there were 20 letters in the alphabet consisting of five vowels and 15 consonants. These were:

a	e	i	o	u
b	k	d	g	h	l	m
n	ng	p	r	s	t	w	y

The consonants were originally referred to with the vowel **a** appended to each letter so that these were pronounced **ba**, **ka**, **da**, and so on. The **ng** consonant was pronounced as **nang**.

In the 1980s, eight more consonants were added to the alphabet. These are **c**, **f**, **j**, **ñ**, **q**, **v**, **x** and **z**. This was done to facilitate the writing of new words and terms borrowed from other languages. The letters of the Tagalog alphabet are now referred to in the same way as the letters in the English alphabet except for **ng** and **ñ** (pronounced *en-ye*) which is of Spanish origin.

Generally, the eight additional consonants are used for proper nouns (names of persons, places, buildings, brand names, the like) such as Fe, Carlos, Santo Niño, Leyte Gulf, Jones Bridge, Jollibee and Louis Vuitton. They are also used for borrowed terms like **zakat** (almsgiving, the third pillar of Islam), indigenous or native terms like **carayab** (an Igorot costume made of tree bark), and medical and scientific terms like zinc and amoxicillin.

There are conventions in the pronunciation of the consonants **ñ** and **ng**. Tagalog words with **ñ** are pronounced as if there is a combination of **n** and **y** consonants instead of one consonant. The first half is the **n** part which takes the sound of the vowel before it while the second half is the **y** part which takes the sound of the vowel after it. For example, the word **Niño** in Santo Niño is pronounced **nin-yo**. Note that **ñ** is between **i** and **o**, thus **n** takes the initial sound of the vowel **i** while **y** takes the sound of the vowel **o**.

The pronunciation of the consonant **ng** is very difficult for foreigners particularly when it appears at the beginning of a word. To produce the sound **ng**, push the tongue back and up—making sure that the back part of the tongue is curled and almost touches the molars and the roof of your mouth to produce a nasal sound, and then add the sound of the vowel after it. The syllable before **ng** usually rides on the nasal **ng** sound.

Another Tagalog consonant that may pose some difficulty for foreigners is the consonant **r**. Unlike the English *r* where the tongue does not touch the sides of the mouth, the Tagalog **r** is produced by quickly tapping the tip of the tongue on the gum ridge behind the upper teeth (like a Spanish *r* but not rolled or trilled).

A Tagalog word is pronounced just as it is spelled, and each syllable is pronounced separately and distinctly. Except for certain vowel and semi-vowel combinations (diphthongs) such as **ay, aw, ey, iw, oy**, and **uy**, foreigners will have minimal difficulty in pronouncing most Tagalog words. However, foreigners may find the **iw** and **uy** combinations a bit hard to pronounce and may likely break up the combinations especially when they appear at the end of words. Some Tagalog examples of these diphthongs are:

agiw	a-giw	cobweb	away	a-way	fight
bitiw	bi-tiw	let go	laway	la-way	saliva
kasuy	ka-suy	cashew	reyna	rey-na	queen
baduy	ba-duy	dowdy	kahoy	ka-hoy	wood
mababaw	ma-ba-baw	shallow	amoy	a-moy	scent
ayaw	a-yaw	do not like			

Foreign Words in Tagalog

When a foreign word is borrowed or assimilated into Tagalog, it is written according to the conventions of Tagalog phonetics. However, the names of persons and places need not be changed. Many foreign words (mostly Spanish and English) have been absorbed into the Tagalog vocabulary and remain foreign when their original spelling and pronunciation is retained. But when changed to conform with the Tagalog alphabet, they become Tagalog words. Although many new English loan words have come into the language in recent years (especially technical and scientific terms), there are still many common, everyday words in the language that were borrowed from Spanish in earlier times. Between the English word *telephone* and the Spanish equivalent *telefono*, for example, the Tagalogs have adopted the latter and write it as **telepono**.

In writing and pronouncing Spanish loan words in Tagalog, be guided by the following:

			SPANISH	TAGALOG	ENGLISH
hard *c*	is changed to **k**	as in	calesa	**kalesa**	rig
soft *c*	is changed to **s**	as in	circo	**sirko**	circus
ch	is changed to **ts**	as in	lechon	**litson**	roast pig
f	is changed to **p**	as in	final	**pinal**	final
soft *j*	is changed to **h**	as in	cajon	**kahon**	box, drawer
	or **s**	as in	jabon	**sabon**	soap
ll	is changed to **ly**	as in	calle	**kalye**	street
q	is changed to **k**	as in	maquina	**makina**	machine
v	is changed to **b**	as in	vapor	**bapor**	ship
z	is changed to **s**	as in	lapiz	**lapis**	pencil

English words also undergo changes when they are assimilated into the Tagalog language. Some words may bear some resemblance to the original English words although others have an added hint of Spanish influence. Still others undergo odd, sometimes comical changes when English sounds are given the nearest Tagalog equivalent such as **kwaliti** for *quality*. Since **kalidad** is another Tagalog loan word (from Spanish), an English word may often have more than one Tagalog equivalent.

A current but debatable issue on the Filipinization of English words has also led to the use of words such as **efektiv** from the English word *effective*, the Tagalog equivalent of which is **mabisa**. Another example is **varayti** from *variety* (or **uri** in Tagalog).

The following lists a few of the rules:

			ENGLISH	TAGALOG
soft *c*	is changed to **s**	as in	cinema	**sine**
hard *c*	is changed to **k**	as in	academic	**akademik**
ck	is changed to **k**	as in	gimmick	**gimik**
ct	is changed to **k**	as in	addict	**adik**
qua or *q*	are changed to **kwa**	as in	quality	**kwaliti**
long *i*	is changed to **ay**	as in	driver	**drayber**
f	is changed to **p**	as in	traffic	**trapik**
v	is changed to **b**	as in	believe	**bilib**
long *o*	is changed to **u**	as in	approve	**aprub**
cle	is changed to **kel**	as in	tricycle	**traysikel**
tion	is changed to **syon**	as in	institution	**institusyon**
x	is changed to **ks**	as in	boxing	**boksing**
j	is changed to **dy**	as in	janitor	**dyanitor**
beginning *s*	is changed to **is**	as in	sport	**isport**
soft *ch*	is changed to **ts**	as in	teacher	**titser**
hard *ch*	is changed to **k**	as in	school	**iskul**

Students should also learn how to write the following foreign words in Tagalog that are very common in everyday conversation. Needless to say, correct pronunciation is very important. Learn to pronounce these words as true Tagalog words by taking particular notice of the accent marks and stresses as discussed in Lesson Two. The remainder of the book will not contain these stress marks to reflect how Tagalog words are currently used in written communication. Repeat the words aloud and take note of the vowels.

alkohol	alcohol	**klub**	club	**silya**	chair
piyano	piano	**sinehan**	movie house	**kompyuter**	computer
radyo	radio	**pelikula**	movie	**pasaporte**	passport
kotse	car	**bentilador**	electric fan	**tiangge**	bazaar
telepono	telephone	**otel**	hotel	**tindahan**	store
bangko	bench	**tabako**	tobacco	**papel**	paper
kape	coffee	**tenis**	tennis	**plastik**	plastic
restawran	restaurant	**sigarilyo**	cigarette	**telebisyon**	television

DAYS OF THE WEEK

Lunes	Monday	**Biyernes**	Friday
Martes	Tuesday	**Sabado**	Saturday
Miyerkules	Wednesday	**Linggo**	Sunday
Huwebes	Thursday		

MONTHS OF THE YEAR

Enero	January	**Hulyo**	July
Pebrero	February	**Agosto**	August
Marso	March	**Setyembre**	September
Abril	April	**Oktubre**	October
Mayo	May	**Nobyembre**	November
Hunyo	June	**Disyembre**	December

Syllables and Stress in Tagalog

I. SYLLABLES IN TAGALOG

A knowledge of the different kinds of syllables (word divisions) in Tagalog will help the learner to articulate the words correctly. There are four kinds of syllables in Tagalog, namely:

1. The simple syllable consisting of only one vowel (V)

as	o	in	tá-o	person
as	a	in	pa-á	foot
as	i	in	i-yák	cry
as	u	in	ú-lo	head

2. The consonant + vowel syllable (CV)

as	ba or sa	in	ba-sa	read
as	ta	in	tá-o	person
as	na	in	i-ná	mother
as	lo	in	ú-lo	head

3. The vowel + consonant syllable (VC)

as	an	in	an-táy	wait
as	am	in	am-bón	shower / drizzle
as	ak	in	ak-yát	climb
as	it	in	ma-pa-ít	bitter

4. The consonant + vowel + consonant syllable (CVC)

as	tak	in	tak-bó	run
as	lak	in	bu-lak-lák	flower
as	lon	in	ta-lón	jump
as	law	in	í-law	light

When pronouncing Tagalog words, there are no hard and fast rules to help you know how to break the syllables (in other words, to know where each syllable starts and ends). An understanding though of the types of syllables that exist and the possible combinations of vowels and consonants that are formed through exposure to the Tagalog language will help the learner pronounce words correctly after some time. In the beginning, however, it is best to simply memorize the stress accents along with the words as you learn them.

Look out as well for prefixes and suffixes which "grab" vowels and consonants from the root word (see Lesson 14 on the **-um-** and **mag-** verbs, and similar discussions on other affixes). An example is **bu-lak-lák** (*flower*) which becomes **bu-lak-lá-kin** (flowery) where the suffix **-in** grabs the final consonant of the root.

A useful rule to remember is not to apply the pronunciation of English words to Tagalog words—for example saying **ku-must-á** rather than **ku-mus-tá** (*how are you*)—since the maximum number of letters in a Tagalog syllable does not exceed three (keeping in mind that **ng** is treated as a single letter). Thus, there is no **must** in **kumustá** although there is **pang** in **pang-ápat** (*fourth*) and **ngin** in **hángin** (*wind*). The syllables **pang** and **ngin** are only made up of three sounds as **ng** is considered a single consonant or letter in the Tagalog alphabet.

Another useful rule for foreigners is not to separate an initial consonant from a vowel, leaving a VC syllable in the middle of a word, as in **bu-má-nat** or *to strike* (which should not be pronounced **bu-má-nat**). VC syllables are mostly found at the beginning of words such as **an-táy** (*wait*) and **ak-yát** (*climb*). VC syllables may also be found at the end of words if the previous syllables end in a vowel as in **pa-ít** (*bitter*) and **la-ot** (*sea*).

As a general rule for the proper pronunciation of Tagalog words, remember to deliver these words in a faster, sharper and less breathy manner than in English (more in the manner of Spanish pronunciation). Do not make any audible breaths (aspirations) in pronouncing the *p*'s, *k*'s, *t*'s and other consonants. Otherwise, you will be branded a "slang," the local term for anyone who speaks Tagalog with an American accent or with too many long *a*'s, long *e*'s and long *o*'s.

EXERCISES

Break the following words correctly into their individual syllables. The first syllable of each word has been given.

1. **magandá**	ma - _____ - _____	beautiful
2. **páaralán**	pa - _____ - _____ - _____	school
3. **pagkáin**	pag- _____ - _____	food
4. **inilutò**	i- _____ - _____ - _____	was cooked
5. **ialís**	i- _____ - _____	to be removed
6. **inalís**	i- _____ - _____	was removed
7. **hángin**	ha- _____	wind
8. **linísin**	li- _____ - _____	to be cleaned
9. **tatló**	tat- _____	three
10. **álaála**	a- _____ - _____ - _____	gift, remembrance

11. **kailángan**	ka- _____ - _____ - _____		needed
12. **násaán**	na- _____ - _____		where
13. **ngayón**	nga- _____		now, today
14. **awítin**	a- _____ - _____		to sing
15. **mabaít**	ma- _____ - _____		good
16. **pangálan**	pa- _____ - _____		name
17. **maliit**	ma- _____ - _____		small
18. **paalám**	pa- _____ - _____		goodbye
19. **maaárì**	ma- _____ - _____ - _____		can be
20. **nag-áaral**	nag- _____ - _____ - _____		studying

Pronounce the words listed in the Exercises on page 21 slowly, syllable by syllable, then repeat them pronouncing each word a bit faster.

II. STRESS

In Tagalog, the use of stress on a particular syllable in a word can make a difference in meaning. **Stress** is the vocal emphasis of a particular syllable. In this section, an accent mark is placed over the vowel of a syllable to indicate which syllable is to be stressed and how the stress is to be sounded.

1. Principal types of stresses
There are four principal types of stresses and in this book, they are marked in the following ways:

a. End Stress
An acute accent mark (´) is placed over the vowel of the last syllable of the word if this syllable receives a stronger emphasis than the others.

anák	**a-NAK**	child
amá	**a-MA**	father
iná	**i-NA**	mother
bulaklák	**bu-lak-LAK**	flower
malakás	**ma-la-KAS**	strong

b. Penultimate Stress
An acute accent mark (´) is also used to indicate a stress on the next to last syllable of a word, by placing the accent above the vowel of that syllable.

babáe	**ba-BA-e**	woman
laláki	**la-LA-ki**	man
maínit	**ma-I-nit**	hot

malínis	ma-LI-nis	clean
táo	TA-o	person

c. Penultimate Stress with a Glottal Catch

A grave accent mark (`) is used above the vowel of the last syllable to indicate a strong emphasis on the next to last syllable. The vowel at the end is pronounced with a glottal catch, which is produced by an abrupt closing of the throat to block the air stream in both the mouth and voice box. The glottal catch is hard to hear and beginners often mistake the sound as that of *k*.

For this particular lesson, however, we shall indicate the pronunciation of the glottal catch with the letter **Q**. Note that this is only a representation of the glottal catch and should not be interpreted as the literal pronunciation of the words (please refer to the online audio to hear how the words are pronounced).

punò	PU-noQ	tree
kandilà	kan-DI-laQ	candle
pusà	PU-saQ	cat
susì	SU-siQ	key
batà	BA-taQ	child

d. End Glottal Catch (no stress)

The circumflex mark (^) is used above the vowel of the last syllable when it is pronounced without a stress but with a glottal catch at the end. The difference with the preceding stress type is that words that fall under this category are pronounced faster and the stress on the last syllable seems lost with the glottal catch.

punô	pu-noQ	full
sampû	sam-puQ	ten
bakyâ	bak-yaQ	wooden shoes
masamâ	ma-sa-maQ	bad
gintô	gin-toQ	gold

Note that longer words may have more than one stressed syllable such as **pinagkákaguluhán** (*being mobbed*) and **mapágsamantalâ** (*opportunistic*).

2. On the use of stress and accents 🔊

There are some important facts that the language learner should also remember about the use of stress and accents in Tagalog. These are the following:

a. A difference in stress can cause a difference in meaning, as in the following examples:

kaibígan	ka-i-BI-gan	friend
kaibigán	ka-i-bi-GAN	desire

káibigán	KA-i-bi-GAN	have mutual understanding with
kaíbigan	ka-I-bi-gan	sweetheart
makaalís	ma-ka-a-LIS	to be able to leave
makáalis	ma-KA-a-lis	to leave unintentionally
matúlog	ma-TU-log	to sleep
matulóg	ma-tu-LOG	to fall asleep unintentionally

b. The glottal catch is lost when a suffix is added after the final vowel.

batà	BA-taQ	child
kabatáan	ka-ba-TA-an	youth
luhà	LU-haQ	tears
luhaán	lu-ha-AN	miserable
punô	pu-noQ	full
punuín	pu-nu-IN	to fill with
susì	SU-siQ	key
susián	su-si-AN	keyhole

c. Monosyllabic words often take on the stress of a preceding word, and the stress in that word is lost. The stress is thus "transferred" to the following single-syllable word.

kumáin	Kumain ká.	Ku-ma-in KA.	You may eat.
hindî	Hindi pá.	Hin-di PA.	Not yet.
ganitó	Ganito bá?	Ga-ni-to BA?	Like this?
malápit	Malapit ná.	Ma-la-pit NA.	It is near.
hindî	Hindi pô.	Hin-di PO.	No, sir / madam.

d. To avoid mispronunciation, a hyphen separates the prefix that ends in a consonant and with a glottal stop from the root that follows which starts with a vowel.

pag-ása	pagQ-A-sa	hope
mag-alís	magQ-a-LIS	to remove
mag-isá	magQ-i-SA	alone
pag-íbig	pagQ-I-big	love

EXERCISES

Practice pronouncing the following words by paying careful attention to the four types of stress and accent marks used to indicate them.

anák	a-NA	child
amá	a-MA	father
iná	i-NA	mother
bulaklák	bu-lak-LAK	flower
malakás	ma-la-KAS	strong
babáe	ba-BA-e	woman
laláki	la-LA-ki	man
maínit	ma-I-nit	hot
táo	TA-o	person
punò	PU-noQ	tree
kandilà	kan-DI-laQ	candle
pusà	PU-saQ	cat
susì	SU-siQ	key
batà	BA-taQ	child
punô	pu-noQ	full
sampû	sam-puQ	ten
bakyâ	bak-yaQ	wooden shoes
masamâ	ma-sa-maQ	bad
gintô	gin-toQ	gold

Greetings and Common Expressions

Nakilala ng manedyer ang bagong assistant niya.
A manager meets her new assistant.

Dumating si Olivia Sy galing sa Hong Kong. Sinalubong siya ni Janice Reyes, isang bagong assistant sa kanilang kompanya.
Olivia Sy arrived from Hong Kong. She was met by Janice Reyes, a new assistant in their company.

JANICE : **Magandang tanghali po. Kumusta po?**
Good afternoon, ma'am! How are you, ma'am?

OLIVIA : **Mabuti naman, salamat. Anong pangalan mo?**
I'm good, thank you. What's your name?

JANICE : **Ako po si Janice Reyes, ma'am. Bagong assistant ninyo. Kumusta po ang biyahe ninyo?**
I'm Janice Reyes, ma'am, your new assistant. How was your trip, ma'am?

OLIVIA : **Mabuti naman. Maayos ang lahat.**
It was all right. Everything was fine.

JANICE : **May reserbasyon po kayo sa Manila Peninsula. Gusto ninyo po bang kumain muna?**
You have a reservation at the Manila Peninsula. Would you like to eat first, ma'am?

OLIVIA : **Mamaya na siguro. Maraming salamat, Janice.**
Perhaps later. Thank you very much, Janice.

JANICE : **Sige po, ma'am. Tayo na po sa opisina.**
Okay, ma'am. Let's go to the office then.

Vocabulary List

tanghali = noon or midday	**salamat** = thank you
kapilya = chapel	**hapon** = afternoon
pangalan = name	**araw** = morning
mabuti = fine	**opo** (or **oho**) = yes (formal)
maganda = beautiful	**biyahe** = trip
gabi = night	**maayos** = fine, good
Kumusta? = How are you?	**kumain** = to eat
paalam = goodbye	**opisina** = office

Aside from the borrowed **Hi** and **Hello**, Tagalogs have other forms of greetings—peppered with speech suffixes that define courtesy and deference.

I. POLITE FORMS OF ADDRESS—**PO** AND **HO**

Tagalog politeness is a trait worthy to be discussed and taught to learners of the language. Younger generations and junior employees include the terms **po** or **ho** at the start or end of their greetings and responses to express respect for older people—parents, older relatives, and other senior individuals—or persons with honorific titles or authority—clergy, teachers, community leaders, employers, and policemen—regardless of age. **Po** and **ho** approximately mean *sir* or *madam* in English and reflect the speaker's good manners and his respect to the one spoken to.

Po is not used by an older person when talking to a younger person such as a father talking to his son or daughter. Neither do equals, such as siblings or friends, use the term.

Short positive responses can be just **oo** or *yes* when speaking to a younger person or a peer in a familiar manner, but when speaking to an older person, you must use either **o-po** or **o-ho**, both of which are the formal or polite versions of *yes*.

II. GREETINGS—GOOD DAY, ETC.

Greetings usually start with **maganda**, which means *beautiful*. The complete greeting is **Maganda ang araw**—often shortened to **Magandang araw**—which literally means *beautiful day*. The most common greetings from morning to evening, in their polite forms, are:

Magandang araw po.	Good day, sir/madam.
Magandang umaga po.	Good morning, sir/madam.
Magandang tanghali po.	Good afternoon, sir/madam.
Magandang hapon po.	Good afternoon, sir/madam.
Magandang gabi po.	Good evening, sir/madam.

Note that **tanghali** is *noon or midday*. The period covers lunch time, from around 11 in the morning to 1 o'clock in the afternoon. This is the time when most Tagalog families prepare and have their lunch.

For equals, it is fine to drop **po** and just say:

Magandang umaga.	Good morning.
Magandang hapon.	Good afternoon.

In addition to the use of **po** or **ho**, another polite way of greeting people is to address them in the plural form by adding **sa inyo**, which means *to you* (plural), and **sa kanila**, which means *to them*, at the end of the greeting. In English, however, a greeting with **sa kanila** at the end still translates to *to you* in Tagalog and not literally *to them*. The plural forms emphasize the greeter's acknowledgment of the seniority or authority of the person being greeted. On the other hand, equals use **sa iyo** or *to you* (singular).

Magandang umaga po sa inyo.	Good morning to you, sir/madam.
Magandang hapon po sa kanila.	Good afternoon to you, sir/madam.
Magandang umaga sa iyo.	Good morning to you.

The usual responses of both older or senior individuals and equals contain **rin** and **naman**, which mean *too*, indicating that the one who received the greeting meant the greeter to have a similar good day.

Magandang umaga rin sa iyo.	Good morning to you, too.
Magandang umaga naman.	Good morning, too.
Magandang tanghali rin po.	Good afternoon, too, sir/madam.

III. GREETINGS—HOW ARE YOU?

The influence of Spanish is evident in the way Filipinos, particularly Tagalogs, greet people. Derived from the Spanish "como esta," Tagalogs use a similar greeting when they meet a friend, a relative or an acquaintance of about their age or stature. Older people also use this greeting toward younger people.

The Tagalog equivalent for the singular pronoun *you* is **ikaw**; it becomes **ka** when the pronoun is used in an inverted or conversational word order (Refer to discussions on sentence formation and pronouns in Lessons Five and Six).

But when greeting an elder or superior, Tagalogs use the plural **kayo** and **sila** instead of **ka**. This is the polite way of greeting and asking how one is. **Kayo** and **sila** are the plural pronouns for *you* and *they*, respectively. **Po** may be dropped if **kayo** and **sila** are used.

Kumusta po kayo?	How are you, sir/madam?
Kumusta sila?	How are you, sir/madam?

Take note that it is not unusual for Tagalogs to ask about one's family—parents, spouse, children, and everyone else in the family—when they see each other, whether the speaker is young, old or at about the same age as the person spoken to. Other cultures should see this as a reflection of the thoughtful nature of Filipinos, young and old alike.

The responses to these greetings usually include **mabuti** which means *fine*, **salamat** which means *thank you*, as well as **rin** and **naman**.

Mabuti naman (po). Salamat (po).	Fine, too, sir/madam.
Mabuti rin (po). Salamat.	Thank you, sir/madam.

Salamat is optional at the end of the sentence, thus **po** or **ho** may be attached to the first half of the response. However, it is never wrong to say **po** again when **salamat** is retained. Foreigners and Tagalog alike could never go wrong with an overuse of the term but will only endear them to older or senior people.

Another peculiarity of the Tagalog is the use of the questions *Where are you going?* or *Where have you been?* in the same context as **Kumusta ka?** when meeting people they know. These very common greetings among Tagalogs should not be taken literally by foreigners. Filipinos are not really asking your itinerary—these are the equivalent of the English *How is it going?* and is simply another way of saying *Hello!* and striking up a conversation.

Saan ka pupunta? (informal)	Where are you going?
Saan kayo pupunta? (formal)	Where are you going, sir/madam?
Saan ka nanggaling? (informal)	Where have you been?
Saan kayo nanggaling? (formal)	Where have you been, sir/madam?

The usual response is **Diyan lamang (po)** which means *Just nearby (sir/madam).* However, you may be specific about the place and say, for example, **Sa Quezon City (po)** which means either *I'm going to Quezon City (sir/madam)* or *I've been to Quezon City (sir/madam).*

IV. VARIOUS WAYS OF SAYING "EXCUSE ME" 🔊

There is no exact equivalent for *excuse me* in Tagalog. However, there are five different ways of expressing it depending on the situation.

1. **Paumanhin po** is used when one apologizes or asks to be excused, or if one bumps into someone else accidentally.
2. **Pakiraan po** is used when one asks for permission to pass through.
3. **Mawalang-galang po** is used when one requests to be heard.
4. **Patawad po** is used when one apologizes for causing physical injury or emotional hurt to someone else.

5. **Pasintabi po** is used when one gives a warning of something that may be offensive or distasteful to others.

In which situations can each of the above be used?

1. When a small group is having a formal discussion or meeting and you need to leave, you may say in a modest tone of voice to the nearest person or to the one presiding the meeting, **Paumanhin (po), aalis na ako** or **Paumanhin (po), lalabas lamang ako sandali.** The statements mean *Excuse me (sir/madam), I will leave now* or *Excuse me (sir/madam), I will go out for a while.* One does not have to say **Paumanhin (po)** in a big meeting where one's absence is not obvious, unless one is the special guest.

   Another situation that calls for **Paumanhin (po)** is when one bumps into someone unintentionally such as at a party or in a crowded area like a shopping mall. This statement is also equivalent to *I'm sorry.*

2. When you want to pass through a passage way or hall that is blocked by two persons talking to one another, you say **Pakiraan po** (*Please let me pass.*) then pass.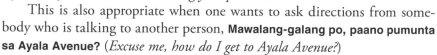

3. When you are in a meeting and wish to voice requests or opinions, or interrupt the speaker to make a comment, you say **Mawalang-galang po** and proceed to make the statement. The phrase literally means *May I lose my courtesy?* but translates as *I beg your pardon.*

   This is also appropriate when one wants to ask directions from somebody who is talking to another person, **Mawalang-galang po, paano pumunta sa Ayala Avenue?** (*Excuse me, how do I get to Ayala Avenue?*)

4. When someone is deeply hurt—either physically or emotionally—by another, the one at fault who realizes his mistake should say **Patawad po** or **Patawarin ninyo ako,** which means *Forgive me.*

5. Some people cannot withstand unpleasant stories or photos. To warn them of a forthcoming offensive situation, one should say **Pasintabi po**. This is commonly used by news reporters when a gruesome film footage is about to be shown on television. The phrase literally means *Please set aside.*

Can one of the above expressions sometimes be used in place of another?
Yes, **Mawalang-galang po** may be used for situations 1 and 2 but not for 4.

Can one use **Paumanhin po** instead of **Patawad po**?

No, **Paumanhin po** may mean *Sorry* but it is is too mild to use in cases of physical or emotional injury.

V. OTHER COMMON EXPRESSIONS

Tagalogs have common everyday expressions that should be memorized by students of this language. The following expressions have shortened forms that are used in everyday speech just as the shortened form of the English *Let's* is used in place of *Let us*. More shortened forms are listed in Lesson Forty-Three.

Saan kayo nakatira?	Where do you live?
Ano ang pangalan mo?	What is your name?
Aywan ko. (shortened: **Ewan ko.**)	I don't know.
Hindi ko alam. (shortened: **Di ko alam.**)	I don't know.
Ayaw ako. (shortened: **Ayoko.**)	I don't like.
Bahala na!	Come what may!
Kaunti lamang. (shortened: **lang**)	Just a little.
Kung minsan.	Once in a while.
Gising na!	Wake up!
Hindi bale!	Never mind!
Hindi naman.	Not so.
Hintay ka! (shortened: **Teka!**)	Wait for a moment.
Huwag na. Salamat.	No more. Thank you.
Bahala ka.	It is up to you.
Magmadali ka. (shortened: **Dali ka!**)	Hurry up! (literally: *Be quick, you!*)
Mamaya na.	For a while.
Salamat.	Thank you.
Maraming salamat.	Thank you very much.
Ano po? (or **Ano?**)	What did you say, sir/madam?
Saka na.	Later.
Sandali lamang. (shortened: **lang**)	Just a moment.
Sige na!	Go on!
Sayang!	What a pity. What a loss.
Tahimik kayo.	Be silent.
Tama na.	It is all right. It is enough.
Tayo na. (shortened: **Tena.**)	Let's go.
Totoo ba? (shortened: **Totoo?**)	Is it true?
Tulog na.	Go to sleep.
Marahil.	Maybe.
Siguro.	Maybe *or* definitely.

Note that the meaning of **siguro** depends on the response to the question being asked. For example, there may be three responses to the question **Siguro ka?** or *Are you sure?*:

Oo, siguro ako.	Yes, I am sure (or *Yes, definitely*).
Hindi ako siguro.	I am not sure.
Siguro.	Maybe.

Remember to include **po** or appropriately change **ka** into **kayo** or **sila** to all the above expressions whenever possible to show respect.

Kataka-taka!	It seems incredible!
Magaling!	Outstanding! (literally: *Skilled*)
Nakayayamot!	It is annoying!
Mabuhay!	Welcome! (literally: *May you live long!*)

Mabuhay, the official greeting of Filipinos to foreign visitors, has also become an expression of collective joy and pride for any occasion, especially when Filipinos are proud of an achievement whether in politics or sports; it may also be used to greet newly weds, **Mabuhay ang bagong kasal!** or literally, *May the newlyweds live long!*

| Maligayang bati (po)! | Congratulations (sir/madam)! (literally: *Happy greetings!* The phrase has now come to be associated with birthday celebrations.) |

EXERCISES

Match a situation from Column B to the appropriate response from column A.

COLUMN A	COLUMN B
Magaling!	1. Your mother calls out that dinner is ready. You are still tidying up your study table as you have just finished doing your homework.
Ano po?	2. Your 2-year old nephew sings the song *Brother John* from start to finish.
Magandang hapon din po.	3. Your grandmother asks a question but you did not understand half of the words she was saying.
Sandali lang po.	4. You are looking for a building along Ayala Avenue. While looking up at one tall building, you bump into somebody.
Paumanhin po.	5. The town mayor is leaving the municipal hall just as you were entering. He greets you good afternoon.

LESSON FOUR

The Articles **Si** and **Ang**

Mga plano pagkatapos ng trabaho
After work plans

Nag-uusap sina Janice at Miguel tungkol sa kanilang mga plano pagkatapos ng trabaho. Kaibigan ni Janice si Miguel sa opisina.
Janice and Miguel are talking about their plans after work. Miguel is Janice's friend at work.

JANICE : **Malayo <u>ang</u> Maginhawa Street!**
Maginwaha street is far!

MIGUEL : **Okay lang. Masarap <u>ang</u> pagkain doon. Mura pa.**
Don't worry. Food there is delicious. And also cheap.

JANICE : **Sige na nga. May kotse naman tayo. Kasama <u>si</u> Chris, <u>ang</u> kaibigan ko.**
Okay, fine. We have a car anyway. Chris, my friend, is going.

MIGUEL : **Lalaki ba o babae <u>si</u> Chris?**
Is Chris male or female?

JANICE : **Babae. Kababata ko <u>si</u> Chris. Mabait siya. Maganda rin.**
Female. Chris is my childhood friend. She's kind. She's also pretty.

MIGUEL : **Talaga?**
Really?

Vocabulary List

marunong = intelligent
bata = young (adj.); child (n.)
lungsod = city
magkapatid = siblings
malinis = clean
sapatos = shoes
lugar = place
mahal = expensive

malayo = far
masarap = delicious
mura = cheap
kaibigan = friend
mabait = kind
maganda = pretty
kababata = childhood friend

Any noun that is used as the subject of a sentence—including names of persons, places, and things—is always preceded by an article, except in direct conversation and in imperative statements.

I. THE ARTICLES SI AND SINA

The singular article **si** is used before the name of a person and the plural article **sina** is used before the names of two or more persons.

Babae si Ruth.	Ruth is a woman.
Lalaki si Peter.	Peter is a man.
Batang babae si Helen.	Helen is a young girl.
Batang lalaki si Tom.	Tom is a young boy.
Maganda si Ruth.	Ruth is pretty.
Marunong si Peter.	Peter is intelligent.
Mababait sina Helen at Tom.	Helen and Tom are good.
Mga bata sina Helen at Tom.	Helen and Tom are children.

Note that Tagalog sentences follow a plurality rule where either the subject or predicate may be made plural. However, the pluralization of both subject and predicate is optional. In the last sentence above, the article **sina** indicates that the subject is plural while **mga** (a plural marker that has no meaning on its own) before **bata** indicates that the noun is plural. Adjectives form their plural by duplicating the first syllable of the root word. For example, **mabait** (or *kind*, root word is **bait**) becomes **mababait**.

II. THE ARTICLES ANG AND ANG MGA

The article **ang** is used before the name of a single thing or place while **ang mga** (pronounced **ma-nga**) is used before the names of two or more things or places.

Mabait ang bata.	The child is good.
Mabait ang aso.	The dog is good.
Mababait ang bata at ang aso.	The child and the dog are good.
Mababait ang mga bata at ang mga aso.	The children and the dogs are good.
Malilinis ang mga sapatos.	The shoes are clean.
Malilinis ang baro at ang sapatos.	The dress and the shoes are clean.
Malilinis ang mga baro at ang mga sapatos.	The dresses and the pairs of shoes are clean.

The article **ang** must always precede the name of a place. However, the article **mga** may be placed before the adjective, which must then take on a plural form if there is more than one name of place in the subject, or before the noun (see underlined words in the examples below).

Maliit ang Pilipinas.
The Philippines is small.

Malaki ang Estados Unidos.
The United States is big.

Isang lungsod ng Pilipinas ang Maynila.
Manila is a city of the Philippines.

Punong-lungsod ng Estados Unidos ang Washington D.C.
Washington D.C. is the capital city of the United States.

Mga lungsod ang Maynila at ang Washington D.C.
Manila and Washington D.C. are cities.

Mga malalamig na lugar ang Baguio at ang Tagaytay.
Malalamig na mga lugar ang Baguio at ang Tagaytay.
Baguio and Tagaytay are cool places.

Note that it is acceptable to delete the second **ang** before the second name of a place and the meaning of the sentence will not change.

Mga lungsod ang Maynila at Washington D.C.
Malalamig na mga lugar ang Baguio at Tagaytay.

EXERCISES

Fill in the blanks with the correct articles:

1. **Malilinis _____ aso at _____ bata.**

2. **Mababait _____ bata at aso.**

3. **Magkapatid _____ Ruth at Peter.**

4. **Malalaki _____ Amerika at Aprika.**

5. **Mababait at marurunong _____ Peter at _____ Ruth.**

6. **Malilinis** _____ **Helen, Tom, Mary at John.**

7. **Magaganda** _____ **bata at** _____ **Helen.**

8. **Mababait** _____ **Tom.** (plural form). Tom and companions are good.

9. **Mababait** _____ **Helen, John, at Peter at** _____ **aso.**

10. **Malalaki** _____ **Amerika at Aprika.**

From the lists of subjects and predicates below, make 15 sentences in the inverse or conversational word order (with the predicate first and the subject last). You can also begin studying how to make a sentence in the subject-predicate order simply by using **ay** to join the subject and predicate, and by adding the correct articles before the subject. More about this on Lesson Five.

SUBJECTS

babae	woman	**maganda**	beautiful
lalaki	man	**marunong**	intelligent
bata	child	**mataba**	fat
bahay	house	**mabait**	kind; good (of character)
bansa	nation	**mabuti**	good (of condition or quality)
tubig	water	**maliit**	small
pagkain	food	**malaki**	big
bulaklak	flower	**mainit**	hot
mesa	table	**malamig**	cold
silya	chair	**malinis**	clean
paaralan	school	**bago**	new
kotse	car	**mura**	cheap
lapis	pencil	**mahal**	dear; expensive
papel	paper	**masarap**	delicious; delightful

PREDICATES

kape	coffee	**malusog**	healthy
isda	fish	**luma**	old (inanimate)
araw	sun; day	**matanda**	old (animate)
hangin	wind	**mataas**	high
aklat	book	**mababa**	low
simbahan	church	**mahirap**	poor; difficult

The sentences in this lesson use the inverted or conversational word order since it is more commonly used in everyday speech by Tagalog speakers. The succeeding lessons will discuss the two different ways sentences are formed in Tagalog.

LESSON FIVE
Sentence Formation

Sa kapihan
At the coffee shop

Pagkatapos ng hapunan, pumunta sina Miguel, Chris at Janice sa isang kapihan. Gusto nilang mag-order ng kape at mga minatamis.
After dinner, Miguel, Chris and Janice went to a coffee shop. They would like to order coffee and desserts.

MIGUEL : **Malinis ang kapihan kahit luma ang mga mesa at silya.**
The cafe is clean even if the tables and chairs are old.

CHRIS : **Maganda ang simbahan sa harap.**
The church in front is beautiful.

MIGUEL : **Ano ang pinakamasarap dito?**
What's the most delicious item here?

JANICE : **Malamig na kape ang gusto ko. Mainit ang panahon.**
I want cold coffee. The weather is hot.

CHRIS : **Masarap ang ensaymada dito. Mag-order tayo ng isa!**
The *ensaymada* here is delicious. Let's order one.

Vocabulary List

bahay = house	**malinis** = clean
aso = dog	**simbahan** = church
kumakain = is/are eating	**pinakamasarap** = (the) most delicious
mainit = hot	**malamig** = cold
pusa = cat	**panahon** = weather
nagluluto = is/are cooking	**ensaymada** = Filipino cheese brioche

---

The following dialogue uses the **ay** sentence form. Notice how the arrangement of the subject and predicate change:

MIGUEL : **Ang kapihan <u>ay</u> malinis kahit ang mga mesa at silya <u>ay</u> luma.**
The cafe is clean even if the tables and chairs are old.

CHRIS : **Ang simbahan sa harap <u>ay</u> maganda.**
The church in front is beautiful.

MIGUEL   :   **Ang pinakamasarap dito <u>ay</u> ano?**
What's the most delicious item here?

JANICE   :   **Ang gusto ko <u>ay</u> malamig na kape. Ang panahon <u>ay</u> mainit.**
I want cold coffee. The weather is hot.

CHRIS   :   **Ang ensaymada dito <u>ay</u> masarap. Tayo ay mag-order ng isa!**
The *ensaymada* here is delicious. Let's order one.

There are two basic ways to form a sentence in Tagalog. These are the **subject-predicate word order** where the subject appears at the beginning of the sentence and the **inverted** or **conversational word** order where the predicate is at the beginning and the subject is at the end of the sentence (or may be omitted). Tagalog speakers tend to use the inverted or conversational word order more often in everyday speech.

> **Note on this edition:** Many of the sentence examples in this revised edition are in the inverted or conversational order so that Tagalog students can learn the form they will most likely use in daily conversations with native speakers. When appropriate, examples with the subject-predicate word order using the **ay** are also shown. Learners should still learn this form, since this is still widely used, especially in written Tagalog such as news articles, essays, stories, formal documents, etc.

I. THE SUBJECT-PREDICATE SENTENCE ORDER

A sentence is in this order when the subject is the most important element in the sentence and it comes first within the sentence. In this order, the word **ay** (which can correspond to the English *is* and *are*) is used.

1. **Ang bahay ay malaki.**
   The house is big.
2. **Si Peter ay mabait.**
   Peter is good.
3. **Sina Peter at Mary ay mga bata.**
   Peter and Mary are children.
4. **Ang bata ay kumakain.**
   The child is eating.
5. **Ang babae at ang lalaki ay nagluluto.**
   The woman and the man are cooking.

The emphasis in this type of sentence is on the subject—meaning that the speaker wishes to focus attention on the subject. The word **ay** in sentences 1, 2, and 3 links the subject to what is said about the subject and is used here as a linking verb. The **ay** in sentences 4 and 5 is a helping verb that accompanies the principal verb, which represents the chief action in the sentence.

II. THE INVERTED OR CONVERSATIONAL SENTENCE ORDER

A sentence is in the inverted or conversational word order when the predicate comes at the beginning of the sentence before the subject. The word **ay** is not used in the inverted or conversational word order sentence. Much of daily speech uses this format.

1. **Malaki ang bahay.**
   Big, the house is. (The house is big.)
2. **Kumakain ang bata.**
   Eating, the child is. (The child is eating.)
3. **Mabait si Peter.**
   Good, Peter is. (Peter is good.)

The focus or emphasis in such sentences is on the predicate rather than on the subject. In inverted word order sentences having plural nouns as their subjects, the word **mga**—not **ang mga**—comes before the first nouns.

Mga bata sina Peter at Mary.	Children, Peter and Mary are.
	Peter and Mary are children.
Mga lungsod ang Maynila at Cebu.	Cities, Manila and Cebu are.
	Manila and Cebu are cities.
Mga babae sina Helen.	Women, Helen and companions are.
	Helen and companions are women.
Mga hayop ang aso't pusa.	Animals, the dog and cat are.
	The dog and cat are animals.

Note that in the last example above, the connective **at** (which means *and* in English) may be shortened to **'t** and attached to a preceding word that ends in a vowel such as **aso**.

EXERCISES

The sentences below are all in the subject-predicate order. Rewrite them in the inverted or conversational order. (Hint: Do you recognize these sentences from Lesson Four? You can simply match them here.)

1. **Si Peter ay lalaki.**

2. **Si Helen ay batang babae.**

3. **Si Ruth ay maganda.**

4. **Si Peter ay marunong.**

5. **Sina Helen at Tom ay mababait.**

6. **Sina Helen at Tom ay mga bata.**

7. **Ang bata at ang aso ay mababait.**

8. **Ang mga bata at ang mga aso ay mababait.**

9. **Ang mga sapatos ay malilinis.**

10. **Ang baro at ang sapatos ay malilinis.**

11. **Ang mga baro at ang mga sapatos ay malilinis.**

12. **Ang Estados Unidos ay malaki.**

13. **Ang Washington D.C. ay punong-lungsod ng Estados Unidos.**

14. **Ang Maynila at Washington D.C. ay mga lungsod.**

15. **Ang Baguio at Tagaytay ay malalamig na lugar.**

The list below is from the second set of exercises in Lesson Four. Change the sentences you made from this list into the subject-predicate order. Use **ay** in between the subject and predicate and the appropriate articles. Remember, this form is still widely used on TV, in the media, newspapers, literature, etc., even if it's not as common in daily speech.

SUBJECTS		PREDICATES	
babae	woman	**maganda**	beautiful
lalaki	man	**marunong**	learned
bata	child	**mataba**	fat
bahay	house	**mabait**	kind; good (of character)
bansa	nation	**mabuti**	good (of condition or quality)
tubig	water	**maliit**	small
pagkain	food	**malaki**	big
bulaklak	flower	**mainit**	hot
mesa	table	**malamig**	cold
silya	chair	**malinis**	clean
paaralan	school	**bago**	new
kotse	car	**mura**	cheap
lapis	pencil	**mahal**	dear; expensive
papel	paper	**masarap**	delicious; delightful
kape	coffee	**malusog**	healthy
isda	fish	**luma**	old (inanimate)
araw	sun; day	**matanda**	old (animate)
hangin	wind	**mataas**	high
aklat	book	**mababa**	low
simbahan	church	**mahirap**	poor; difficult

Personal and Demonstrative Pronouns

Nakita ni Janice at ng mga kaibigan niya si Robert.
Janice and her friends run into Robert.

Lumabas ang tatlong magkaibigan sa kapihan at nakita ni Janice si Robert sa kalye. Pinsan ni Janice si Robert.
The three friends left the coffee shop and Janice saw Robert in the street. Robert is Janice's cousin.

JANICE : **Robert, nandito <u>ka</u> pala!**
Robert, I didn't realize you're here!

ROBERT : **Kumusta <u>ka</u>? Sino ang mga kasama <u>mo</u>?**
How are you? Who are you with?

JANICE : **Si Miguel <u>ito</u>. Kaibigan <u>ko siya</u> sa trabaho.**
This is Miguel. He's my friend from work.

MIGUEL : **Kumusta. <u>Ito</u> si Chris.**
How is it going? This is Chris.

CHRIS : **Kapitbahay <u>ko</u> si Janice noong bata <u>kami</u>.**
Janice was my neighbor when we were kids.

JANICE : **Kumain at nagkape <u>kami</u> sa kalye Maginhawa. <u>Ikaw</u>?**
We ate and had coffee at Maginhawa Street. You?

ROBERT : **Nagsimba <u>ako</u> sa simbahang <u>iyon</u>.**
I attended mass at that church.

JANICE : **Ganoon ba? Malapit <u>iyon</u> sa kapihan.**
Is that so? That's near the cafe.

Vocabulary List

masipag = industrious
magkaibigan = friends
magkapatid = siblings
mahirap = poor
marami = plenty
naniniwala = believe

kapitbahay = neighbor
nagkape = drank/had coffee
nagsimba = attended mass
malapit = near
trabaho = work

A pronoun replaces a noun in a Tagalog sentence to make the sentence less repetitive. Two important types of Tagalog pronouns that are often used are personal pronouns (**ako, kami, tayo, ikaw, kayo, siya** and **sila**) and demonstrative pronouns (**ito, iyan** and **iyon**).

I. PERSONAL PRONOUNS

The following pronouns are nominative in form and can only be used as the subject of a verb in a sentence.

1. The personal pronoun ako (meaning *I*)

The pronoun **ako** is the equivalent of the English pronoun *I* and, when used as a subject, can come at the beginning of the sentence before the verb or, in the inverted or conversational word order, after the predicate, as in the following examples

Si John ako.	**Ako ay si John.**	I am John.
Lalaki ako.	**Ako ay lalaki.**	I am a man.
Masipag ako.	**Ako ay masipag.**	Industrious I am. (I am industrious.)
Malusog ako.	**Ako ay malusog.**	Healthy I am. (I am healthy.)

Ako is linked by **ay** to the predicate in the first two sentences above using the subject-predicate word order. Note that in this type of sentence, **ay** may be shortened to **'y** when the preceding word ends in a vowel. The shortened form **'y** is also used after **kami** (*we* including *he/she, and I*), **tayo** (*we* including *you, he/she, and I*), and other pronouns ending in vowels.

Ako'y si John.	I am John.
Ako'y lalaki.	I am a man.
Ako'y nag-aaral.	I am studying.

2. The personal pronouns kami and tayo (meaning *we* – kami as "exclusive *we*" and tayo as "inclusive *we*"; explained more below)

The pronoun *we* is expressed by **kami** and **tayo** in Tagalog. **Kami** means *we* in the sense of *he/she and I* excluding the person spoken to, whereas **tayo** means *we* in the sense of *you, he/she and I,* or *you and I* ("you" as the person spoken to).

Sina John at Helen kami.	We are John and Helen.
Kami'y magkapatid.	We are brothers and sisters.
Mababait kami.	Good we are. (We are good.)
Mahihirap kami.	Poor we are. (We are poor.)

It is important to remember that pronouns may come at the beginning of the sentence before the verb or at the end of the sentence after the predicate depending on the word order.

Sina John at Mary tayo.	We are John and Mary.
Magkaibigan tayo.	We are friends.
Mababait tayo.	Good we are. (We are good.)
Masisipag tayo.	Industrious we are. (We are industrious.)

3. The personal pronouns **ikaw** and **kayo** (meaning *you*)
The pronoun **ikaw** is used to express *you* when it is used at the beginning of the inverted or conversational word order where the subject comes after the predicate, it is shortened to **ka**.

Ikaw ay si Mary.	You are Mary.
Ikaw ay babae.	You are a woman.
Masipag ka.	Industrious you are. (You are industrious.)
Malusog ka.	Healthy you are. (You are healthy.)

Kayo is the plural form of **ikaw** excluding the speaker.

Sina John at Helen kayo.	You are John and Helen.
Magkapatid kayo.	You are brother and sister. (or siblings)
Malulusog kayo.	Healthy you are. (You are healthy.)

4. The personal pronouns **siya** and **sila** (meaning *he/she* and *they*)
The pronoun **siya** is singular meaning *he* or *she*.

Si Peter siya.	He is Peter.
Isang bata siya.	He is a child.
Marunong siya.	Intelligent he is. (He is intelligent.)
Mabait siya.	Good she is. (She is good.)

The plural form of **siya** is **sila** meaning *they*.

Sina John at Mary sila.	They are John and Mary.
Magkaibigan sila.	They are friends.
Marurunong sila.	Intelligent they are. (They are intelligent.)

In a polite or formal situation, either one of the plural pronouns **kayo** and **sila** may replace the singular pronoun **ikaw** or **ka** in sentences and questions to indicate respect (see Lesson Three on Greetings and Common Expressions.)

Guro po ba kayo?	Are you a teacher, sir/madam?
Guro po ba sila?	Are you a teacher, sir/madam?
Mabait kayo.	You (plural) are kind.

EXERCISES

Fill in the blanks with the proper pronouns in the third sentence in each set of sentences by combining the pronouns mentioned in the first two sentences. For example, the answer in the first set of sentences is the combination of **kayo** + **ako**.

1. **Bumili kayo ng pagkain. Bumili ako ng pagkain. Bumili _____ ng pagkain.**
2. **Mabait ka. Mabait siya. Mabait _____.**
3. **Nag-aral si Maria. Nag-aral si Tino. Nag-aral _____.**
4. **Ako'y naniniwala kay Delia. Sila'y naniniwala kay Delia. _____'y naniniwala kay Delia.**
5. **Nakakasulat na si Gizelle. Nakakasulat na ako. Nakakasulat na _____.**

Translate the following sentences into Tagalog:

1. We (exclusive) are studying Tagalog.
2. I am Mary. He is John.
3. We (inclusive) are clean and good.
4. They are healthy and intelligent.
5. You are a teacher. (polite)
6. You (plural) are Filipinos.
7. She is playing. (**naglalaro**)
8. I believe (**naniniwala**) you.

II. THE DEMONSTRATIVES **ITO**, **IYAN** AND **IYON**

The English demonstrative pronouns *this* and *that* have equivalents in the Tagalog language: **ito**, **iyan**, and **iyon**.

1. The demonstrative **ito** (*this*)
The demonstrative **ito** (pronounced **i-TO**) is used to refer to a thing that is very near or close to the person speaking. It is followed by the linking verb **ay** in a subject-predicate sentence word order. The linking verb **ay** may be shortened to **'y** as it follows the word **ito**. In an inverted or conversational word order sentence where the predicate comes at the beginning, such as the sentence **Maliit ito**, the linking verb **ay** is dropped.

Ito ay si John.	This is John.
Ito'y si John.	This is John.
Ito'y bata.	This is a child.
Ito'y pagkain.	This is food.
Maliit ito.	This is small.
Malaki ito.	This is big.

2. The demonstrative **iyan** (*that*)
The demonstrative **iyan** (pronounced **i-YAN**) is used to refer to a thing that is near the person spoken to. It is followed by **ay** in the subject-predicate order.

Si Mary iyan. Iyan ay si Mary.	That is Mary.
Pagkain iyan. Iyan ay pagkain.	That is food.
Pagkain ni Mary iyan.	That is Mary's food.
Marami iyan. Iyan ay marami.	That is plenty.
Mainit iyan.	That is hot.

3. The demonstrative **iyon** (*that, over there*)
The demonstrative **iyon** (pronounced **i-YON**) is used to refer to a thing that is far from both the person speaking and the one spoken to.

Ilog Pasig iyon.	That is Pasig River.
Mahaba iyon.	That is long.
Malinis at mahaba iyon.	That is clean and long.
Malinis iyon.	That is clean.
Mahaba iyon.	That is long.

4. Plural forms of **ito**, **iyan** and **iyon**
Note that since Tagalog sentences follow a plurality rule and either or both the subject or predicate may be made plural, sentences containing the plural forms of **ito**, **iyan**, and **iyon** may be marked by the plural marker **ang mga**. The singular forms of **ito**, **iyan**, and **iyon** are not preceded by **ang**; but the plural forms of these words are preceded by the plural article **ang mga**. *This* and *that* thus become *these* and *those*.

Mababait ang mga ito.	These are good.
Malalaki ang mga iyan.	Those are big.
Malilinis ang mga iyon.	Those are clean.

As discussed in Lesson Four, the pluralization of both subject and predicate is optional, and will still produce correct sentences (as in the three sentences above). However, the third sentence may be restructured into **Malinis ang mga iyon** (plural subject) or **Malilinis iyon** (plural predicate).

5. *This* and *that* as modifiers
The demonstratives **ito**, **iyan**, and **iyon** can also be used as modifiers to point out or specify the subject of a sentence. It is interesting to note that when used as modifiers, these demonstratives are placed before the noun and may also be repeated for emphasis before the linking verb **ay** in a subject-predicate sentence (see first example) or at the end of an inverted or conversational word order sentence (see

second example below). Either sentence structure is acceptable but the first one is more formal and the second is more colloquial.

Ang mesang ito ay malinis.
Itong mesang ito ay malinis.

This table is clean.

Malaki ang bahay na iyon.
Malaki iyong bahay na iyon.

That house is big.

Maganda ang suot mong iyan.
Maganda iyang suot mong iyan.

Your clothes are beautiful.

Observe the use of **-ng**, **-g** and **na** in the following phrases:

ito<u>ng</u> mesa<u>ng</u> ito
iyang suot mo<u>ng</u> iyan
iyong bahay <u>na</u> iyon

In these phrases, the connective **-ng** is attached to the modifier **ito**, the noun **mesa**, and the pronoun **mo**; the connective **-g** is attached to the modifiers **iyan** and **iyon**; and the connective **na** comes after the noun **bahay**.

The purpose of these three connectives or ligatures, to be discussed in the next lesson is to connect the following:
— a demonstrative and a noun (**ito<u>ng</u> mesa, iyang suot, iyong bahay**)
— a noun and a demonstrative (**bahay <u>na</u> iyon, mesa<u>ng</u> ito**)
— a possessive pronoun and a demonstrative (**mo<u>ng</u> iyan**)

In a sentence containing the demonstratives **ito**, **iyan**, and **iyon** and the marker **sa** (which means *in*, *at*, *on* or *to*, and is used to denote the location of an action), the demonstratives **ito**, **iyan**, or **iyon** always appear after the noun at the end of the sentence.

Kumain ang bata <u>sa mesang ito</u>.	The child ate <u>on this table</u>.
Pumunta kami <u>sa bahay na iyan</u>.	We went <u>to that house</u>.
Sumakay sila <u>sa bus na iyon</u>.	They rode <u>on that bus</u>.

EXERCISES

You are in front of the class behind the teacher's desk pointing out where things are in the classroom. Show where the following things are by filling in the blanks below with the proper singular or plural forms of the demonstratives **ito**, **iyan**, or **iyon**.

1. _____ **ang aking lamesa.** (table)

2. (Pointing to a student's seat) **Upuan ng estudyante** _____.

3. **Nasa likod** (at the back) **ang malaking pisara** (blackboard). **Susulatan ko** _____ **ng mga takdang-aralin** (homework).

4. **Nasa kanan** (to the right) **ang mga libro. Babasahin natin** _____.

5. **Nasa kaliwa** (to your left) **ninyo ang mga bintana. Palaging nakabukas** _____. (always open)

Make five sentences each using **ito**, **iyan**, and **iyon** following the sample sentence patterns given.

1. **Ito** as the subject at the end of the sentence.
   Sentence pattern: **Aklat ko ito.** This is my book.

2. **Iyan** as the subject at the end of the sentence.
   Sentence pattern: **Bahay na malaki iyan.** That is a big house.

3. **Iyon** as the subject at the end of the sentence.
   Sentence pattern: **Paaralan ko iyon.** That is my school.

Make five sentences with **ito**, **iyan**, and **iyon** as a modifier of a subject in both subject-predicate and inverted or conversational word order sentences.

Sentence patterns:
Ang aklat na ito ay mabuting basahin.   This book is good to read.
Mabuti ang aklat na ito.

Words That Link and Describe

Pagbalik sa trabaho sa Lunes
Returning to work on Monday

Tapos na ang Sabado at Linggo. Babalik na sa trabaho sina Chris, Janice, Miguel at Olivia Sy. Nagtuturo si Chris sa elementarya. Nagtatrabaho sa malaking korporasyon sina Janice, Miguel at Olivia.

The weekend is done. Chris, Jance, Miguel and Olivia Sy will go back to work. Chris teaches at an elementary school. Janice, Miguel and Olivia work in a big corporation.

OLIVIA : **Masipag na manedyer si Olivia. Mabilis na kakain dahil maaga ang pulong niya.**
Olivia is an industrious manager. She'll eat quickly because her work meeting is early.

CHRIS : **Papasok sa malaking paaralan si Chris. Isa siyang mahusay na guro.**
Chris will work at a big school. She's a great teacher.

JANICE : **Sasakay sa lumang bus si Janice papunta sa trabaho. May sariwang prutas siya sa bag.**
Janice will ride on an old bus to go to work. She has fresh fruit in her bag.

MIGUEL : **Huli na naman si Miguel. Binatang puyat kasi.**
Miguel is late again. He's a sleep-deprived bachelor, that's why.

Kasama nila ang maraming tao sa maingay at matrapik na Maynila ngayong Lunes.
They're with a lot of people in a noisy and congested Manila this Monday.

Vocabulary List

mapagbigay = generous	**masipag** = hardworking
hangal = fool	**mabilis** = fast
pagod = tired	**maaga** = early
inapi = maltreated	**pulong** = meeting
sariwa = fresh	**malaki** = big
maasim = sour	**sariwa** = fresh
tahimik = quiet	**binata** = single man
malinaw = clear	**puyat** = sleep-deprived
matapang = brave	**maingay** = noisy
bundok = mountain	

A peculiar but noteworthy feature of the Tagalog language is the use of connectives or ligatures to "link together" two adjacent words. The ligature suffixes **-ng** and **-g** are attached to the end of the first word in a sequence whereas the ligature word **na** is placed between the two words.

These ligatures have no particular meaning of their own, but merely indicate that there is a close relationship between the two words and that, generally, one modifies the other.

I. THE RULES FOR USING EACH TYPE OF LIGATURE

1. The suffix ligature **-ng**
The ligature **-ng** is attached as a suffix to the end of words that end in vowels.

Isang paaralan ang malaking bahay.	(**malaki** + **-ng** + **bahay**)
The big house is a school.	big house
Marunong ang batang mabait.	(**bata** + **-ng** + **mabait**)
The good child is intelligent.	good child

2. The suffix ligature **-g**
The ligature **-g** is attached as a suffix to the end of words that end in the consonant **n**.

Mapagbigay ang mayamang lalaki.	(**mayaman** + **-g** + **lalaki**)
The rich man is generous.	rich man
Malamig ang hanging malakas.	(**hangin** + **-g** + **malakas**)
The strong wind is cold.	wind strong

3. The ligature **na**
The ligature word **na** is used after words that end in consonants other than **n**.

Kumain siya ng <u>maasim na mangga</u>.	(**maasim** + **na** + **mangga**)
He/She ate a sour mango.	sour mango
Maganda ang <u>tahimik na bata</u>.	(**tahimik** + **na** + **bata**)
The quiet child is beautiful.	quiet child

Note that the above sequences are made up of adjective + noun or noun + adjective. In a series of more than one adjective before a noun, only the last adjective has a ligature, for example, **mabait at masunuring aso.**

II. OTHER WORD SEQUENCES THAT NEED LIGATURES

1. Noun + noun

Natulog ang <u>batang babae</u>.	The <u>young girl</u> slept.
<u>Matandang lalaki</u> ang lolo ko.	My grandfather is an <u>old man</u>.

2. Noun + verb (or verb + noun)

Binaril ang <u>ibong lumilipad</u>.   The flying bird was shot.
Binaril ang <u>lumilipad na ibon</u>.

3. Adjective + verb (or verb + adjective)

<u>Pagod na dumating</u> si tatay sa bahay.   My father arrived home tired.
<u>Dumating na pagod</u> si tatay sa bahay.

4. Verb + adverb (or adverb + verb)

<u>Kumaing mabilis</u> si Pablo.   Pablo ate quickly.
<u>Mabilis na kumain</u> si Pablo.

5. Noun + adverb (or adverb + noun)

Iwasan ang <u>pag-aaway na matagal</u>.   Avoid the long feud.
Iwasan ang <u>matagal na pag-aaway</u>.

6. Adjective + adverb (or adverb + adjective)

<u>Mahal na totoo</u> ang relo mo.   Your watch is truly expensive.
<u>Totooong mahal</u> ang relo mo.

7. Conjunction + adverb

<u>Samantalang wala</u>, magtiis tayo.   While [we have] none, let us be
                                                  patient.
<u>Sakaling dumating</u>, paghintayin ang   If he/she comes, make the
  mensahero.   messenger wait.

However, the conjunctive **kung** (which means *if*) does not need a ligature.

Kung wala pa ako, mauna na kayo.   If I am not around yet, you may
                                              go ahead.

8. Verb + verb

<u>Hinayaang umalis</u> ang bata.   The child was allowed to leave.
<u>Namatay na lumalaban</u> ang sundalo.   The soldier died fighting.

Exceptions to this rule include the following:

a. Verb-verb sequences that result in an adjectival expression

Mamatay-mabuhay ang relo ko.   My watch stops periodically.
                                          (literally, dies and lives)

b. Helping verb and main verb sequences

Ayaw kumain ng maysakit.   The sick person does not want to eat.

9. Adverb + adverb sequences where the adverb is repeated for emphasis

<u>**Gabing-gabi**</u> **na siya umuwi.**   He/She came home very late.
<u>**Bukas na bukas**</u> **talaga ay babalik ako.**   I shall certainly return tomorrow.

10. Adjective + adjective sequences where the adjective is repeated to create a
     superlative

<u>**Malinaw na malinaw**</u> **ang utos niya.**   His/her command is very clear.
<u>**Mabait na mabait**</u> **ang guro ko.**   My teacher is very kind.

11. Noun + pronoun (or pronoun + noun)

Akin ang <u>**bahay na iyan**</u>**.**   <u>That house</u> is mine.
Ito ang <u>**aking lupa**</u>**.**   This is <u>my land</u>.

An exception to this sequence is the noun + possessive pronoun (**ko**, **namin**,
nila and others) combination as the possessive pronoun changes forms when it is
placed after nouns. Examples include **aklat ko**, **bahay namin**, and **lupa nila**.

12. Pronoun + adjective (or adjective + pronoun)

<u>**Ikaw na marunong**</u> **ay magsalita.**   <u>You who are learned</u> should speak.
Umiiyak ang <u>**hangal**</u> **na ito.**   <u>This fool</u> is crying.

An exception to the pronoun + adjective or adjective + pronoun sequence is
the adjective + nominative pronoun sequence. A nominative pronoun such as **ka**
and **kayo** is a personal pronoun (see Lesson Six) that can be used as the subject
of a sentence.

Marunong ka.   You are intelligent (or learned).
Mababait kayo.   You (plural) are kind.

13. Verb + pronoun (or pronoun + verb)

Tatawaging ano ang bata?	By what name shall the child be called?
Natuto tayong <u>kanilang inapi</u>.	We, whom they maltreated, learned.

 The verb + pronoun (or pronoun + verb) sequence below is the exception to the list of rules as most combinations of this type do not need ligatures, such as:

Liligaya tayo.	We shall be happy.
Kinuha ko ito.	I took this.

14. Pronoun + pronoun

Kinuha ninyo <u>yaong amin</u>.	You took that which is ours.
Natuto <u>tayong kanilang</u> inapi.	We, whom they maltreated, learned.

(**<u>kanilang inapi</u>** is also an example of a pronoun + verb sequence)

 Exceptions to the above sequence include those in sentences in the subjunctive mood (see the first sentence) as well as two successive pronouns that form a complete sentence by themselves.

Kung <u>ako</u> [ay] <u>ikaw</u>, aalis ako.	If I were you, I will leave.
Kaniya ito.	This is his/hers.

 Observe that, generally, the exceptions in the last four sequences contain either a possessive personal pronoun that comes after a noun such as **ko**, **mo**, **niya**, **namin**, **natin**, **ninyo**, **nila** or a nominative personal pronoun (see list in Lesson Six) that changes form when used in an inverted or conversational word order sentence such as **ka**, **kayo**, **kami**, **tayo**, **siya**, and **sila**. Some sequences not mentioned above also do not need a ligature and these will be pointed out later.

 Also note that changing the sequence of nouns, adjectives, verbs and adverbs does not change the meaning of the phrases or the position of the ligatures, which still come after the first word. And the resulting sequences still follow the rules for using the ligatures **-ng**, **-g**, and **na**.

batang babae or **babaeng bata**	young girl
matabang lalaki or **lalaking mataba**	fat man
ibong lumilipad or **lumilipad na ibon**	flying bird
pagod na dumating or **dumating na pagod**	arrived tired
kumaing mabilis or **mabilis na kumain**	ate quickly
matagal na pag-aaway or **pag-aaway na matagal**	long feud
mahal na totoo or **totoong mahal**	truly expensive

Below are more examples of subjects and modifiers:

NOUNS		MODIFIERS	
binata	bachelor	marami	many; much
dalaga	unmarried woman	masipag	industrious
damit	cloth; dress	mabilis	fast
gabi	night	marumi	dirty
araw	day; sun	madilim	dark
gamot	medicine	luto	cooked
gulay	vegetable	mayaman	rich
guro	teacher	mahusay	efficient
ibon	bird	sariwa	fresh
isda	fish	payat	thin
lamok	mosquito	mataba	fat
tubig	water	maitim	black
pagkain	food	maputi	whitish
dagat	sea	matapang	brave
langit	sky	maingay	noisy
bundok	mountain	tahimik	quiet
dahon	leaf	tamad	lazy
bulaklak	flower	matamis	sweet (food)

EXERCISES

Give the formula for attaching ligatures to the following pairs of words. The first one has been given as an example.

1. rich man

   mayamang lalaki (mayaman + -g + lalaki)
   lalaking mayaman (lalaki + -ng + mayaman)

2. clean food

   _____

   _____

3. poor woman

   _____

   _____

4. dirty shoes

   _____

   _____

5. strong boy

   _____

   _____

From the nouns and the descriptive words in the previous page, construct 15 sentences in the inverted word order. Use the words in the second column as modifiers of the subjects, not as predicates. This is to practice the correct use of ligatures. Note that in the inverted or conversational order, there is no **ay**.

Translate each of the following pairs of English words into Tagalog in two different ways (noun + adjective, then adjective + noun) and use them in sentences.

fresh fish	new dress	pretty girl
small child	good teacher	small flower
noisy Manila		

Words That Show Possession

May bagong estudyante.
There's a new student.

Magkaklase sina Antonio, Marta at Ricky. Nag-uusap sila sa recess. Bagong estudyante si Ricky.

Antonio, Marta and Ricky are classmates. They're talking at recess. Ricky is a new student.

ANTONIO : **Ako si Antonio.**
My name is Antonio.

MARTA : **Ako si Marta.**
My name is Marta.

RICKY : **Ako si Ricky. Galing ako sa Bulacan.**
I am Ricky. I came from Bulacan.

ANTONIO : **Bakit ka lumipat sa Maynila?**
Why did you transfer to Manila?

RICKY : **Mas malapit <u>ang trabaho ng tatay ko dito</u>. Malayo ang bahay namin sa Bulacan.**
My father's work is nearer here. Our house in Bulacan is far.

MARTA : **Bago <u>ang mga libro ni Ricky</u>!**
Ricky's books are so new!

RICKY : **Oo, kasi nagsimula ako kahapon.**
Yes, since I started yesterday.

ANTONIO : **Masarap <u>ang meryenda ng nanay ko</u>. Gusto ninyo ba?**
My mom's snack is delicious. Would you like some?

MARTA : **Hindi na. Mag-aaral pa ako. Mahirap <u>ang mga eksamen ni Ms. Castro</u>.**
No, thank you. I will study more. Ms. Castro's tests are difficult.

Vocabulary List

damit = clothes
kotse = car
gamot = medicine
pagkain = food
luma = old
paaralan = school
malamig = cold

madumi = dirty
galing sa = from
lumipat = transfer
mga libro = books
meryenda = snack
mag-aaral = will study
mahirap = difficult (also, financially poor)

Certain words in Tagalog are used to indicate possession. These include the words **ni** and **ng**; possessive pronouns such as **akin**; as well as **nito**, **niyan** and **niyon**, which are the possessive counterparts of the demonstratives *this* and *that*.

I. THE POSSESSIVE WORDS **NI** AND **NG**

To indicate ownership, the possessive word **ni** is placed before a proper noun such as Maria or Pedro while the word **ng** is placed before a common noun such as **guro** (*teacher*) or **babae** (*woman*). **Ni** and **ng** both mean *of* in English. Note that in Tagalog sentences, the object that is possessed must always come before the owner as in the following examples:

ang bahay ni Maria	the house of Maria or Maria's house
ang baro ni Juan	the shirt of Juan or Juan's shirt
ang lapis ni Helen	the pencil of Helen or Helen's pencil
ang sapatos ni Berto	the shoes of Berto or Berto's shoes
ang aklat ni Paulo	the book of Paulo or Paulo's book
ang bahay ng lalaki	the house of the man or the man's house
ang baro ng sanggol	the dress of the baby or the baby's dress
ang lapis ng guro	the pencil of the teacher or the teacher's pencil
ang sapatos ng bata	the shoes of the child or the child's shoes
ang aklat ng babae	the book of the woman or the woman's book

Based on the plurality rule, when the owner or the thing that is possessed is more than one, the plural forms of **ni** and **ng** are used. The plural form of **ni** is **nina** while that of **ng** is **ng mga**.

ang bahay nina Maria at Pedro	the house of Maria and Pedro
ang lapis nina Helen	the pencil of Helen and company
ang bahay ng mga lalaki	the house of the men
ang mga damit ng mga bata	the clothes of the children

EXERCISES

Give four things or qualities possessed by a mother (**ina**), qualities possessed by a book (**libro**), and things or qualities possessed by a man named Juan. Afterwards, give the plural forms for #1–8.

1. _____ ina

2. _____ ina

3. _____ **ina**

4. _____ **ina**

5. _____ **libro**

6. _____ **libro**

7. _____ **libro**

8. _____ **libro**

9. _____ **Juan**

10. _____ **Juan**

11. _____ **Juan**

12. _____ **Juan**

II. THE POSSESSIVE PRONOUNS **AKIN**, **IYO**, **KANIYA**, ETC.

The following possessive pronouns are used in Tagalog:

Table 1. List of possessive pronouns

	Singular	Plural
First person	**akin** (*my*)	**amin** or *our* in the sense of *his/her and mine* (excluding the person spoken to) **atin** or *our* in the sense of *yours, his/her and mine* (including the speaker and person spoken to)
Second person	**iyo** (*your*)	**inyo** (*your*)
Third person	**kaniya** (*his/her*)	**kanila** (*their*)

These possessive pronouns are used either (1) before a noun or (2) after a noun. When the pronouns are used before a noun, note that the ligatures **-ng**, **-g** and **na** are needed. Possessive pronouns placed after the noun change their forms as seen in the examples below.

1. **Akin(g)** becomes **ko** when placed after the noun.
   Malaki ang aking bahay.   My house is big.
   Malaki ang bahay ko.

2. **Iyo(ng)** becomes **mo** when placed after the noun.
   Bago ang iyong baro.   Your dress is new.
   Bago ang baro mo.

3. **Kaniya(ng)**, which may be shortened to **kanya**, becomes **niya** when placed after the noun.
   Malinis ang kaniyang sapatos.   His/Her shoes are clean.
   Malinis ang sapatos niya.

4. **Amin(g)** (or *his/her and mine*) becomes **namin** when placed after the noun.
   Luma ang aming kotse.   Our car is old.
   Luma ang kotse namin.

5. **Atin(g)** (or *yours, his/her, and mine*) becomes **natin** when placed after the noun.
   Malaki ang ating bahay.   Our house is big.
   Malaki ang bahay natin.

6. **Inyo(ng)** becomes **ninyo** when placed after the noun.
   Masipag ang inyong ama.   Your father is industrious. (plural)
   Masipag ang ama ninyo.

7. **Kanila(ng)** becomes **nila** when placed after the noun.
   Mahaba ang kanilang lapis.   Their pencil is long.
   Mahaba ang lapis nila.

Remember the following changes when pronouns are placed after nouns:

Table 2. Changes in possessive pronouns

	Singular	Plural
First person	**akin** becomes **ko**	**amin** becomes **namin** **atin** becomes **natin**
Second person	**iyo** becomes **mo**	**inyo** becomes **ninyo**
Third person	**kaniya** becomes **niya**	**kanila** becomes **nila**

In cases where two pronouns are used in a sentence, a combination of the two styles (possessive pronouns used before and after the nouns) instead of only one style for both pronouns, will produce a better sentence. For example, the sentence *Her mother went to her house* uses the pronoun *her* twice. Sticking to one style will produce the following awkward sentences:

Not Good: **Pumunta sa kanyang bahay ang kanyang ina.**
Not Good: **Pumunta sa bahay niya ang ina niya.**

The two sentences above use similar possessive pronouns, thus producing redundant sounds of either **niya** or **kaniya**.

However, a combination of two different possessive pronouns, one placed before the first noun and another placed after the second noun, will produce better sounding sentences.

Good: **Pumunta sa kanyang bahay ang ina niya.**
Good: **Pumunta sa bahay niya ang kanyang ina.**

Each sentence above uses two different versions of the possessive pronoun to avoid the repetition of either **niya** or **kanya** in the same sentence. However, the first sentence has the tongue-twisting phrase **ina niya**. The second sentence sounds better as it eliminates the phrase by pairing **ina** with **kanya** and **bahay** with **niya**. Both sentences, however, are correct.

In other words, it is better if the same form of a possessive pronoun is not used twice in the same sentence. In this case, Tagalog speakers prefer to use two different forms of the same possessive pronoun (one appearing before and one after the nouns they modify).

In the case of plural nouns, the possessive personal pronouns are placed between **ang** and **mga**. Similarly, the adjectives should be in their plural forms as well.

Right: **Mababait ang <u>aking mga anak.</u>**
Wrong: **Mababait ang <u>mga aking anak.</u>**
My children are good.

EXERCISES

Fill in the blanks with the appropriate possessive pronouns.

1. **Kakulay ng _____ baro ang pitaka _____.** (*you, singular*)
   Your dress has the same color as your wallet.

2. **Pumunta sa _____ bahay ang guro _____.** (*our,* "*exclusive*" *our, i.e.*
   excludes the person spoken to.)
   Our teacher went to our house.

3. **Naghanap ang _____ anak na babae ng regalo para sa _____ kapatid
   na babae.** (*my*) My daughter looked for my gift for her sister. (literal)

4. **Mahaba ang pasensiya _____ sa _____ ama.** (*their*) They have long
   patience for their father.

5. **Ang pang-unawa _____ ay mas mahalaga sa _____ abuloy.**
   (*you, plural*) Your understanding is more important than your contribution.

Translate the following sentences into Tagalog using both the subject-predicate
word order and the inverted or conversational order.
1. The man's shoes are new.
2. Their house is big.
3. The child's dress is dirty.
4. Peter's book is clean.
5. Your food is cold.

III. THE POSSESSIVES **NITO, NIYAN** AND **NIYON**

Ito, iyan and **iyon** are similar to *this* and *that*; they indicate where an object is in
relation to the speaker. As possessives, they change into **nito** (*of this person*), **niyan**
and **niyon** (*of that person*) and point to a possession belonging to a person near or
far from the speaker or persons spoken to. When **nito, niyan,** and **niyon** are used,
the speaker assumes that the person he/she is talking to also recognizes the owner.

Note that in contrast with the preceding examples using possessive personal
pronouns, the possessives **nito, niyan,** and **niyon** are always used in the same place
after the noun, even in an inverted sentence.

> **Ang bahay nito ay malaki.**
> **Malaki ang bahay nito.**
> The house of this (person) is big.
> (Owner of house is near the speaker)

Ang bahay niyan ay maliit.
Maliit ang bahay niyan.
The house of that (person) is small.
(Owner of the house is near the person spoken to)

Ang bahay niyon ay maliit.
Maliit ang bahay niyon.
The house of that (person) is small.
(Owner of the house is far from the persons talking)

As previously mentioned in Lesson Four, Tagalog sentences follow the plurality rule. In the case of possessive pronouns, their plural forms are formed by adding **ng mga** to the demonstratives **ito**, **iyan**, **iyon**; and not to the possessives **nito**, **niyan** and **niyon**. As **ng** is already a possessive word, **ng mga niyan**, for example, is both wrong and redundant.

ang bahay ng mga ito	the house of these people
ang bahay ng mga iyan	the house of those people
ang bahay ng mga iyon	the house of those people

EXERCISES

Translate the following sentences into Tagalog using the inverted or conversational word order to indicate that the owner is near, far from the listener, and far from both you and the listener. Follow the sentence patterns of the first sentence.

1. Robert's dog is intelligent.
   Matalino ang aso nito.
   Matalino ang aso niyan.
   Matalino ang aso niyon.

2. The baby's medicine is effective (**mabisa**).
3. The girl's dress is pretty.
4. Peter's book is clean.
5. Her school is big.
6. The man's shoes are new.

Convert all your Tagalog sentences above into subject-predicate sentences. Remember to use **ay** to separate your subject and predicate.

LESSON NINE

Asking Questions

Sa Palengke
At the Market

Nagpunta sa palengke sina Janice at Chris. Magkakaroon sila ng munting salu-salo para sa mga kaibigan nila. Gusto nilang bumili ng mga sariwang prutas at gulay sa palengke.

Janice and Christ went to the market. They will have a small party for their friends. They want to buy fresh fruits and vegetables in the market.

JANICE : **<u>Saan</u> ba galing ang mga mangga ninyo?**
Where do your mangoes come from?

TINDERO : **Sa Pangasinan ho.**
From Pangasinan, ma'am.

CHRIS : **Matamis <u>ba</u> ang mga ito?**
Are these sweet?

TINDERO : **Matamis ho.**
They're sweet, ma'am.

CHRIS : **Bibili <u>ba</u> tayo ng pakwan?**
Are we buying watermelon?

JANICE : **Oo, gustong-gusto ko ang pakwan.**
Yes, I like watermelon very much.

CHRIS : **<u>Paano ba</u> malalaman kung hinog ang pakwan?**
How will one know if the watermelon is ripe?

CHRIS : **Sa tunog. Hinog ang mga ito.**
With its sound. These here are ripe.

TINDERO : **<u>Ilan</u> ho ang gusto ninyo?**
How many would you like?

JANICE : **Dalawa lang. <u>Magkano</u> ang lahat?**
Just two. How much for everything?

TINDERO : **Dalawang daan ho para sa lahat.**
Two hundred for all these, ma'am.

CHRIS : **Heto ang bayad. Salamat.**
Here's the payment. Thank you.

Vocabulary List

malaman = to know	**galit** = angry	**matamis** = sweet
gusto = to like	**dumating** = arrived	**pakwan** = watermelon
nakatira = live/reside	**tao** = person	**malalaman** = will know
simbahan = church	**pelikula** = movie	**bayad** = payment

I. QUESTION WORDS IN TAGALOG

There are 14 different question words in the Tagalog language that correspond to the English question words *who, what, which, how, why, when, where* and *whose*. These are:

sino	*who*	**Sino ba kayo?** Who are you?
ano	*what*	**Ano ba ang pangalan ninyo?** What is your name?
alin	*which*	**Alin ba ang iyong gusto?** Which do you like?
gaano	*how*	**Gaano kalaki ang Pilipinas?** How large is the Philippines? (requires a response expressing degree or quality)
paano	*how*	**Paano mo malalaman?** How will you know? (requires a response detailing a process)
bakit	*why*	**Bakit siya galit?** Why is he/she angry?
kailan	*when*	**Kailan kayo dumating sa Pilipinas?** When did you arrive in the Philippines?
nasaan	*where*	**Nasaan siya?** Where is he/she? (when asking for the location of a person or thing)
saan	*where*	**Saan kayo nakatira?** Where do you live? (when asking for the location of an action)
ilan	*how many*	**Ilan ang anak ninyo?** How many children do you have?
magkano	*how much*	**Magkano ang aklat?** How much is the book?
kanino	*whose*	**Kanino ang bahay na iyan?** Whose house is that?

Questions beginning with **kanino** require responses that point to **akin** (*mine*), **kaniya** (*his* or *her*), **kanila** (*their*) or other possessive pronouns.

para sa kanino	*for whom*	**Para sa kanino iyan?** For whom is that?
sa kanino	*with/to whom*	**Sa kanino iyan?** To whom does that belong?

II. THE PLURAL FORMS OF QUESTION WORDS

In Lesson Four, the pluralization of either or both the predicate and subject of a sentence has been pointed out. Plural markers such as **sina**, **nina**, **ng mga** and **ang mga** have also been introduced. Question words are not exempt from the plurality rule either.

The plural forms of these interrogatives are formed by duplicating the question words or certain syllables of the question words based on the following rules:

1. When a word is composed of two syllables, the whole word is duplicated:
    alin becomes **alin-alin**   **sino** becomes **sinu-sino**

2. When a word has three or more syllables, only the first two syllables are duplicated:
    kanino becomes **kani-kanino**   **magkano** becomes **magka-magkano**

3. The **o** in the last syllable becomes **u** in the first half of the new duplicated word.
    ano becomes **anu-ano**   **sino** becomes **sinu-sino**

The plural forms of these interrogative words are used when more than one thing is being referred to and when an answer in the plural form is expected. The interrogatives **nasaan** and **bakit** are never duplicated for the simple reason that nothing or no one can be in more than one place at the same time nor can there be more than one explanation for an event or action.

The following are examples of questions using duplicated interrogatives.

Sinu-sino ang inyong mga anak?	Which of the children are yours?
Anu-ano ang mga pangalan ninyo?	What are your names?
Kani-kanino ang mga bahay na iyan?	Whose houses are those?
Saan-saan kayo nakatira?	Where do you (plural) live?
Magka-magkano ang mga aklat?	How much are each of the books?
Ilan-ilan ang mga anak nila?	How many children do they have?

In the **ilan-ilan** question above, the speaker is referring to the total number of children of more than one couple or parent. The question may be translated to *Between those two (or three) couples (or parents), how many children do they have in all?*

Kai-kailan kayo dumating sa Pilipinas?
When (plural, referring to several dates) did you (plural) arrive in the Philippines?

Note that **kai-kailan** *is* very infrequently used nowadays and is mostly confined in rural Tagalog areas or regions.

III. CONTRACTED FORMS OF QUESTIONS

Contracted and shortened forms of a word or two words together are very common in spoken Tagalog, as in English. In the case of interrogatives, ligatures may produce another version of a question. Both **iyan** and **ito** may also be shortened to **'yan** and **'to**. They lose the stresses on the second syllable as both become mono-syllabic modifiers. Note the differences in the following Tagalog questions.

Sino ang taong iyan?	Who is that person?
Sinong tao iyan?	
Sino 'yan?	Who is that (person)?
(Speaker is pointing to someone)	

Kanino ang aklat na ito?	Whose book is this?
Kaninong aklat ito?	
Kanino 'to?	Whose (book) is this?
(Speaker is pointing to or holding a book)	

Ano ang simbahang iyan?	What church is that?
Anong simbahan iyan?	
Ano 'yan?	What (church) is that?
(Speaker is pointing to a church)	

IV. COMMON EVERYDAY QUESTIONS

Other common questions aside from the ones mentioned above that need to be committed to memory are the following. Note the presence of **ba** (the use of **ba** is discussed in the next lesson) in these questions.

Kilala mo ba siya?	Do you know her/him?
Sasama ka ba?	Are you coming along?
Gusto mo ba ito?	Do you like this?

Uuwi ka na ba?	Are you going home already?
Gusto mo bang manood ng sine?	Do you like to watch a movie?
Tama ba ito?	Is this correct?
Tama ba ako?	Am I right?
Ano ba 'yan?	What's that?
Ano'ng gusto mo?	What do you like?
Saan ka pupunta?	Where are you going?
Sino ba siya?	Who's she/he?
Nasaan siya?	Where's she/he?

EXERCISES

Answer the first seven questions from the previous page with complete sentences. The *yes* and *no* responses have been preselected.

1. **Oo,** _____.

2. **Hindi,** _____.

3. **Oo,** _____.

4. **Hindi,** _____.

5. **Oo,** _____.

6. **Hindi,** _____.

7. **Oo,** _____.

Create fictional answers to these questions.

1. **Ano ba 'yan?**	What's that?
2. **Ano ang gusto mo?**	What do you like?
3. **Saan ka pupunta?**	Where are you going?
4. **Sino ba siya?**	Who's she/he?
5. **Nasaan siya?**	Where's she/he?

LESSON TEN

The Question Word **Ba**

Sa salu-salo nina Janice at Chris
At Janice's and Chris's party

JANICE : <u>Kailan</u> darating ang mga bisita?
When will the guests arrive?

CHRIS : Dumating na sina Robert at Miguel.
Robert and Miguel have arrived.

JANICE : Tuloy kayo. Gutom ba kayo? <u>Anong</u> gusto ninyo?
Come in. Are you hungry? What would you like?

MIGUEL : May malamig na Coke <u>ba</u>? Busog pa ako. Mamaya ako kakain.
Is there cold Coke? I'm still full. I'll eat later.

CHRIS : Oo, may Coke kami. Gusto mo <u>ba</u> ng yelo?
Yes, we have Coke. Would you like some ice?

MIGUEL : Sige, salamat. <u>Nasaan</u> si Robert?
Sure, thank you. Where's Robert?

JANICE : May kausap sa telepono.
He's on a phone call with someone.

CHRIS : <u>Sino</u> ang kausap?
Who is on the phone with him?

JANICE : Kapatid niya ang kausap niya.
He's talking with his sibling.

Vocabulary List

aalis = is/are leaving
magkano = how much
kaibigan = friend
matapang = brave
kasama = companion
magsalita = to speak up
radyo = radio
marumi = dirty
darating = will arrive

dumating = arrived
kapatid = sibling
busog = full (with food)
gutom = hungry
mamaya = later
telepono = telephone
yelo = ice
tuloy = come in

Certain words unique to the Tagalog language give a particular meaning or sentiment that a speaker may wish to convey in his/her sentences and questions. These words spice up the language. Curiosity, frustration, irritation and other emotions pepper everyday Tagalog speech and a learner of this language will do well to understand these nuances.

One example is the question word **ba**. The word has no specific meaning and cannot be translated in English except that it serves as a spoken question mark to indicate clearly that the speaker is asking a question.

Questions do not necessarily need **ba** but without the **ba**, a question may be mistaken for a statement, especially when pronounced wrongly, as in the following examples:

Aalis na sila.	They will leave now.
Aalis na ba sila?	Are they leaving now?
	(Remember to raise the tone of voice at the end of a question to differentiate it from a statement.)

The question above written as **Aalis na ba sila?** emphasizes that the action **aalis** as being confirmed or awaited by the speaker. In **Sila ba ay aalis na?**, which is the subject-predicate order, the focus is on the subject, which is **sila**, rather than on the action of leaving.

What are the rules for using **ba**?

1. To change a sentence in the subject-predicate word order into a question, place **ba** immediately after the subject and just before **ay**. The sequence **ba + ay** is then often shortened into **ba'y**.

Sila ay aalis na.	They will leave already.
Sila ba ay aalis na?	Are they leaving now?
Sila ba'y aalis na?	
Ang babae ay mabait.	The woman is good.
Ang babae ba ay mabait?	Is the woman good?
Ang babae ba'y mabait?	
Si Pedro ay marunong.	Pedro is intelligent.
Si Pedro ba ay marunong?	Is Pedro intelligent?
Si Pedro ba'y marunong?	

2. To change a sentence in the inverted or conversational word order into a question, place **ba** immediately after the predicate.

Aalis sila.	They will leave.
Aalis ba sila?	Will they leave?
Mabait ang babae.	The woman is good
Mabait ba ang babae?	Is the woman good?
Kakain ako.	I shall eat.
Kakain ba ako?	Shall I eat?

3. In questions that start with interrogatives, always place **ba** immediately after the interrogative pronoun. This sequence is not answerable by *yes* or *no* unlike the examples in the first two rules in using **ba**.

Sino ba ang kasama mo?	Who is your companion?
Ano ba ang gusto mo?	What do you like?
Saan ba kayo pupunta?	Where are you going?
Kailan ba kayo aalis?	When are you leaving?
Magkano ba ito?	How much is this?

There are cases where monosyllabic words—such as the personal pronouns **ka**, **ko**, and **mo** as well as the Tagalog particles **na**, **pa**, **din**, **daw**, **po**, **ho**, **nga**, and others—are inserted for emphasis. They follow the interrogatives and push **ba** further toward the end of the question.

Ba actually belongs to the same group as the Tagalog particles **na**, **pa**, **din**, **daw**, and others, which are optional in sentences and questions but gives emphasis to statements. The other monosyllabic particles have the following meanings:

— **Na** means *already* or *now*, and expresses finality
— **Pa** means *still, yet* or *more*
— **Din** means *too* and *also*; placed after words ending in consonants (**Ikaw din ba?** *You too?*); **rin** is placed after words ending in vowels (**Ako rin ba?** *Me too?*)
— **Daw** means *they say* or *reportedly*; expresses that the information relayed by the speaker is from another source; placed after words ending in consonants (**Ikaw daw.** *They say it is you.*); **rin** is placed after words ending in vowels (**Ako raw.** *They say it is I.*)
— **Nga** means *indeed*; also puts emphasis to the word before it

Aalis na ba sila?	Will they leave already?
Aalis ka na ba?	Will you leave already?
Maganda rin ba ang babae?	Is the woman pretty too?
Malinis daw ba ang bata?	Is the child clean as they say?
Marumi raw ba ang bata?	Is the child dirty as they say?
Marumi pa ba siya?	Is he/she still dirty?

4. In questions that start with pseudo verbs such as **gusto**, **ayaw**, **ibig**, **puwede**, **maaari**, and others, which help the main verb to express moods (see Lesson Seventeen on Pseudo Verbs), place **ba** between the pseudo verb and the main verb and attach the ligature **-ng** to **ba**.

Gusto bang kumain ng bata?	Does the child like to eat?
Ibig bang umalis ng lalaki?	Does the man like to leave?
Ayaw bang umalis ng babae?	Doesn't the woman want to leave?

However, if a pronoun comes before the main verb (usually an **-um-** or **mag-**verb, see Lesson Fourteen), the ligature **-ng** is attached to the pronouns **siya**, **kami**, **sila** and **tayo** rather than to **ba**.

Dapat ba <u>siyang</u> magsalita?	Should he/she speak?
Puwede ba akong umalis?	Can I go?
Maaari ba kaming magtiwala sa iyo?	Should we trust you?

Note that in some Tagalog-speaking provinces, **baga** is used instead of **ba**. In asking questions, raise your voice at the end if the answer is either *yes* or *no*; if not, bring down the voice at the end.

<u>**Aalis ka ba?** Oo/Hindi.</u>	Are you leaving? Yes/No.
<u>**Sino ka ba?** Ako si Mary.</u>	Who are you? I am Mary.

EXERCISES

Form questions using the following statements by inserting **ba** in the appropriate places.

1. Si Herbert ang kaibigan ko.
2. Pupunta sila sa kapilya.
3. Ako ay guro.
4. Marunong ng Tagalog si Peter.
5. Mabait na bata siya.
6. Kanila ang magagandang bahay.
7. Sila ay magsasalita sa radyo.
8. Ang mga mababait ay sina Helen at Mary.
9. Kakain ka na.
10. Mabait din si Robert.

Answer the following questions.

1. Ano ba ang inyong pangalan? (formal)
2. Saan ba kayo nakatira? (formal)
3. Sino ba ang inyong kaibigan dito? (formal)
4. Mabait ba siya?
5. Amerikano ba siya?
6. Saan-saan kayo pumunta (went)?
7. Malaki ba ang bahay nila?
8. Marunong ba si Rizal?*
9. Si Bonifacio* ba ay matapang?
10. Gusto ba ninyo sa Pilipinas?

* Jose P. Rizal (1861–1896) is the national hero of the Philippines. He is a writer, poet, physician, sociologist and nationalist, among others. Andres Bonifacio (1863–1896) is the father of the revolutionary movement called **Katipunan** and led the revolt of the masses against Spain.

Making Comparisons

Nasa mall sina Janice at Chris para bumili ng damit.
Janice and Chris are at a mall to buy a dress.

Kailangan ni Janice ng bagong damit para sa isang kasalan at tinutulungan siyang pumili ni Chris.
Janice needs a new dress for a wedding and Chris is helping her choose.

CHRIS : **<u>Maganda</u> ito sa iyo. <u>Modernong-moderno</u>.**
This looks nice on you. Very modern.

JANICE : **<u>Napakamahal</u> ng bestidang ito. May <u>mas mura</u> ba?**
This dress is very expensive. Is there something more affordable?

CHRIS : **Subukan mo ito. <u>Magkasinghaba</u> at <u>magkasingayos</u> ang dalawang damit pero <u>mas mura ito.</u>**
Try this one. The two dresses are equally long and well-made but this one is more affordable.

JANICE : **Sige ito na lang. Pumunta rin tayo sa department store.**
I'll go with this one. Let's also go in the department store.

CHRIS : **<u>Bagsak-presyo</u> ang mga sapatos. Baka makabili tayo.**
Prices on shoes were slashed. Maybe we'll find a pair.

JANICE : **Ay naku! Lumalaki ang gastos!**
Oh my! It's getting more expensive!

CHRIS : **Okay lang, basta ikaw ang <u>pinakamagandang bisita</u> sa kasal.**
That's okay, as long as you're the prettiest guest at the wedding.

Vocabulary List

makabago = modern
lalo, higit na, mas = more
pareho, gaya = similar to, like
gaya ng pusa = like a cat
modernong-moderno = very modern
napakamahal = very expensive
mas mura = cheaper
bestida / damit = dress

gastos = expense
magkasing + haba = equally long
magkasing + ayos = equally good, well-made
pinakamaganda = the most beautiful
bisita = guest
kasal = wedding

People and things have qualities or attributes that may be compared to one another. These qualities are expressed by an adjective, which can indicate if two people or things are equal or not equal, or if a person or thing has a high degree of a certain quality—if not the highest among all others.

In the Tagalog language, as in English, there are various ways of comparing things according to the different levels or degrees.

I. EQUALITY (A = B)

To express equality between two nouns (A and B) in terms of one quality, either attach the prefixes **kasing-** or **magkasing-,** which by themselves mean *as*, to the root word of an adjective; or use the words **pareho, katulad** or **gaya,** all of which mean *similar to* or *like*.

1. A is as [adjective] as B
Formula: A prefix **kasing-** + adjective + **ni** (or **ng**) B
This phrase means *as* + adjective + *as* as seen in the following examples, and the order can also be reversed with **kasing-** + adjective at the beginning of the sentence.

Kasingganda ni Elena si Maria.	Maria is <u>as beautiful as</u> Elena.
Kasinggaling ni Rizal si Bonifacio.	<u>As good as</u> Rizal, Bonifacio is. (lit.)
	Bonifacio is as good as Rizal.

2. A and B are equally [adjective]
Formula: prefix **magkasing-** + adjective
Unlike the previous formula, subjects being compared using **magkasing-** are mentioned side by side. An optional pronoun or article introducing the name or names of subject or subjects is needed if **magkasing-** is placed at the beginning of the sentence (see second and third sentences).

Magkasingganda sina Maria at Elena.	Maria and Elena <u>are equally beautiful</u>.
Magkasinggaling sina Rizal at Bonifacio.	Rizal and Bonifacio <u>are equally good</u>.
Magkasintaas kami.	We are equally tall.

Note how the following prefixes are attached to the adjectives:
a. **kasing-** or **magkasing-** is attached to roots that begin in **a, e, i, o, u, k, g, h, m, n, w,** and **y** (for example: **kasingkulot** meaning *as curly as*)
b. **kasin-** or **magkasin-** is attached to roots that begin with **d, l, r, s,** and **t** (for example: **kasindumi** meaning *as dirty as*)
c. **kasim-** or **magkasim-** is attached to roots that begins with **b** and **p** (for example: **magkasimbaho** meaning *as foul-smelling as*)

Remember also that names of people must be preceded by the articles **ni/nina** and **si/sina** while names of things or places use the articles **ng/ng mga**.

3. A is [adjective] like B
Formula: A + adjective + **pareho ni/ng, katulad ni/ng** or **gaya ni/ng** + B
These phrases mean *similar to* or *like* on their own and but translate to the first formula (*as* + adjective + *as*) when used to compare the qualities of nouns.

> **Maganda si Maria pareho ni Elena.**
> **Maganda si Maria gaya ni Elena.**
> Maria is beautiful like (as beautiful as) Elena.

II. INEQUALITY (A = B)

1. A is better than B
To express that something is better than something else, the formula is:
A + **lalong** (or **higit na** or **mas**) + [adjective] + **kaysa kay** (or **kaysa sa**) + B

The first noun is usually the one with the higher degree of quality. **Lalong** (**lalo** + the ligature **-ng**), **higit na** (**higit** + the ligature **na**) or **mas** all mean *more* while **kaysa** means *than*. Similar to the possessive words **ni** and **ng**, **kaysa kay** is followed by the name of a person while **kaysa sa** is followed by the name of a place or thing. **Kaysa sa** may be shortened to **kesa**.

> **Lalong marunong si Peter kaysa kay John.**
> **Higit na marunong si Peter kaysa kay John.**
> Peter is brighter than John.

> **Lalong masipag kaysa sa bata ang matanda.**
> **Mas masipag ang matanda kaysa sa bata.**
> The old is more diligent than the young.

2. A is worse than B
To express a lower quality or lesser degree, the formula is:
A + **hindi kasing-** + [adjective] + **ni /ng** + B

The resulting phrase *not as* [adjective] *as* means that the quality of the first noun is lower or lesser than that of the second noun.

> **Hindi kasindunong ni Peter si John.**
> **Hindi kasimbait ng anak niya ang aking anak.**

John is not as bright as Peter.
My child is not as good as his/her child.

III. INTENSIVES: A IS VERY [ADJECTIVE]

The intensive degree expresses a quality of a noun in a more forceful and emphatic way by using a phrase that starts with *very*. There are many ways to express the intensity of the qualities in Tagalog but the most common are the following:

1. By duplicating the adjective and attaching an appropriate ligature (**-ng**, **-g** or **na**):

magandang-maganda	very beautiful
matandang-matanda	very old
pangit na pangit	very ugly
masipag na masipag	very industrious

2. By attaching the prefix **napaka-** (which means *very*) to the adjective:

napakapangit	very ugly
napakasipag	very industrious
napakatanda	very old
napakaganda	very beautiful

IV. SUPERLATIVES: A IS THE MOST [ADJECTIVE]

Superlatives express the quality of something to the highest degree (the greatest, the best, the most). It uses the prefix **pinaka-** (which means *most*) attached to adjectives, resulting in such words as the following:

pinakapangit	the ugliest
pinakamalinis	cleanest
pinakamasipag	most industrious
pinakamatanda	oldest
pinakamaganda	most beautiful

EXERCISES

Compare the singing skills of two famous singers you like based on the following criteria using the different degrees of adjectives you have just learned. Use the adjectives given for each category to describe the similarity of or the differences in their skills.

1. rhythm (**indayog**)		**mabilis**	fast
2. style (**istilo**)		**makabago**	modern
3. voice (**boses** or **tono**)		**malawak**	broad
4. kind of music (**uri ng tugtugin**)		**maganda**	beautiful

Describe a quality or feature of the following nouns, using the superlative form.

1. **bahay**	house	6. **yelo**	ice
2. **babae**	woman	7. **bundok**	mountain
3. **araw**	sun	8. **ilog**	river
4. **gabi**	night	9. **radyo**	radio
5. **simbahan**	church	10. **langit**	sky

Use the following adjectives and write down examples for each of the levels discussed in this lesson.

1. **bait**
2. **taba**
3. **dunong**
4. **sama**
5. **laki**
6. **hirap**
7. **sipag**
8. **yaman**
9. **ayos**

LESSON TWELVE
Using **May** and **Mayroon**

Ano ang regalo natin sa mga ikakasal?
What's our gift to the bride and groom?

Nagpaplano ang magpinsan na si Janice at Robert tungkol sa kasal nina Anna at David. Gaganapin ito sa Tagaytay, sa labas ng Maynila.

The cousins Janice and Robert are talking about Anna and David's wedding. This will happen in Tagaytay, outside of Manila.

ROBERT : **<u>May regalo</u> ka ba para kina Anna at David?**
Do you have a gift for Anna and David?

JANICE : **<u>Wala pa</u>. Pero <u>may pangarap</u> sila na magbakasyon sa Paris, kaya magsisimula ako ng travel fund para sa kanila.**
Not yet. But they have a dream to travel to Paris so I'll start a travel fund for them.

ROBERT : **Talaga? Ang galing naman. Sasali din ako sa regalong iyan.**
Really? That's great. I'll join in that gift too.

JANICE : **Teka, paano ka pupunta sa Tagaytay? <u>Meron</u> ka bang sasakyan?**
By the way, how will you get to Tagaytay? Do you have a ride?

ROBERT : **Oo, <u>meron</u>! Sabay ka sa akin. <u>Wala</u> akong kasama.**
Yes, I do! You can go with me. I don't have anyone with me.

Vocabulary List

silid = room
bago = new
masarap = delicious
punongkahoy = trees
mayroon = has/have
wala = none

regalo = gift
pangarap = dream
magbakasyon = to go on vacation
magsisimula = will start
sasali = will join
sasakyan = vehicle

Sentences with the words **may** or **mayroon** (pronounced as **may-ro-on**) point to the existence (*there is* or *there are*) or possession (*has* or *have*) of things. Although both can mean *there is/there are* and *has/have*, the two words cannot be used interchangeably as there are certain rules to follow.

I. HOW TO USE **MAY** (THERE IS/THERE ARE, HAS/HAVE)

1. **May** is followed immediately by a noun, in either the subject-predicate or inverted or conversational order sentence, to show possession or existence (see last sentence). **May** sentences often do not explicitly mention the possessor.

   Ako ay may <u>kaibigan</u> sa Quezon City.   I have a friend in Quezon City.
   May <u>kaibigan</u> ako sa Quezon City.

   Kami ay may <u>bahay</u> sa Maynila.   We have a house in Manila.
   May <u>bahay</u> kami sa Maynila.

   May <u>tao</u> sa labas.   There is someone outside.

2. **May** is followed immediately by an adjective or numeral in either type of word order sentence, to indicate possession or existence.

   Siya'y may <u>magandang</u> bahay.   He/She has a nice house.
   May <u>dalawang</u> aso sa kulungan.   There are two dogs in the cage.

3. When referring to more than one thing in possession or in existence, **may** is followed immediately by **mga** then the noun.

   May <u>mga</u> punong-kahoy sila.   They have trees.
   May <u>mga</u> tao sa labas.   There are men outside.

4. **May** is followed immediately by a verb to indicate the existence of someone or something.

   May <u>natutulog</u> na tao sa silid.   There is a person sleeping in the room.

II. HOW TO USE **MAYROON** (HAS/HAVE)

1. **Mayroon** is followed by monosyllabic words like **ka**, **na**, **nang**, **pa**, **ba**, **din** and **daw** (see Lesson Ten for a discussion of these words). Ligatures are then attached to the monosyllabic words nearest to the nouns or adjectives. **Mayroon** may be shortened to **meron**.

Mayroon pang trabaho si Lucio.	Lucio still has a job.
Meron ka bang bagong aklat?	Do you have a new book?

2. **Mayroon** is followed by a personal pronoun such as **ako, ka, tayo, kami, kayo,** and **sila** in inverted sentences to indicate possession. The suffix ligature **-ng** is attached to these pronouns as they end in vowels. To change a **may** sentence into a **mayroon** sentence, simply rearrange the **may** + noun + possessive pronoun sequence into a **mayroon** + possessive pronoun + **-ng** sequence.

May bahay kami sa Maynila.	We have a house in Manila.
Mayroon <u>kami</u>ng bahay sa Maynila.	

3. **Mayroon** alone is an answer to a question. The word **oo** (*yes*) at the start of a sentence as well as the noun or pronoun after **mayroon** is optional.

May bagong sapatos ba si Bob?	Does Bob have a new pair of shoes?
(Oo), mayroon (siya).	(Yes), he has.

The **ma-** prefix that is attached to root words to form other words is actually a contracted form of **may**—for example, **marami** (*many*) is **may dami** (*there are many*), **mataas** (*tall*) is **may taas** (literally, *there is height*) and **malinis** (*clean*) is **may linis** (*there is clean*).

In short, with abstract nouns, **ma-** means *there is/are*. With concrete nouns, **ma-** means *having many*, such as **mabuto** (*bony*; literally, *having many bones*).

III. HOW TO USE **WALÂ** (THERE IS/THERE ARE NO, DO/DOES NOT HAVE, NONE)

To negate the existence or possession of a thing, replace **may** and **mayroon** with the word **wala**, which contradicts possession or existence. **Wala** changes *there is/are* into *there is/there are no* and changes *has/have* into *does not/do not have*. **Wala** also means *none* on its own or as a response to a **mayroon** question. To use **wala**, follow these three simple rules based on the **may** and **mayroon** rules:

1. **Wala** is usually used at the beginning of a sentence and is followed by a possessive pronoun or a monosyllabic word. The suffix ligature **-ng** is added to the pronoun or the monosyllabic word or the monosyllabic word that come after it.

Wala <u>ako</u>ng kaibigan sa Quezon.	I do not have a friend in Quezon.
Wala silang mga punong-kahoy.	They do not have trees.
Wala pang bagong aklat.	There is no new book yet.
Wala nang trabaho si Lucio.	Lucio does not have a job now (or anymore).

2. **Wala** with the suffix ligature **-ng** is used before numerals or adjectives, nouns, the article **mga** and verbs.

Walang <u>dalawang</u> aso sa kulungan.	There are no two dogs in the cage.
Walang tao sa labas.	There is no one outside.
Walang mga tao sa labas.	There are no men outside.
Walang natutulog na tao sa silid.	No one is sleeping in the room.

3. **Wala** by itself is a negative response to a question using **may** or **mayroon** and means *none*. **Hindi** (or *no*) is an incorrect answer to this type of question. **Wala** also changes a positive question into a negative one.

May bagong sapatos ba si Bob?	Does Bob have a new pair of shoes?
Wala.	None.
May kotse ba sila? Wala.	Do they have a car? None.
Mayroon ka bang pagkain?	Do you have food?
Wala ka bang pagkain?	Don't you have food?

EXERCISES

Fill in the blanks with **may**, **mayroon** or **wala**. Note that **wala** may be used in most of the sentences.

1. _____ mabait na anak ako.

2. _____ magandang bulaklak si Mary.

3. _____ bang aklat si John?

4. _____ pera ba kayo?

5. _____ damit ang batang mahirap.

6. _____ masayang Pasko ang mga tao.

7. **Ang bahay ay** _____ lamok.

8. _____ kaming masayang buhay.

9. _____ kumakaing bata sa silid (room).

10. _____ aklat ako sa Tagalog.

Translate the following sentences into Tagalog.

1. Yes, I have.
2. We have good boys and girls in school.
3. Do you have delicious food there?
4. None. We do not have delicious food.
5. I have a pretty sister.
6. They have many books in the library (**sa aklatan**).

LESSON THIRTEEN

Numbers

Sa kasalan nina Anna at David 🔊
At the wedding of Anna and David

Marami ang bisita sa kasal nina Anna at David. Masarap ang mga pagkain at nasiyahan ang lahat.

There are a lot of guests at the wedding of Anna and David. The food is delicious and everyone enjoyed themselves.

BISITA # 1 : **May mga isang daan ang bisita nila.**
They have about a hundred guests.

BISITA # 2 : **Malaki ang pamilya ni Anna. Anim ang kapatid niya.**
Anna's family is big. She has six siblings.

BISITA # 1 : **Ikailan siyang anak?**
Which child is she?

BISITA # 2 : **Ika-pito. Bunso siya.**
Seventh. She's the youngest.

BISITA # 1 : **Ilang taon sina Anna at David?**
How old are Anna and David?

BISITA # 2 : **Pareho silang tatlumpu. Panganay si David sa pamilya niya.**
They are both thirty. David is the oldest in his family.

Vocabulary List 🔊

limampu = fifty
labindalawa = twelve
una = first
kalahati = half
sandaan = one hundred
isang libo = one thousand
huli = last

ikapu = tenth
ikailan = which (in terms of order)
pamilya = family
kapatid = sibling
bunso = youngest child
panganay = eldest child
bisita = visitor/guest

When learning the Tagalog names of numbers, it is also useful to learn the Spanish ones as well (spelled according to the conventions of Tagalog phonetics) since these are still commonly used, especially among the older generations. So in this lesson, we give the Spanish equivalents of numbers if they are commonly used by Filipinos.

I. CARDINAL NUMBERS

Tagalog numbers have equivalents in Spanish (written according to Tagalog orthography) and these are commonly used by older people, especially in buying and selling.

	TAGALOG	SPANISH
1	**isa**	uno
2	**dalawa**	dos
3	**tatlo**	tres
4	**apat**	kuwatro
5	**lima**	sinko
6	**anim**	seis
7	**pito**	siyete
8	**walo**	otso
9	**siyam**	nuwebe
10	**sampu**	diyes
11	**labing-isa**	onse
12	**labindalawa**	dose
13	**labintatlo**	trese
14	**labing-apat**	katorse
15	**labinlima**	kinse
16	**labing-anim**	disiseis
17	**labimpito**	disisiyete
18	**labingwalo**	disiotso
19	**labinsiyam**	disinuwebe
20	**dalawampu**	beynte
21	**dalawampu't isa**	beynte uno
25	**dalawampu't lima**	beynte sinko
30	**tatlumpu**	treynta
36	**tatlumpu't anim**	treynta'y seis
40	**apatnapu**	kuwarenta
47	**apatnapu't pito**	kuwarenta'y siyete
50	**limampu**	sinkuwenta
55	**limampu't lima**	sinkuwenta'y sinko
60	**animnapu**	sesenta
70	**pitumpu**	setenta

TAGALOG		SPANISH
80	walumpu	otsenta
90	siyamnapu	nobenta
100	sandaan	siyento
110	sandaa't sampu	siyento diyes
200	dalawang daan	dos siyentos
300	tatlong daan	tres siyentos
400	apat na raan	kwatro siyentos
500	limang daan	kinyentos
1,000	isang libo	mil

Sample Sentences

Ang lima at anim ay labing-isa.	Five and six are eleven.
Marurunong ang dalawang kapatid ko.	My two siblings are intelligent.
Sampung tao ang umawit sa palatuntunan.	Ten people sang in the program.
May mga isang daang bata ang nag-aaral dito.	About a hundred children are studying here.
May labindalawang buwan sa isang taon.	There are twelve months in a year.
Ilang taon ka na?	How old are you?
Dalawampu't limang taon na ako.	I am 25 years old (already).

Approximate or estimated numbers may be expressed by using **mga** before a number such as **mga sampu**, which means *about ten*.

II. ORDINAL NUMBERS

An ordinal number indicates the place occupied by an item in an ordered sequence. Tagalog ordinals are easy to put together and remember. The prefix **ika-** is added to the cardinal numbers. There are a few irregularities, however—first and last are always **una** and **huli**, respectively, and the removal of the first two letters of **dalawa** and **tatlo** before attaching the prefix **ika-**.

una	first
ikalawa	second
ikatlo	third
ikaapat	fourth
ikalima	fifth
ikaanim (ikanim)	sixth
ikapito	seventh
ikawalo	eighth
ikasiyam	ninth

ikasampu	tenth
ikalabing-isa	eleventh
ikadalawampu	twentieth
ikasandaan	one hundredth
huli	last

Sample Sentences

Ikailan kang anak?	Which child are you?
Ikalima ako.	I am the fifth.
Sino ba ang una?	Who is the first?
Si Peter ang una.	Peter is the first.
Ikaw ba ay panganay?	Are you the first child?
Hindi, bunso ako.	No, I am the youngest child.
Nasa ikaanim na grado siya.	He/She is in th e sixth grade.

III. FRACTIONS

One part of a whole is expressed by adding the prefix **ka-** (shortened form of **ika-**) to the denominator (the lower number in the fraction). The word **bahagi** (meaning *part*) is often added also for clarity. The term **kalahati**, however, is a set name for *one half*.

kalahati (or **kalahating bahagi**)	one half
katlo (or **ikatlong bahagi**)	one third
kapat (or **ikapat na bahagi**)	one fourth
kalima (or **ikalimang bahagi**)	one fifth
kanim (or **ika-anim na bahagi**)	one sixth
kapito (or **ikapitong bahagi**)	one seventh
kawalo (or **ikawalong bahagi**)	one eighth
kasiyam (or **ikasiyam na bahagi**)	one ninth
kapulo (or **ikasampung bahagi** or **ikapu**)	one tenth

Bigger fractions are formed by adding a multiple in front:

dalawang-katlo	two-thirds
katlong-kapat	three-fourths

Note that the use of fractions today seems to be limited to schools and is not common in everyday speech. An exception is the word **kalahati** which can be regularly heard in markets and even in homes.

Sample Sentences

Kalahati ng mansanas ito.	This is half of an apple.
Para sa iyo ang dalawang-katlo ng aking salapi.	Two-thirds of my money is for you.
Maglagay ng tatlong-kapat ng kutsaritang asin sa pagkain.	Put three-fourths teaspoon of salt in the food.
Pareho ng dalawang-kapat ang apat na kawalo.	Four-eighths is equivalent to two-fourths.

IV. PRICES AND MONEY

Tagalog and Spanish numbers are used interchangeably in buying and selling, with sellers often giving preference to the Spanish numbers because these are faster to say to prospective buyers. This is logical as the local market scene is fast-paced. To understand market vendors better, you need to know both.

The unit of exchange in the Philippines is the *peso* or **piso** in Tagalog and coins are in *centavos* or **sentimo** or **pera**. One peso is **isang piso** or simply **piso** while the others are:

	TAGALOG	SPANISH
₱ 1.20	**isang piso at dalawampung sentimo** (or **isang piso't dalawampung sentimo**)	uno beinte
₱ 2.30	**dalawang piso't tatlumpung sentimo**	dos treinta
₱ 3.40	**tatlong piso't apatnapung sentimo**	tres kuwarenta
₱ 4.50	**apat na piso't limampung sentimo**	kuwatro sinkuwenta
₱ 5.60	**limang piso't animnapung sentimo**	sinko sesenta
₱ 6.70	**anim na piso't pitumpung sentimo**	scis sctcnta
₱ 7.80	**pitong piso't walumpung sentimo**	siyctc otscnta
₱ 8.90	**walong piso't siyamnapung sentimo**	otso nobenta
₱ 9.00	**siyam na piso**	nuwebe pesos
₱ 10.00	**sampung piso't sampung sentimo**	diyes-diyes

Sample Sentences

Nagkakahalaga ang aking sapatos ng pitong daan at limampung piso.
My pair of shoes costs seven hundred and fifty pesos.

Walong daan siyamnapu't siyam na piso at pitumpu't limang pera ang halaga ng kanyang damit.
The cost of her dress is eight hundred ninety-nine pesos and seventy-five centavos.

Dalawang libong piso ang halaga ng silya.
The chair costs two thousand pesos.

In writing Tagalog cardinals above ten, bear the following in mind:

1. The prefix **labing-** (might be a contracted form of **labis ng** or *excess of,* thus a prefix meaning *excess of ten*) is added to the cardinals **isa** (*one*) to **siyam** (*nine*) to create numbers above ten. The prefix, however, becomes **labin-** when attached to **dalawa** (*two*), **tatlo** (*three*), **lima** (*five*) and **siyam** (*nine*). The prefix becomes **labim-** when attached to **pito** (*seven*).

2. In writing tens, the particle **puo** (meaning *ten*) is added as suffix to numbers from one to nine but is written as **-pu**. For example, ten is basically **isang puo**. The ligatures **-ng** and **-g** after the cardinals are then changed to **-m** to adjust phonetically to **-pu**. Thus, **isang puo** becomes **sampu**.

3. Basically, the numbers above **siyam** (*nine*) all have ligatures as these numbers are combinations of several words. For those above **siyam** (*nine*) but below one hundred, the numbers are written as one word such as **siyamnapu** (*ninety*). On the other hand, a number word higher than a hundred is written as separate words such as **siyam na raan** (*nine hundred*). In addition, **daan** (*hundred*) is used after numbers ending in consonants or after the suffix **-ng** while **raan** is used after numbers ending in consonants or the suffix **na**.

4. The connective **at** (shortened to **'t**) is only used between the last two numbers in a series of numbers and words such as **tatlong libo sandaa't siyam** (*three thousand one hundred nine*).

5. Other numbers and their equivalents are:

ten	**puo**	hundred	**daan**
thousand	**libo**	ten thousand	**laksa**
hundred thousand	**yuta**	million	**angaw**

EXERCISES

Write down all the numbers from 1 to 30. Make sure that the rules on pages 100–101 are followed.

Tell something about yourself and focus on details that involve numbers (your age, your mother's age, the number of siblings you have, your place in the family, others), fractions (percentage of your life you have lived in a certain place, heritage, others) and prices (cost of sending you or your kids to school, others).

LESSON FOURTEEN
-Um- and Mag- Verb Forms

Sa isang pulong sa opisina
At a meeting in the office

OLIVIA : **<u>Dumating</u> ba si Miguel? Kailangan ko ang ulat para sa pulong.**
Has Miguel arrived? I need the report for the meeting.

JANICE : **Hindi pa ho. <u>Tatawag</u> ho ako sa kanya para malaman kung nasaan siya.**
Not yet, ma'am. I'll call him to know where he is.

(sa telepono) Nasaan ka? <u>Nagtatanong</u> si Ma'am Sy tungkol sa report.
Where are you? Ma'am Sy is asking about the report.

MIGUEL : **<u>Naglalakad</u> ako papunta sa elevator. Natrapik ako. <u>Nagsulat</u> ako ng mga bagong ulat sa bahay.**
I'm walking towards the elevator. I got stuck in traffic. I even wrote new reports at home.

JANICE : **Kung ako sa iyo, <u>tumakbo</u> ka na. <u>Pumunta</u> sa pulong si Ma'am Sy. <u>Nagmamadali</u> siya.**
If I were you, run. Ma'am Sy just went to the meeting. She was in a hurry.

MIGUEL : **<u>Hihingi</u> ako ng paumanhin sa kanya. <u>Mag-usap</u> tayo pagkatapos.**
I'll apologize to her. Let's talk afterwards.

Vocabulary List

magtanong = to ask a question
aral = study
uminom = drank
magsayaw = to dance
magbayad = to pay
tumawag = called
dumating = arrived
ulat = report

pulong = meeting
tatawag = will call
nagtatanong = is asking
naglalakad = is walking
tumakbo = run
nagmamadali = is hurrying
paumanhin = apology

Sentences using -um- and **mag-** verbs are generally similar to sentences in the active voice in English, where the subject is the actor although many sentences in English using the active voice would be translated by Tagalog speakers into the equivalent of the passive voice. This is because Tagalogs prefer to construct sentences in the inverted or conversational word order where the predicate containing the verb is found at the beginning of the sentence, because to them, that is the more important part of the sentence.

The most commonly used verbs in subject-focused sentences have an -um- infix or **mag-** prefix (an infix is inserted in the middle of a root word to form a new word whereas a prefix is attached at the front of the root word). These verbs emphasize the doer of the action or the act itself. These verb forms may be used in sentences that do not require an object to complete the meaning or in sentences with an object when the emphasis is on the doer

Some verb roots occur only with an -um- (an example is **alis** which means *to go*) while others occur with **mag-** alone (an example is **laba** which means *to wash*). Some occur with both (such as **hingi** which means *to ask for*) although the derivatives (the new words formed from roots and affixes) formed have different meanings. Usually, when a verb takes both forms, its -um- form expresses non-intensive or casual action (an example is **kumakain** or *is/are eating*) while its **mag-** form expresses frequency and intensity of action (an example is **nagkakakain** or *to always be eating* or *to continually be eating*). With regards to action, the -um- form expresses action toward the doer (such as **bumibili** or *is/are buying*) while the **mag-** form expresses action away from the doer (such as **magbibili** or *is/are selling*).

Forming **-Um-** and **Mag-** Derivatives

I. **-UM-** VERB FORMS

1. For verb roots beginning with vowels, attach -um- to the front of the root directly as a prefix.

   Example: **alis**   leave
   Infinitive: **umalis**   (-um- + root) to leave
   Imperative: **umalis**   (same)
   Past: **umalis**   (same) left
   Present: **umaalis**   (-um- + duplicate first syllable + root) is/are leaving
   Future: **aalis**   (duplicate first syllable + root) will leave

2. For verb roots beginning with consonants, attach -um- as an infix to the root immediately following the initial consonant.

   Example: **kain**   eat
   Infinitive: **kumain**   (infix -um- after initial consonant) to eat

Imperative: **kumain**	(same)
Past: **kumain**	(same) ate
Present: **kumakain**	(duplicated first syllable, infix **-um-** between initial consonant and succeeding vowel + root) is/are eating
Future: **kakain**	(duplicated first syllable + root) will eat

II. **MAG-** VERB FORMS

1. For verb roots beginning with vowels, attach **mag-** followed by a hyphen before the verb root. The hyphen denotes a glottal stop after **mag-**.

Example: **aral**	study
Infinitive: **mag-aral**	(**mag-** + hyphen + root) to study
Imperative: **mag-aral**	(**mag-** + hyphen + root)
Past: **nag-aral**	(change **mag-** to **nag-** + hyphen + root) studied
Present: **nag-aaral**	(**nag-** + hyphen + duplicated first syllable + root) is/are studying
Future: **mag-aaral**	(**mag-** + hyphen + duplicated first syllable + root) will study

2. For verb roots beginning with consonants, attach **mag-** in front of the root.

Example: **luto**	cook
Infinitive: **magluto**	(**mag-** + root) to cook
Imperative: **magluto**	(same)
Past: **nagluto**	(change **mag-** to **nag-**) cooked
Present: **nagluluto**	(**nag-** + duplicated first syllable + root) is/are cooking
Future: **magluluto**	(**mag-** + duplicated first syllable + root) will cook

Note that the present tense denotes habitual and ongoing action. For verbs whose first syllables have three letters such as **sampay** (*to hang something*), duplicate the first two letters only (thus, **magsasampay**).

EXAMPLES OF **-UM-** AND **MAG-** VERBS

pumunta	to go to a place
umalis	to leave
dumating	to arrive
kumain	to eat
umupo	to sit
sumulat	to write
bumasa	to read
humingi	to ask for
gumawa	to do or make something

lumangoy	to swim
umiyak	to cry
bumili	to buy
kumanta }	to sing
umawit	
tumugtog	to play an instrument
uminom	to drink
magsalita	to speak
mag-usap	to converse
magsulat	to write
magluto	to cook
mag-aral	to study
maglaro	to play
mag-away	to quarrel with one another
maglakad	to walk
magbayad	to pay
magtanim	to plant
magsayaw	to dance
mag-isip	to think
maglinis	to clean
magpunta	to go
magtanong	to ask a question
magbili	to sell

EXERCISES

Write the roots of the following **-um-** and **mag-** verbs.

magtanong	to ask a question	_____
magpunta	to go	_____
magbili	to sell	_____
umalis	to leave	_____
dumating	to arrive	_____
kumain	to eat	_____
mag-away	to quarrel with one another	_____
maglakad	to walk	_____
magbayad	to pay	_____
magtanim	to plant	_____

magsayaw	to dance	_____
mag-isip	to think	_____
maglinis	to clean	_____
umupo	to sit	_____
sumulat	to write	_____
bumasa	to read	_____
humingi	to ask for	_____
gumawa	to do or make something	_____

Affix **-um-** to the following roots.

pasok	enter	_____
balik	go back	_____
tawag	call	_____
sakay	ride	_____
tayo	stand	_____
upa	rent	_____
isip	think	_____
ulan	rain	_____
dating	arrive	_____
ibig	love	_____
tawa	laugh	_____
kuha	get	_____
uwi	go home	_____
sama	go with	_____

Sentence Patterns

There are two different sentence patterns for **-um-** and **mag-** verbs where the doer or subject occupies different positions within the sentences. In both of these patterns, the verb comes first. But in the first pattern the subject comes next whereas in the second pattern the object or modifier comes next.

I. FIRST SENTENCE PATTERN USING **-UM-** AND **MAG-** VERBS

VERB	DOER OR SUBJECT	OBJECT OR MODIFIER
1. **Kumain**	si Peter	ng kanin.

Peter ate rice.

2. **Pumasok**	ang bata	sa paaralan.

The child went to school.
(**pumasok** means *entered* but translates to *went* when used with school or office)

3. **Sumulat**	siya	ng kuwento.

He/She wrote a story.

4. **Naglakad**	si Mary	kahapon.

Mary walked yesterday.

5. **Nagluto**	sila	ng gulay.

They cooked vegetables.

II. SECOND SENTENCE PATTERN USING **-UM-** AND **MAG-** VERBS

VERB	OBJECT OR MODIFIER	DOER OR SUBJECT
1. **Kumain**	ng kanin	si Peter.

Peter ate rice.

2. **Pumasok**	sa paaralan	ang bata.

The child went to school.

3. **Sumulat**	ng kuwento	siya.

He/She wrote a story.

4. **Naglakad**	kahapon	si Mary.

Mary walked yesterday.

5. **Nagluto**	ng gulay	sila.

They cooked vegetables.

Both sentence patterns are correct but in sentences with pronouns such as **siya** and **sila** as the subject, the first structural pattern is preferred.

Sample Sentences

Dumating si Helen kahapon.	Helen arrived yesterday.
Sumusulat si Gng. Smith.	Mrs. Smith is writing.
Nagsasalita ang bata.	The child is talking.
Naglalaro ang aking mga anak.	My children are playing.
Nagluto ba kayo ng kanin?	Did you cook rice?
Bumasa tayo ng isang kuwento.	Let us read a story.
Uminom kayo ng kape.	You (plural) drink coffee.
Umiinom ng gatas ang bata.	The child is drinking milk.
	The child drinks milk.

EXERCISES

Write sentences using the **-um-** and **mag-** verbs in the imperative mood and in the three tenses (past, present, and future).

Read the following paragraphs aloud. Observe a slight pause at the end of every phrase as marked by the slanting line.

    Sina G. at Gng. Smith / ay mga Amerikano. / Dumating sila rito sa Pilipinas / noong isang buwan. / Nag-aaral ng Tagalog / sina G. at Gng. Smith /. / Nag-aaral silang magsalita / ng wika ng Pilipinas.

    May dalawang anak sila. / Peter at Mary ang mga pangalan / ng kanilang mga anak. / Sila ay magaganda / at malulusog. / Umiinom sila / ng maraming gatas / araw-araw. / Si Gng. Smith ang nagluluto / ng kanilang pagkain. / Nagluluto siya / ng gulay / at karne. / Mabuti ang gulay / para sa mga bata. / Ang gatas / ay mabuti rin. / Sina Peter at Mary / ay umiinom ng maraming gatas / araw-araw / kaya sila'y malulusog. / Sina G. at Gng. Smith / ay masasayang magulang. / Masaya rin / ang mga anak nila. /

Pick out all the action words from the two paragraphs above and give their tenses or forms.

Use the following phrases and words to make your own sentences:

1. **noong isang buwan**   last month
2. **wika**   language
3. **gatas**   milk
4. **karne**   beef
5. **kaya**   thus/so
6. **masasaya**   happy
7. **magulang**   parents

-In- Verb Forms

Ano ang <u>ginawa</u> ninyo sa museo?
What did you do at the museum?

<u>Tinatanong</u> ni Mr. and Mrs. Alvarez si Ricky tungkol sa Museo Pambata. Nagpunta ang klase ni Miss Chris Castro doon.

Mr. and Mrs. Alvarez is asking Ricky about the Children's Museum. Miss Chris Castro's class went there.

MR. ALVAREZ : **Kumusta ang Museo Pambata, Ricky?**
How was the Children's Museum, Ricky?

RICKY : **Masaya po, Itay. <u>Dinala</u> kami ni Miss Castro sa mga exhibit.**
It was fun, dad. Miss Castro took us to the exhibits.

MRS. ALVAREZ : **At pagkatapos, anong <u>ginawa</u> ninyo?**
And after, what did you do?

RICKY : **<u>Binisita</u> namin ang giftshop.**
We visited the gift shop!

MR. ALVAREZ : **Ano ang <u>binili</u> mo doon?**
What did you buy there?

RICKY : **Bumili ako ng libro. At mga pasalubong para sa inyo!**
I bought a book. And presents for you both!

MRS. ALVAREZ : **Ang ganda ng t-shirt! Salamat, anak.**
The t-shirt is great! Thank you, son.

Vocabulary List

sabihin = to tell	**dinala** = brought
baguhin = to change	**ginawa** = did
pasukin = to enter	**binili** = bought
gisingin = to awaken	**bumili** = bought
masaya = fun	**pasalubong** = gift from a trip or outing

Unlike the active **-um-** and **mag-** verbs which emphasize the doer of the action or the action itself, the **-in-** verbs are passive in the sense that they emphasize the object or receiver of the action. The receiver of the action then becomes the subject of the passive sentence. **-In-** verbs indicate an action expressed by the root on the subject without necessarily naming the doer of the action.

A similar meaning can be conveyed by an active sentence with **-um-** and **mag-** verbs (for example, **Bumasa ako ng libro** or *I read a book*) where an object is not necessary to complete the meaning (for example, **Bumasa ako** or *I read*) and by a passive form of the verb with **-in-** or its alternant **-hin** (for example, **Binasa ko ang libro** or *I read the book*).

The main difference is that in the latter, the object (**ang libro**) is necessary and cannot be omitted. And the emphasis is on the object (**ang libro**) rather than the subject (**ko**). You will find that Tagalogs generally prefer the second form using **-in-** verbs.

Forming **-In-** Derivatives

-In- verbs are formed in the following ways:

I. FOR A VERB BEGINNING WITH A VOWEL

-In- is either added at the end or the front of the root form depending on the tense.

Example: **alis**	remove
Infinitive: **alisin**	(root + suffix **-in**) to remove
Imperative: **alisin**	(root + suffix **-in**)
Past: **inalis**	(prefix **-in** + root) was/were removed
Present: **inaalis**	(prefix **-in** + root and duplicated first syllable) is/are removing
Future: **aalisin**	(duplicated first syllable + root + suffix **-in**) will remove

II. FOR A VERB WITH AN END GLOTTAL CATCH BEGINNING WITH A CONSONANT

-In- is either added at the end or after the first consonant, depending on the tense.

Example: **basa**	wet
Infinitive: **basain**	(root + suffix **-in**) to wet
Imperative: **basain**	(root + suffix **-in**)
Past: **binasa**	(infix **-in-** after initial consonant) wet
Present: **binabasa**	(duplicated first syllable, infix **-in-** between initial consonant and succeeding vowel + root) is/are wetting
Future: **babasain**	(duplicated first syllable + root + suffix **-in**) will wet

III. FOR A VERB BEGINNING WITH A CONSONANT

-In- is added after the first consonant but becomes **-hin** when added at the end of the verb.

Example: **basa**   read
Infinitive: **basahin**   (root + alternant suffix **-hin**) to read
Imperative: **basahin**   (root + alternant suffix **-hin**)
Past: **binasa**   (infix **-in-** after initial consonant) read
Present: **binabasa**   (duplicated first syllable, infix **-in-** between initial consonant and succeeding vowel + root) is/are reading
Future: **babasahin**   (duplicated first syllable + root + suffix **-hin**) will read

Conventions Used in Forming **-In-** Verbs

-In- is usually suffixed to verbs and its alternant (or variant form) **-hin** may take its place under certain circumstances. However, there are irregular cases where these conventions are ignored.

I. REGULAR VERB FORMATIONS USING **-IN-**

1. **-In-** is suffixed to
   a. a root word that ends in a consonant

   alis   = **alisin** (*to remove*)   **pasok**   = **pasukin** (*to enter*)

   b. a root word with an end glottal catch that ends in a vowel

   sira   = **sirain** (*to break*)   **puno**   = **punuin** (*to fill*)

2. **-Hin** is suffixed to a root word without a glottal catch that ends in a vowel.

   basa   = **basahin** (*to read*)   **bili**   = **bilhin** (*to buy*)
   sabi   = **sabihin** (*to tell*)

II. IRREGULAR VERB FORMATIONS USING **-IN-**

1. After verb roots with an end syllable stress, the final vowel is omitted before adding the suffix **-hin**.

   bili   = **bilhin** (*to buy*)   **dala**   = **dalhin** (*to bring*)

2. After verb roots whose last syllable is a VC or CVC syllable (see Lesson Two) containing the vowels **i** or **o**, the **i** or **o** of the last syllable is omitted before adding the suffix **-in-**.

> **kain** = **kainin** (*to eat*)   **sunod** = **sundin** (*to obey*)
> **dakip** = **dakpin** (*to capture*)

3. Before root verbs that begin with an **l**, **w** or **y**, the infix **-in-** becomes a prefix **ni-** to form the past and present tenses.

> **luto** (*cook*)   = **niluto**   **walis** (*sweep*)   = **niwalis**
> **yari** (*made of*)   = **niyari**

Note that for the infinitive, imperative and future forms of a root verb whose last syllable is CVC containing **o**, the **o** changes to **u** and follows the regular pattern.

> **gamot** (*to cure or treat*)   = **gamutin, gagamutin**
> **inom** (*to drink*)   = **inumin, iinumin**

EXAMPLES OF **-IN-** VERBS

awit	= **awitin**	to sing
luto	= **lutuin**	to cook (irregular)
sabi	= **sabihin**	to tell
sulat	= **sulatin**	to write
mahal	= **mahalin**	to love
bago	= **baguhin**	to change
laro	= **laruin**	to play
gamot	= **gamutin**	to cure
gising	= **gisingin**	to awaken
inom	= **inumin**	to drink
tawag	= **tawagin**	to call

EXAMPLES OF **-IN-** VERBS

kain	= **kainin**	to eat (irregular)
dala	= **dalhin**	to bring or carry (irregular)
patay	= **patayin**	to kill to put out light or flame (colloquial)
bati	= **batiin**	to greet
puri	= **purihin**	to praise
linis	= **linisin**	to clean
bilang	= **bilangin**	to count

Sentence Patterns for **-In-** Verbs

In sentences with **-in-** verb forms, the doer is always expressed in the possessive form such as **ni Peter, ng bata, ko, niya, iyo, kanya, akin, atin,** and **kanila**. The doer may also be **kita** (*we*), a pronoun equivalent to **ikaw** (*you*) and **ko** (*I*) exclusively.

The verb always comes first, followed immediately by the doer or subject, then the object.

ACTION	DOER/SUBJECT (in possessive form)	OBJECT

1. **Pinili**   **ng bata**   **ang aklat.**
   Was chosen   by the child   the book
   The child chose the book.
2. **Binasa**   **ko**   **ang sulat.**
   Was read   by me   the letter.
   I read the letter.
3. **Kakanin**   **ni Peter**   **ang isda.**
   Will be eaten   by Peter   the fish
   Peter will eat the fish.
4. **Ibinili**   **kita**   **ng prutas.**
   Was bought   for you by me   the fruit
   I bought you a fruit.

Sample Sentences 🔊

Aawitin ng mga bata ang Bahay Kubo.
Bahay Kubo will be sung by the children.

Ginagamot ng doktor ang aking sakit.
My sickness is being treated by a doctor.

Nilinis ni Marta ang kanilang bahay.
Their house is being cleaned by Marta.

Lulutuin ng katulong ang gulay.
The vegetables will be cooked by the helper.

Babasahin ko ang aklat ni Dr. Rizal.
The book by Dr. Rizal will be read by me.

Kakanin ba nila ang mga saging?
Will the bananas be eaten by them?

Aalisin niya ang kanyang sapatos.
His/Her shoes will e removed by him/her.

Dinadala namin ang aklat ng Tagalog sa paaralan.
The Tagalog book is brought by us to school.

Sinira ni Lucio ang papel.
The paper was torn by Lucio.

Bilangin natin ang pera.
Let the money be counted by us.

EXERCISES

Give the three tenses of each of the following verbs:

awit	**awitin**	to sing
past	_____	
present	_____	
future	_____	

luto	**lutuin**	to cook (irregular)
past	_____	
present	_____	
future	_____	

sabi	**sabihin**	to tell or say
past	_____	
present	_____	
future	_____	

sulat	**sulatin**	to write
past	_____	
present	_____	
future	_____	

tawag	**tawagin**	to call
past	_____	
present	_____	
future	_____	

kain   **kainin**   to eat (irregular)

past   _____

present   _____

future   _____

dala   **dalhin**   to bring or carry (irregular)

past   _____

present   _____

future   _____

Change the following active sentences using **-um-** and **mag-** forms of the verbs into passive sentences using the **-in-** forms. Then translate the sentences into English.

1. **Ang aming katulong ay nagluto ng manok** (chicken).
2. **Umaawit ng kundiman** (a Tagalog love song) **ang mga bata.**
3. **Nagbago sila ng baro.**
4. **Tayo ay umiinom ng gatas araw-araw** (everyday).
5. **Nagbabasa ako ng pahayagan** (newspaper) **sa umaga.**
6. **Naglaro ang mga batang lalaki ng patintero** (a native game).
7. **Nagpatay na ng ilaw** (light) **ang aking ina.**
8. **Nagbasa ng paa ang magsasaka** (farmer).
9. **Kumain ng masarap na gulay ang malusog** (healthy) **na bata.**
10. **Bumilang** (count) **ka ng sampung piso.**

Use the imperative forms of the seven **-in-** verbs from the first exercises to create sentences.

Change the following sentences from the passive into the active forms. Do not change the tense nor the person and number.

Aawitin ng mga bata ang Bahay Kubo.	*Bahay Kubo* will be sung by the children.
Lulutuin ng katulong ang gulay.	The vegetables will be cooked by the helper.
Kakainin ba nila ang mga saging?	Will the bananas be eaten by them?
Aalisin niya ang kanyang sapatos.	His/Her shoes will be removed by him/her.
Dinadala namin ang aklat ng Tagalog sa paaralan.	The Tagalog book is brought by us to school.

The Articles **Ang** and **Ng**

Sino ang iinom <u>ng</u> tsaa?
Who will drink tea?

Gumagawa <u>ng</u> school project sina Antonio at Ricky sa bahay. Kakain sila ng meryenda. Nagluto ng turon si Mrs. Alvarez.

Antonio and Ricky are doing a school project at home. They're about to eat a snack. Mrs. Alvarez cooked banana fritter.

ANTONIO : **Masarap <u>ang</u> turon <u>ng</u> nanay mo!**
Your mom's *turon* is delicious!

RICKY : **Siyempre! Ako <u>ang</u> bumili <u>ng</u> saging.**
Of course! I was the one who bought the plantains.

MRS. ALVAREZ : **Masipag <u>ang</u> anak ko.**
My son is hard-working.

ANTONIO : **Oo. At mabait pa.**
Yes. And also kind.

MR. ALVAREZ : **Umiinom si Ricky ng tsaa kapag may turon.**
Ricky drinks tea when there's *turon*.

RICKY : **Umiinom ka rin ba <u>ng</u> tsaa?**
Do you also drink tea?

MRS. ALVAREZ : **Minsan, umiiom ako <u>ng</u> gatas sa meryenda, pero hindi tsaa.**
Sometimes, I drink milk during snack time, but not tea.

Vocabulary List

dalaga = young woman
palengke = market
magkakapatid = siblings
kapitbahay = neighbor
maysakit = sick
kuwento = story
lola = grandmother
tinapay = bread

turon = banana fritter
bumili = bought
saging = banana
masipag = hard-working
mabait = kind
tsaa = tea
umiinom = drinks, is drinking
gatas = milk

Two of the most commonly used words in the Tagalog language are the articles **ang** and **ng** (introduced in Lesson Eight along with **ni** as a word that shows possession). The word **ang** functions like the English definite article *the* and introduces the main character in a sentence, while **ng** introduces the other minor characters, among other things, and may be translated using the English preposition *of* or the indefinite articles *a* and *an*.

For many non-Tagalog speakers, when to use the articles **ang** and **ng** is a source of confusion. They use **ang** where **ng** should be used, and **ng** where **ang** should be used. The following rules should help to differentiate the usage of one from the other.

I. RULES FOR USING **ANG** AND **NG**

1. **Ang** is used:

a. To introduce a common noun as the subject of a sentence (**ang** is similar to the English definite article *the* in this case)

Mabait at masipag <u>ang bata</u>.	The child is good and diligent.
Kumakain ng mangga <u>ang dalaga</u>.	The young woman is eating a mango.

b. Place **ay** to emphasize the identity of or mark the doer

<u>Ako</u> ay sumulat ng kuwento.	I wrote a story.
<u>Ako ang</u> sumulat ng kuwento.	I was the one who wrote the story.
Ang bata ay maysakit.	The child is sick.
Ang <u>bata ang</u> maysakit.	The child is the one who is sick.

2. **Ng** is used:

a. To introduce the receiver of an action

Bumili <u>ng pagkain</u> ang babae.	The woman bought food.
Si Elena ay nagluto <u>ng manok</u>.	Elena cooked the chicken.

b. To indicate association or possession

Nagpunta sa palengke ang <u>ina ng bata</u>.	The child's mother went to the market.
Bago ang <u>bahay ng lalaki</u>.	The man's house is new.

c. To introduce the doer of the passive action (observe the **-in-** verb forms)

Kinain <u>ng aso</u> ang tinapay.	The dog ate the bread.
Binili <u>ng batang babae</u> ang aklat.	The girl bought the book.

II. THE PLURAL FORMS OF **ANG** AND **NG**

As Tagalog sentences follow the plurality rule initially mentioned in Lesson Four, plural words need to be introduced by the plural forms of **ang** and **ng**. Thus, **ang** becomes **ang mga** and **ng** becomes **ng mga**:

Ang mga bahay ng magkakapatid (denotes two or more siblings) **na babae ay malalaki.**
The sisters' houses are big.

Bumili ng mga prutas ang lola.
The grandmother bought fruits.

EXERCISES

Fill in the blanks with **ang, ng, ang mga** or **ng mga** and then translate the sentences into English.

1. **Nasa Quezon City _____ bahay _____aking kaibigan.**

2. **Nasa Taft Avenue _____ paralan _____ babae.**

3. **John _____ pangalan _____ aking asawa.**

4. **_____ pangalan _____ kapatid ko ay Peter at Mary.**

5. **Kumakain _____ gulay _____ malusog na bata.**

6. **Uminom _____ gatas _____ anak _____ aking kapithahay.**

7. **Si Peter _____ kumain _____ prutas _____ punong-kahoy.**

8. **Magkano ba _____ isang kilo _____ asukal?**

9. **Ilan _____ nag-aaral sa klase _____ Tagalog?**

10. **Kinain _____ bata _____ isang man**

Pseudo Verbs—**Dapat**, **Gusto** and Others

Marunong ka bang magluto?
Do you know how to cook?

<u>Gustong magluto</u> ni Miguel para kay Chris. Naghanap siya ng recipe para sa lechon manok pero nahihirapan siya sa kusina.

Miguel wants to cook for Chris. He looked for a recipe for roasted chicken, but he's having a hard time at the kitchen.

MIGUEL : **Simple lang ang recipe. <u>Kailangan</u> ko ng bawang, kaunting paminta at asin.**
The recipe is simple. I need garlic, a bit of pepper, and salt.

CHRIS : **Buti walang sili. <u>Ayaw kong kumain</u> ng maanghang.**
Good thing there's no chili. I don't want to eat spicy food.

MIGUEL : **<u>Dapat lutuin</u> ang mga patatas, pero hindi ko alam kung paano.**
The potatoes need to be cooked but I don't know how.

CHRIS : **<u>Gusto kong tumulong</u>. <u>Pwede kong hiwain</u> ang mga patatas.**
I would like to help. I can slice the potatoes.

MIGUEL : **Nakakahiya. Bisita ka pa naman! <u>Dapat umupo</u> ka lang.**
How embarrassing. You're the guest! You should sit back and relax.

CHRIS : **Ayos lang. Kung hindi ako tutulong, baka bukas na tayo makakain!**
Don't worry. If I don't help, we may have to wait until tomorrow to eat!

Vocabulary List

mag-aral = to learn	**paminta** = pepper
estudyante = student	**asin** = salt
tinapay = bread	**sili** = chili pepper
baka = cow or beef	**maanghang** = spicy
balut = steamed duck embryo	**patatas** = potato
kaibigan = friend	**nakakahiya** = embarassing
magulang = parent	**umupo** = to sit down
dalandan = orange fruit	**bukas** = tomorrow
bawang = garlic	**kailangan** = need

In the Tagalog language, there are pseudo verbs that accompany principal verbs and express the chief action in the sentence. These include **dapat**, **maaari**, **puwede**, **kailangan**, **ibig**, **gusto** and **ayaw**. Their individual meanings are:

dapat	must, should, would, has/have to
maaari or **puwede**	can, may, could
kailangan	needs to, is necessary to
ibig or **gusto**	likes, desires, wants
ayaw	does not like

These pseudo verbs shift the meaning of the main verb to indicate that an action should have been done or should not have been done, or can be carried out or cannot be carried out, etc.

Dapat kumain ng gulay ang mga bata.
The children <u>should eat</u> [their] vegetables.

Puwedeng lutuin ang baka.
(You) <u>may cook</u> the beef.

Maaari kayong lumakad na.
You (plural) <u>may go</u> already.

Ayaw nilang uminom ng gatas.
They <u>do not like to drink</u> milk.

Kailangang maligo tayo araw-araw.
We <u>need to take a bath</u> everyday.

Ibig kong mag-aral ng Tagalog.
Gusto kong mag-aral ng Tagalog.
I <u>like to learn</u> Tagalog.

Rules for Using Pseudo Verbs

1. Use only the infinitive form of the main verb with any of the following affixes: **-um-**, **mag-**, **-in-**, and **-hin**.

Correct: **Dapat <u>kumain</u> ng gulay ang mga bata.**
          The children must eat [their] vegetables.

Incorrect: **Dapat kumakain ng gulay ang mga bata.**

Incorrect: **Dapat kakain ng gulay ang mga bata.**

Correct: **Kailangang <u>punuin</u> mo ng bato ang paso.**
You must fill up the claypot with stones.

Incorrect: **Kailangang pupunuin mo ng bato ang paso.**

Incorrect: **Kailangang napuno mo ng bato ang paso.**

Note the use of the ligature **-g** above to link **kailangan** with the main verb **punuin**. This applies to other pseudo verbs although with **ibig**, **ayaw** and **dapat** before a main verb, a ligature is not necessary. However, all pseudo verbs followed by a pronoun, such as **siya** and **niya**, require ligatures after the pronoun.

2. For **ibig** and **gusto** pseudo verbs, use the form of possessive pronoun that comes after a subject (such as **ko** and **mo**, refer to Lesson Eight) and attach the appropriate ligature. Place the pronoun between the pseudo verb and the principal verb, whether the principal verb is active (with an **-um-** or **mag-** verb) or passive (with an **-in-** verb).

Correct: **Ibig kong mag-aral ng Tagalog.**
I want to learn Tagalog.

Incorrect: **Ibig mag-aral ko ng Tagalog.**

Incorrect: **Ibig mag-aral ng Tagalog ako.**

Correct: **Gusto kong aralin ang Tagalog.**
I want to learn Tagalog.

Incorrect: **Gusto aralin ko ng Tagalog.**

Incorrect: **Gusto aralin ng Tagalog ako.**

3. Except for **ibig** and **gusto**, all other pseudo verbs require a nominative pronoun (such as **ako** and **siya**) with the appropriate ligature attached when used with an active **-um-** or **mag-** verb (see first example).

Correct: **Dapat <u>siyang uminom</u> ng gatas.**

Incorrect: **Dapat siyang inumin ang gatas.**

Similarly, a pseudo verb requires a possessive pronoun (such as **niya**) with the appropriate ligature attached when used with a passive **-in** verb (see example below).

Correct: **Dapat <u>niyang inumin</u> ang gatas.**

Incorrect: **Dapat <u>niyang uminom</u> ng gatas.**

4. A pseudo verb that ends in a consonant other than **n** does not need a suffix. Those ending in vowels need suffixes.

Correct:	**Ibig uminom ng gatas ang bata.**
Correct:	**Gustong uminom ng gatas ang bata.**
Incorrect:	**Gusto uminom ng gatas ang bata.**

Sample Sentences

Dapat akong sumulat sa aking kaibigan sa Estados Unidos.
I must write to my friend in the United States.

Dapat sulatin ni Peter ang kanyang kuwento ngayong gabi.
His/Her story must be written by Peter tonight.

Maaari bang linisin mo ang aking sapatos?
Could my shoes be cleaned by you?

Maaari akong maglinis ng iyong sapatos.
I can clean your shoes.

Kailangang mag-aral ang mga estudyante araw-araw.
Students need to study every day.

Ibig nilang magsalita ng Tagalog.
They like to speak in Tagalog.

Ayaw niyang kainin ang balut.
He/She does not like *balut* (steamed duck embryo) to be eaten.

Ayaw siyang kumain ng balut.
He/She does not like to eat *balut*.

EXERCISES

Each of the exercise below has three words (a pseudo verb, an object, and a subject). Think of an appropriate main verb and use its proper form following the grammatical rules in this lesson to create a logical sentence. Translate the sentences into English.

1. **dapat**   **libro**   **estudyante**

   _____.

2. **lumipad**   **ibig**   **bata**

   _____.

3. **kailangan**   **lola**   **gamot**

   _____.

4. **ayaw**   **pangako**   **dalaga**

   _____.

5. **maaari**   **pritong manok**   **kuya** (elder brother)

   _____.

Translate the following phrases into Tagalog.

1. We must eat vegetables every day.
2. Do you like to buy oranges (**dalandan**)?
3. The sick person needs to sleep.
4. It is necessary to take a bath every day.
5. He does not like to swim.
6. The child can eat now.
7. You need to clean the house.
8. I like to write stories.
9. We should love our parents.

Ma- and Maka- Verb Forms

Magbakasyon na tayo!
Let's go on vacation!

Sa wakas, <u>nakaipon</u> ng pera ang mga bagong ikinasal. <u>Makakapunta</u> na sa Paris sina Anna at David. Nagpaplano sila kasama ang isang travel agent.

Finally, the newlyweds have been able to save money. Anna and David will now be able to go to Paris. They're planning with a travel agent.

ANNA	:	**Kailan namin <u>matatanggap</u> ang mga pasaporte namin?** When will we receive our passports?
TRAVEL AGENT	:	**Darating ang mga pasaporte ninyo sa Biyernes. <u>Makakabalik</u> ba kayo dito?** Your passports will arrive on Friday. Will you be able to come back?
DAVID	:	**<u>Makakapunta</u> kami pagkatapos ng trabaho.** We will be able to come after work.
ANNA	:	**<u>Maginaw</u> sa Paris kapag Pebrero. <u>Magagawa</u> ba namin ang river cruise?** It's cold in Paris in February. Can we still do the river cruise?
TRAVEL AGENT	:	**Oo naman. <u>Nabili</u> ko ang mga tiket ninyo. Tuloy na tuloy na.** Yes, sure! I was able to buy your tickets already. It's pushing through.
ANNA	:	**Ang saya-saya naman! Hindi ako <u>makakatulog</u> sa tuwa!** How exciting! I will be unable to sleep from excitement!

Vocabulary List

pag-asa = hope	**matatanggap** = will receive
mabasag = to be broken	**makakabalik** = will be able to return
nakahiga = lying down	**maginaw** = cold
maysakit = sick	**makakatulog** = will be able to sleep
araw-araw = every day	**nabili** = was able to buy
putok = explosion	

Ma- is a prefix that is attached to the beginning of a verb root. In general, a verb with a **ma-** indicates capability to do something. A **ma-** verb has two types: active and passive. When **ma-** is used with an intransitive verb (verb does not take an object), it is in the active form and takes a noun or a nominative pronoun (such as **siya** and **ikaw**) as the subject similar to **-um-** and **mag-** verb forms. If it is attached to a transitive verb (a verb which needs an object to complete its meaning), the **ma-** form is passive and requires a subject in the possessive form (such as **niya** and **mo**) similar to the **-in-** verb.

Maka- has the same meaning as **ma-** except that **maka-** is always active and takes a noun or a nominative pronoun (such as **siya** and **ikaw**) as its subject. While a **ma-** verb can be formed from a verb showing emotion or feeling, a **maka-** verb can only be formed from a verb showing action. Thus, not all **ma-** verb forms have their equivalent in **maka-** verb forms.

Transitive and Intransitive **Ma-** and **Maka-** Verb Forms

I. INTRANSITIVE VERBS USING **MA-**

An intransitive verb with **ma-** does not need any other element besides the subject to form a sentence. Its derivatives are formed as follows:

Example: **tulog**	sleep
Infinitive: **matulog**	(**ma-** + root) to sleep
Imperative: **matulog**	(**ma-** + root)
Past: **natulog**	(**ma-** becomes **na-** + root) slept
Present: **natutulog**	(**ma-** becomes **na-** + duplicated first syllable + root) sleeps/sleep
Future: **matutulog**	(**ma-** + duplicated first syllable + root) will sleep

EXAMPLES OF INTRANSITIVE VERBS USING **MA-**

matulog	= to sleep	**maligo**	= to take a bath
magutom	= to be hungry	**magalit**	= to be angry
makinig	= to listen to	**mahiya**	= to be ashamed
mahiga	= to lie down	**maupo**	= to sit
matuwa	= to be delighted	**matakot**	= to be afraid
mamatay	= to die	**malungkot**	= to be sad

II. TRANSITIVE VERBS USING **MA-**

A transitive verb needs an object to complete its meaning. Its derivatives are formed similar to an intransitive verb except its imperative form.

Example: **kita**   see
Infinitive: **makita**   (**ma-** + root) to be seen
Imperative: none
Past: **nakita**   (**ma-** becomes **na-** + root) saw
Present: **nakikita**   (**ma-** becomes **na-** + duplicated first syllable + root)
                                  sees/see
Future: **makikita**   (**ma-** + duplicated first syllable + root) will see

EXAMPLES OF TRANSITIVE VERBS USING **MA**

makita	to be seen
makain	to be able to eat
maalala	to be remembered
makuha	to be able to get
marinig	to be heard
mabili	to be able to buy
masunog	to be burned
mabasa	to be able to read
mabasag	to be broken

III. VERBS USING **MAKA-**

Generally, adding **maka-** to a verb expresses the capability to do something. It does not have an imperative form.

Example: **tulog**   sleep
Infinitive: **makatulog**   (**maka-** + root) to be able to sleep
Imperative: none
Past: **nakatulog**   (**maka-** becomes **naka-** + root) was/were able to sleep
Present: **nakatutulog**   (**maka-** becomes **naka-** + duplicated first syllable +
                                  root) is/are able to sleep
Future: **makatutulog**   (**maka-** + duplicated first syllable + root) will be
                                  able to sleep

EXAMPLES OF **MAKA-** VERBS

makatulog	to be able to sleep	makaalala	to be able to remember
makaligo	to be able to bathe	makakuha	to be able to get
makahiga	to be able to lie down	makarinig	to be able to hear
makaupo	to be able to sit	makabili	to be able to buy
makabuhay	to be able to give life	makasunog	to be able to burn
makakita	to be able to see	makabasa	to be able to read
makakain	to be able to eat	makabasag	to be able to break

Sample Sentences 🔊

Dapat matulog nang maaga ang mga bata.
Children should sleep early.

Nagutom ako kagabi pagkatapos mag-aral.
I got hungry last night after studying.

Nagagalit ang aking ina sa mga batang matigas ang ulo.
My mother gets angry with hard-headed (or stubborn) children.

Nakita ko si Mary sa palengke kahapon.
I saw Mary in the market yesterday.

Makukuha mo na ang iyong suweldo.
You can get your salary now.

Nakatulog kagabi ang maysakit.
The sick person was able to sleep last night.

Hindi ako makaligo kung malamig.
I cannot take a bath when it is cold.

Ang mga bata ay nakahiga sa lupa.
The children are able to lie on the ground.

Ang pag-asa ay nakabubuhay.
Hope is able to give life.

Naaalala ko ang aking anak sa gabi bago matulog.
I think of my child at night before sleeping.

EXERCISES

Fill in the blanks with the appropriate tenses or forms of the verbs using **ma-** and **maka-** found in this lesson and underlined in the English translations below.

1. _____ **ang mga bata sa dadalhin mong regalo.**
   The children <u>will be delighted</u> with the gift you will bring.

2. _____ **kami sa pagkawala ng iyong singsing.**
   We <u>were saddened</u> by the loss of your ring.

3. **Sa kabilang palengke** _____ **si Tess ng gulay.**
   Tess <u>was able to get</u> vegetables from the other market.

4. _____ **na mag-isa ang aking bunso.**
   My youngest <u>can</u> now <u>take a bath</u> alone.

3. **Kung malakas ang tugtog mo, hindi ka** _____.
   If your music is loud, you <u>will</u> not <u>be heard</u>.

Ma- and Maka- Verb Forms

To express unintentional or accidental actions, attach **ma-** and **maka-** to the beginning of verbs. The resulting verbs convey the performance of an act beyond the control of the doer or the receiver. These verbs do not have imperative forms and **ma-** and **maka-** verb forms are retained in all tense forms. Not all **ma-** verb forms have **maka-** counterparts.

I. VERBS USING **MA-**

In forming a verb using **ma-**, the second syllable of the prefix is duplicated in the present and future tenses.

> Example: **tulog**   sleep
> Infinitive: **matulog**   (**ma** + root) to sleep unintentionally
> Imperative: none
> Past: **natulog**   (**ma-** becomes **na-** + root) slept unintentionally
> Present: **natutulog**   (**ma-** becomes **na-** + duplicated first syllable + root) sleeps unintentionally
> Future: **matutulog**   (**ma-** + duplicated first syllable + root) will sleep unintentionally

EXAMPLES OF VERBS WITH **MA-**

> **matulog**   to sleep unintentionally
> **makita**   to be seen accidentally
> **makain**   to be eaten accidentally
> **mabasa**   to be read unintentionally
> **marinig**   to be heard accidentally
> **mainom**   to be drank accidentally
> **mabangga**   to be bumped unintentionally
> **mabaril**   to be shot accidentally
> **mapatay**   to be killed unintentionally

II. VERBS USING **MAKA-**

In forming a verb using **maka-**, the second syllable of the prefix is duplicated in the present and future tenses.

> Example: **tulog**   sleep
> Infinitive: **makatulog**   (**maka-** + root) to sleep unintentionally
> Imperative: none
> Past: **nakatulog**   (**maka-** becomes **naka-** + root) slept unintentionally
> Present: **nakakatulog**   (**maka-** becomes **naka-** + duplicated **ka** + root) sleeps/sleep unintentionally
> Future: **makakatulog**   (**maka-** + duplicated **ka-** + root) will sleep unintentionally

Example: **ligo**   bathe
Infinitive: **makaligo**   (**maka-** + root) bathe unintentionally
Imperative: none
Past: **nakaligo**   (**maka-** becomes **naka-** + root) bathed unintentionally
Present: **nakakaligo**   (**maka-** becomes **naka-** + duplicate **ka** + root) bathe/
                             bathes unintentionally
Future: **makakaligo**   (**maka-** + duplicate **ka-** + root) will bathe unintentionally

EXAMPLES OF VERBS WITH **MAKA-**

makabili	to buy without previous intention
makabaril	to shoot accidentally
makakita	to see by chance, involuntarily
makakain	to eat accidentally
makainom	to drink accidentally
makabangga	to bump against accidentally
makarinig	to hear unintentionally
makapulot	to pick up something accidentally
makapatay	to kill accidentally
makadalaw	to visit without previous intention

Sample Sentences

Nakita ko siya sa palengke.
I saw her (by chance) at the market.

Nakain ko ang lumang tinapay.
I (accidentally) ate the stale bread.

Narinig namin ang kanilang awit.
We heard (by chance) their song.

Nabangga ang kotse sa pader.
The car (accidentally) bumped against the wall.

Nakabaril ng pulis ang magnanakaw.
The robber (accidentally) shot the policeman.

Nakapulot ang bata ng sampung piso.
The child (by chance) picked up ten pesos.

Nakarinig siya ng putok.
He heard (by chance) an explosion.

Nakadalaw si Maria sa kaniyang ina.
Maria visited her mother (without meaning to).

Natulog ang lalaki sa loob ng simbahan.
The man fell asleep (without meaning to) inside the church.

Nakabili siya ng magandang sapatos sa Marikina.
She bought (without previous intention) pretty shoes in Marikina.

EXERCISES

Look for the correct **ma-** and **maka-** verb forms needed to translate the following sentences and write them on the blanks.

1. _____

   The sick man is now able to eat.

2. _____

   I was seen by my teacher in the church.

3. _____

   I can now read the Tagalog Bible.

4. _____   _____

   The old woman can take a bath now if (**kung**) the water is not cold (**malamig**).

5. _____

   I shall be able to leave tomorrow.

6. _____

   The baby (**sanggol**) can now take the medicine.

7. _____

   We were able to visit her (by chance) in the hospital.

8. _____

   The man shot his companion accidentally in the hand.

9. _____

My father bought an expensive dress for me without planning to.

10. _____

I cannot sit.

Use the present tense forms of the following accented **ma-** and **maka-** verb forms in sentences. Read the sentences aloud afterwards.

1. **makainom**   to drink unintentionally
2. **makabangga**   to bump against accidentally
3. **makarinig**   to hear unintentionally
4. **makapatay**   to kill by accident
5. **makadalaw**   to visit without previous intention

LESSON NINETEEN
Maging—*To Be* or *To Become*

Magiging guro ako!
I'll become a teacher!

Nasa pulong si Chris at ang mga magulang ni Ricky, sina Mr. at Mrs. Alvarez. Nag-uusap sila tungkol sa mga grado at ugali ni Ricky sa klase.

Chris and Ricky's parents, Mr. and Mrs. Alvarez, are in a meeting. They're talking about Ricky's grades and behavior in class.

CHRIS : <u>**Magiging mas mataas**</u> **ang mga grado mo kung mag-aaaral ka, Ricky.**
Your grades will be higher if you study, Ricky.

RICKY : **Sige po, Miss Castro, <u>magiging mas masipag</u> ako.**
Okay, Miss Castro, I will become more diligent.

MRS. ALVAREZ : **Tama iyan, anak. Gusto mo <u>maging duktor</u>, hindi ba? <u>Magiging mas mahirap</u> ang mga klase mo sa high school.**
That's right, son. Didn't you want to be a doctor? Your classes in high school will be more difficult.

RICKY : **Gusto ko ho <u>maging guro</u>!**
I would like to be a teacher!

MR. ALVAREZ : **Kumusta ang ugali niya sa klase?**
And how is his behavior in class?

CHRIS : **Maayos ho. <u>Naging</u> kaibigan agad ni Ricky sina Marta at Antonio dahil mabait siya.**
It's great. Marta and Antonio became fast friends with Ricky because he's kind.

Vocabulary List

kapitbahay = neighbor
panahon = weather
malusog = healthy
maingay = noisy
tahimik = quiet/peaceful

bulag = blind
mas mataas = higher
ugali = behavior
guro = teacher

When the word **maging** (meaning *to be* or *to become*) is placed before a noun or adjective, the phrase expresses the speaker's or the subject's desire to change from one state or condition to another. **Maging** is in fact a very common helping verb in Tagalog. Examples of **maging** phrases include the following:

maging mabait	to become good (or to be good)
maging Pilipino	to become a Filipino (or to be a Filipino)
maging masama	to become bad (or to be bad)
maging guro	to become a teacher (or to be a teacher)
maging abugado	to become a lawyer (or to be a lawyer)
maging tahimik	to become quiet (or to be quiet)
maging mayaman	to become rich (or to be rich)
maging bulag	to become blind (or to be blind)

Forming Phrases with **Maging**

Example: **bait**   kindness
Infinitive: **maging mabait**   (**maging** + **ma-** attached to root) to be kind
Imperative: **maging mabait**   (**maging** + **ma-** attached to root) Be kind!
Past: **naging mabait**   (**maging** becomes **naging** + **ma-** attached to root) became kind
Present: **nagiging mabait**   (**maging** becomes **nagiging** + **ma-** attached to root) become kind
Future: **magiging mabait**   (**maging** becomes **magiging** + **ma-** attached to root) will become kind

Sample Sentences

Nagiging mabait na ngayon ang anak niya.
Her/His child is becoming good now. (literal)
Her/His child is better behaved now.

Ang aking kaibigan ay magiging mayaman na.
My friend will soon get rich.

Kailangang maging malusog ang lahat ng mga bata.
All children need to be healthy.

Nagiging tahimik na ang aming bahay.
Our house is becoming quiet now.

Naging kapitbahay namin sila.
They were once our neighbors.

Gusto kong maging guro.
I want to become a teacher.

Ayaw mo bang maging doktor?
Don't you want to become a doctor?

Nagiging masama ang panahon.
The weather is going bad. (literal)
The weather is getting worse.

Mahirap maging bulag.
It is difficult to go blind.

EXERCISES

Translate the following phrases into Tagalog and use them in sentences.

1. becoming noisy _____

2. will become poor _____

3. became a hero _____

4. becoming industrious _____

5. will be a lawyer _____

6. became dirty _____

7. becoming dark _____

8. will be rainy _____

9. was a teacher _____

10. will be happy _____

Select five names of friends and describe what they wanted to become when they were still young. Compare this to what they are now or what they want to be five years from now.

Magkaroon—*To Have*

Nagkasakit si Chris!
Chris got sick!

Nasa klinika ng duktor si Chris. <u>Nagkaroon siya ng ubo</u> dahil malamig ang panahon. <u>Nagkasakit</u> din ang maraming estudyante sa klase niya.
Chris is in the doctor's clinic. She got a cough because the weather is cold. A lot of students in her class also got sick.

DUKTOR : **Kailan ka <u>nagkasakit</u>?**
When did you get sick?

CHRIS : **Noong Sabado pa. Nahawa yata ako sa mga estudyante ko.**
Since Saturday. I may have gotten infected from my students.

DUKTOR : **Baka <u>magkaroon ka rin ng lagnat</u>. Huwag kang magtrabaho bukas.**
You might get a fever. Don't go to work tomorrow.

CHRIS : **Naku! <u>Magkakabisita</u> ako ngayong Biyernes.**
Oh dear, I will have guests this Friday.

DUKTOR : **Ang payo ko, magpahinga ka hanggang Lunes.**
My advice is to rest until Monday.

CHRIS : **Sige ho doc. Ayaw kong maging malala ang ubo ko.**
Okay, doctor. I don't want my cough to get worse.

Vocabulary List

anak na kambal = twins	**tanim** = plant (noun); to plant (verb)
ubo = cough	**nagkasakit** = became or got sick
bisita = visitor	**nahawa** = got infected
radyo = radio	**lagnat** = fever
trabaho = work	**magpahinga** = to rest
anay = termite	**malala** = grave or worse

The word **magkaroon** means *to have*. It is usually placed before a noun to indicate to have what the noun expresses. **Magkaroon** may be shortened to **magka-** and is similar in meaning to **may** and **mayroon** (see Lesson Twelve) which also express existence and/or actual possession. However, **magkaroon** has tense forms—past, present and future—while **may** and **mayroon** do not have any except when **may** is followed by a verb.

Forming Phrases and Words with **Magkaroon**

To create a **magkaroon** phrase or form a **magka-** word, follow the formulas below:
magkaroon + article **ng** + noun
or **magka-** + noun

Example:	**magkaroon ng pera**	to have money
	or **magkapera**	
Past:	**nagkaroon ng pera**	(**magkaroon** becomes **nagkaroon**)
	or **nagkapera**	(**nagka** + noun) had money
Present:	**nagkakaroon ng pera**	(**magkaroon** becomes **nagkakaroon**)
	or **nagkakapera**	(**nagkaka** + noun) has money
Future:	**magkakaroon ng pera**	(**magkaroon** becomes **magkakaroon**)
	or **magkakapera**	(**magkaka** + noun) will have money

The subject of a sentence using **magkaroon** or a **magka-** word is introduced by **si** or **ang** or is indicated by a nominative pronoun such as **siya**. A pronoun subject is always placed after **magkaroon** while a subject introduced by **si** or **ang** may be inserted after **magkaroon** or after the object. The meaning, however, does not change.

Nagkaroon <u>si Maria</u> ng aso.	Had Maria a dog. (literal)
	Maria had a dog.
Nagkaroon ng aso <u>si Maria</u>.	Maria had a dog.

To state the negative of **magkaroon**, the word **hindi** (meaning *not* within a sentence or *no* when used as a response) is placed before the word **magkaroon**. For example, **Hindi nagkaroon si Maria ng aso** (*Maria did not have a dog*).

Sample Sentences

Past:	**Nagkaroon siya ng anak na kambal.**	She had twins.
	Nagkaanak siya ng kambal.	
Present:	**Nagkakaroon ako ng ubo kapag malamig.**	I have a cough when the weather is cold.
	Nagkakaubo ako kapag malamig.	
Future:	**Magkakaroon kami ng bisita.**	We will have visitors.
	Magkakabisita kami.	
Past:	**Nagkaroon ng sakit ang bata.**	The child got sick.
	Nagkasakit ang bata.	
Present:	**Nagkakaroon ng anay ang bahay.**	The house has termites.
	Nagkakaanay ang bahay.	

Future: **Magkakaroon si Pedro ng trabaho.**   Pedro will have a job.
          Magkakatrabaho na si Pedro.

Negative: **Hindi nagkakaroon ng bulaklak ang tanim.** The plant does not bear
          Hindi nagkakabulaklak ang tanim.   flowers.

Negative: **Hindi sila nagkaroon ng bahay.**   They did not have a house.
          Hindi sila nagkabahay.

Negative: **Hindi kami magkakaroon ng radyo.**   We will not have a radio.
          Hindi kami magkakaradyo.

EXERCISES

Write the correct tense forms of the **magkaroon** and **magka-** phrases and words in the blanks. Afterwards, translate these sentences into Tagalog.

1. _____
   They will have a pretty house in Quezon City.

2. _____
   Did you get sick last year?

3. _____
   We are having a grand time (**kasiya-siyang panahon**) on the beach (**dalampasigan**).

4. _____
   He will have a car next month (**susunod na buwan**).

5. _____
   His business does not have plenty of money.

6. _____
   My child will have a friend.

7. _____
   We shall have a good teacher.

8. _____
   The rich man will have a new car.

9. _____
   I would like to have a good friend.

Think of what you will or would like to have in a few years from now, and form 10 other examples of **magkaroon** and **magka-** phrases and words not found in this lesson.

LESSON TWENTY-ONE

Expressing Thoughts and Actions

Sa palagay ko, mananalo ang team ko.
I think my team will win.

Nanonood ng basketbol sina Robert at Miguel. Magaling lahat, kaya mahigpit ang laban.

Robert and Miguel are watching basketball. Everyone is good, so the competition is tight.

MIGUEL : **<u>Sa palagay mo</u>, sino ang mananalo?**
In your opinion, who will win?

ROBERT : **<u>Tila</u> ang Eagle Team.**
Maybe Team Eagle.

MIGUEL : **Tama ka. <u>Sa akala ko</u>, mananalo ang Lion Team, pero mas magaling ang Eagle Team.**
You're right. I thought Lion Team will win, but Eagle Team is better.

ROBERT : **<u>Mag-isip ka</u> ng plano natin pagkatpos ng laro.**
Think about our plan after the game.

MIGUEL : **Pumunta tayo kay Janice.**
Let's go visit Janice.

ROBERT : **Sige, <u>sa tingin ko</u>, matutuwa siya.**
Sure, I think she'll enjoy that.

Vocabulary List

paraan = way
langoy = to swim
dumalaw = visited
pupunta = will go
tabing-dagat = beach
maysakit = sick
mananalo = will win

palagay = opinion
mananalo = will win
mas magaling = better/more skilled
mag-isip = to think
matutuwa = will enjoy/will be happy
about something

When expressing their thoughts and actions, Filipinos make use of the words **tila**, **akala**, and **isip** (all of which simply mean *to think* in English) as well as **pumunta** (means *to go*) and a multitude of other verbs to indicate what they did, are doing and will do.

I. TO THINK 🔊

1. Tila, sa akala and sa palagay

The English word *to think* may be translated in three ways in Tagalog but all three indicate opinions, ideas and assumptions. Basically, they all mean the same— *I think, He/She thinks, They/We think*—when used in sentences but individually, they have the following definitions:

tila	= an adverb that means *it seems*
sa akala or **sa palagay**	= to my thinking (literal), a preposition meaning *to assume or to have an opinion*

Tila, sa akala and **sa palagay** phrases are formed this way:
tila + verb or adjective or nominative pronoun such as **sila** or **ikaw**
particle **sa** + **akala** or **palagay** + possessive noun or pronoun (**ni Jay, ko, niya, nila, mo, ng lahat** *or of everybody*)

Tila is placed mostly at the beginning of a sentence in common conversations and always implies the speaker's own perception.

Tila uulan.	It seems it will rain.
Ang sagot niya ay tila mali.	His/Her answer seems wrong.
Tila siya'y lalong maganda ngayon.	She seems prettier now.

On the other hand, **sa akala** or **sa palagay** is followed by a noun or a pronoun in the possessive form such as (**ni Coi, niya** or **mo**).

Sa akala ko matalino ka.
To my thinking, you are an intelligent man. (literal)
I think you are an intelligent man.

Sa palagay ko ay mananalo tayo.
To my thinking, we will win. (literal)
I think we will win.

Sa akala nila, may sakit siya.
To their thinking, he is sick. (literal)
They think he is sick.

Sa palagay ni Gem ay tama ako.
To Gem's thinking, I am right. (literal)
Gem thinks I am right.

To a Tagalog speaker, a sentence with **sa akala** leaves room for validation or contradiction as the speaker's assumptions may be proven wrong. For example, **Sa akala ko ikaw ay matalino** (*I thought you were intelligent*) somehow negates the subject's intelligence as perceived by the speaker. On the other hand, the statement **Akala ko Amerikano siya** (*I thought he is an American*) invalidates a previous assumption. Note that Tagalog speakers may sometimes omit **sa** before **akala**, replace **sa** with **ang** as well as omit the linking verb **ay**. Such practices result in the following sentences, which are brief and still correct:

Sa akala ko ay Amerikano siya.
To my thinking, he is an American.

Akala ko Amerikano siya.
To my thinking, he is an American.

Ang akala ko Amerikano siya.
My assumption is that he is an American.

On the other hand, **sa palagay** voices a personal opinion. An informal translation of *to think* similar to **sa palagay [ko]** is **sa tingin [ko]** which roughly means *in [my] view*.

2. **Isip**

When used to mean *to do some real thinking* or *to ponder over something*, the equivalent of *to think* in Tagalog is **umisip** or **mag-isip** (active form) or **isipin** (passive form).

Umiisip siya ng lalong mabuting paraan.
He is thinking of a better way.

Iniisip niya ang kanyang mga sinasabi.
She thinks about what she says.

Mag-isip ka ng magagawa.
(You) Think of what can be done.

II. TO GO

1. Common usage of the word *to go*

To simply indicate direction or itinerary, the verb **pumunta** is the exact translation of the English word *to go* although **pumunta** can also mean *to come* (see first sample of an imperative sentence below). When used in this sense, **pumunta** has an imperative form and all tenses of the **-um-** and **mag-** forms.

Imperative: **Pumunta ka dito.**	Come here.
Imperative: **Pumunta ka doon.**	Go there.
Future: **Pupunta kami sa simbahan.**	We will go to church.
Past: **Pumunta sila sa tabing-dagat.**	They went to the beach.
Present: **Pumupunta sya sa Maynila araw-araw.**	He/She goes to Manila everyday.

2. *To go* plus verb

The other use of the word *to go* beyond *to go to a place* has no exact translation in Tagalog but will depend on the verb immediately following *to go*. For example, the phrase *went swimming* translates into **lumangoy** only whereas the phrase *will go to sleep* translates into **matutulog**. The imperative form and various tenses of the second verb are used in this sense. These sentences are usual responses to the questions **Ano ang ginawa mo? Ano ang ginagawa mo? Ano ang gagawin mo?** (*What did you do? What are you doing? What will you do?*) and other similar questions. Note that the English sentences use the various tenses of the word *to go* plus the *-ing* form or various tenses of the verb but the Tagalog translations mention the tenses of the verb only. The Tagalog language does not really use **pumunta** along with another verb in the same way that the English language uses *to go* as an auxiliary to another verb.

Imperative: **Maglakad ka.**	You go to walk (or You walk).
Future: **Lalangoy kami.**	We will go swimming.
Past: **Dumalaw kami sa isang kaibigan.**	We went to visit a friend.
Present: **Natutulog sila sa kabilang kuwarto.**	They are sleeping in the next room.

EXERCISES

Fill in the blanks with **tila**, **akala**, or **palagay** and the correct Tagalog forms of the English nouns or pronouns given at the end of each sentence. Afterwards, translate the sentences into English.

1. _____, nasa bahay _____.
   (*everybody, I*)

2. _____ ay umalis na _____.
   (*they, we* excluding person spoken to)

3. _____ mali ang _____ iniisip.
   (*our* including person spoken to)

4. **Teka, _____ nawawala _____.**
   (*we* including person spoken to)

Fill in the blanks with the appropriate tenses or forms of *to go* in Tagalog based on the available list of verbs:

aral (*study*)   **tanong** (*ask*)   **sulat** (*write*)

laro (*play*)   **tanim** (*plant*)

1. _____ kami sa bahay ng guro.

2. _____ tayo ng mga halaman sa hardin.

3. _____ sila kung hindi nila alam ang lugar.

4. _____ ba ang mga basketbolista?

5. _____ ako ng isang kuwento.

Expressing Emotions

Gustong-gusto ko ang Paris!
I like Paris very much!

Nag-uusap sina Anna at David tungkol sa bakasyon nila. Masayang-masaya ang bagong kasal.

Anna and David are talking about their vacation. The newly-weds are very happy.

ANNA : **<u>Gustong-gusto</u> ko ang Paris!**
I really like Paris!

DAVID : **<u>Mahal</u> ang regalong ito.**
This gift is expensive.

ANNA : **<u>Mahal</u> kasi ako ng mga pinsan ko.**
My cousins love me, that's why.

DAVID : **<u>Mas mahal kita!</u>**
I love you more!

ANNA : **Alam ko. <u>Iniibig</u> din kita.**
I know. I'm in love with you too.

DAVID : **<u>Gusto kong maglakad</u> sa buong Paris.**
I would like to walk in all of Paris.

ANNA : **Ako naman, <u>gusto kong makita</u> ang Eiffel Tower sa gabi.**
As for me, I'd like to see the Eiffel Tower at night.

Vocabulary List

bunso = youngest child
bayan = country
binata = bachelor
ulan = rain
magkakapatid = siblings

bago = before
maglakad = to walk
makita = to see
gabi = night

I. TO LOVE 🔊

The English word *to love* has two rather different meanings in Tagalog, as expressed by **mahalin** or **ibigin**. The root words are **mahal** and **ibig**, respectively.

Mahal literally means *noble* and *expensive* (a derivative is **mahalaga** or *important*). As a term of endearment, it means *dear* or *beloved*. **Mahal** implies that someone values something or someone.

On the other hand, **ibig** means *a fondness for someone or something*; it can also mean *affection, desire, purpose, whim,* and *love*. The emotions it captures range from the simple (*caprice*) to the complex (*love*).

Mahal kita.
I love you.

Minamahal niya ang kanyang aso.
He/She loves his/her dog.

Minamahal nila ang kanilang guro.
They love their teacher.

Dapat nating mahalin ang ating bayan.
We should love our country.

Minamahal ko ang aking mga magulang.
I love my parents.

Minamahal niya ang kanyang bunso nang higit sa lahat.
He/She loves his/her youngest child the most.

What is the difference between **mahalin** and **ibigin**?

When you are referring to a sensual love between a man and a woman, use **ibig**. Thus, the mutual feelings a man and a woman may share are called **pag-iibigan** (*mutual love*) and they **pag-ibig** (*love*) for each other. You may also use a weaker term—but nonetheless implying strong affection—**pagmamahalan** (*bond of love*).

However, for the filial love that exists between a parent and a child, between siblings, between friends or in all other types of relationships, the various forms of the verb **mahal** are used instead. Thus, either **pagmamahal** or **pagmamahalan** (both of which means *love*) is used.

Proper:	**Minamahal ko ang aking anak.**	I love my child.
Improper:	**Iniibig ko ang aking anak.**	

Proper:	**Minamahal nila ang kanilang ama.**	They love their father.
Improper:	**Iniibig nila ang kanilang ama.**	

An exception to this is the poetic and patriotic use of the noun **pag-ibig** when referring to the love for one's country (or **pag-ibig sa tinubuang lupa**, as used by Filipino heroes Dr. Jose Rizal and Andres Bonifacio in their writings for their fellowmen in the late 19th century, refer to appendices).

II. TO LIKE

The English word *to like* indicates fondness for someone or for doing certain activities. Its Tagalog equivalent is either **gusto** or **ibig**, which may be used interchangeably.

The ligatures **-ng** or **-g** are attached to possessive pronouns such as **niya**, **ko**, and **namin** in sentences containing **gusto** or **ibig**, and the possessive word **ni** (or **ng**, see Lesson Eight) and the ligature **na** are used to conform to the usual rules. Also take note of the usage of the articles **si** (which precedes a name such as Claudette), **sina** (if the noun is plural), **ng** (which should precede the name of a thing), and **sa** (which should precede the name of a place).

Gusto (or **ibig**) **niyang lumangoy.**	He/She loves to swim.
Gusto kong magluto.	I love to cook.
Gusto ko si Claudette.	I love Claudette.
Gusto nila sa Tagaytay.	They like Tagaytay.
Gusto naming lumakad sa ulan.	We love to walk in the rain.
Gusto kong magbasa bago matulog.	I love to read before going to bed.
Gusto ni Tom na basahin ang libro.	Tom likes to read the book.

Gusto may be duplicated—as in **gustong-gusto**—to indicate an intense feeling or desire for something or someone.

EXERCISES

Compose a paragraph made up of not less than six sentences that detail the things you like and the activities you like to do.

Translate the following sentences into Tagalog.

1. I love to walk in the rain.
2. Peter's dog loves him very much.
3. God loves us all.
4. I love my brother more than my sister.
5. Are you in love with that man?
6. Do you like this?
7. I love to play the piano.
8. The rich bachelor loves the poor girl.

LESSON TWENTY-THREE
Who, Which and *That*

Magaling ang palabas na sinulat niya.
The show she wrote is good.

Nasa teatro sina Mr. and Mrs. Alvarez. Gustong-gusto nila ang palabas.
Mr. and Mrs. Alvarez are in the theater. They like the show very much.

MR. ALVAREZ : **Sino ang nag-imbita sa atin?**
Who invited us?

MRS. ALVAREZ : **<u>Iyong nasa harap</u>. Kaklase ko siya sa kolehiyo.**
That one in front. She was a college classmate.

MR. ALVAREZ : **Siya ba ang nag-sulat? Maganda ang <u>kwentong sinulat</u> niya.**
Is she the writer? The story that she wrote is good.

MRS. ALVAREZ : **Oo. At magaling din ang <u>artistang kinuha</u> nila.**
Yes. And the actress that they got is also good.

MR. ALVAREZ : **Ang lapit natin sa entablado!**
We're so near the stage!

MRS. ALVAREZ : **Kitang-kita natin ang <u>lahat na nangyayari</u>.**
We can see everything that is happening.

Vocabulary List

nasunog = burned	**kaklase** = classmate
tinanggap = received	**kolehiyo** = college
ginigising = being awakened	**kwento** = story
niluto = cooked	**sinulat** = wrote
inaabala = being disturbed	**artista** = actor/actress
tinatawag = being called	**entablado** = stage
nag-imbita = invited	**lahat** = everything/all

An English sentence may contain any of the following relative pronouns—such as *who, which* or *that*. This type of pronoun establishes a connection with a preceding noun. A similar relationship is found in Tagalog sentences. A ligature (**-ng, -g** and **na**) connects the noun or pronoun to a verb (or vice-versa) and results in a phrase that acts as a relative pronoun.

In the phrases below, the underlined ligatures stand for *who, which* and *that.* The rules in using these ligatures are laid out in Lesson Seven (Words that Link and Describe). Note that changing the sequence of the noun or pronoun and the verb does not change the meaning of the phrase (see Lesson Seven).

ang bata<u>ng</u> kumakain or ang <u>ku</u>makain<u>g</u> bata   the child <u>who</u> is eating

ang bahay <u>na</u> nasunog or ang nasunog <u>na</u> bahay   the house <u>which</u> was burned

ang pagkaing niluto or ang niluto<u>ng</u> pagkain   the food <u>that</u> was cooked

Sample Sentences

Ang sulat na tinanggap ko ay kanya.
The letter that I received was his/hers.

Maliit ang sapatos na binili ko.
The shoes that I bought were small.

Kaming nag-aaral ang inaabala mo.
We who are studying are being disturbed by you. (literal)

Magaganda ang mga babaeng umaawit.
The women who are singing are beautiful.

Ginigising ng bata ang lalaking natutulog
The man who is sleeping is being awakened by the child.

Iyong mga umaalis ang mga tinatawag mo.
The ones that you are calling are those who are leaving.

In case of names of persons as subjects, it is not wrong to say:

Kaibigan ko si Pedrong umaawit.
Pedro, the one who sings, is my friend.

Si <u>Juang sumulat</u> nitong kuwento ay may sakit.
Juan, the who wrote this story, is sick.

Note however, that the use of the ligature **na** after a name of a person is more common, as in:
Kaibigan ko si Pedro na umaawit.
Si <u>Juan na sumulat</u> nito ay may sakit.

EXERCISES

Translate the underlined words into Tagalog. Alternate between subject-predicate and inverse or conversational order, so you can practice with both sentence forms.

1. The <u>man who is talking</u> is my father.

    _____

2. The <u>pair of shoes that I bought</u> was very large.

    _____

3. The <u>boy who eats</u> vegetables is healthy.

    _____

4. The <u>dog which we bought</u> is very pretty.

    _____

5. The <u>book which I read</u> was written by Romulo.

    _____

6. The <u>child who was sick</u> was taken to the hospital.

    _____

7. The <u>chicken that I ate</u> was delicious.

    _____

8. <u>They, who are sleeping,</u> are lazy.

    _____

9. The <u>dress which she will wear</u> (**isusuot**) is expensive.

    _____

10. The <u>chair that he broke</u> is old.

    _____

LESSON TWENTY-FOUR

Saying *Please*

Pakidala ang sulat ko sa Amerika.
Please bring my letter to America.

Pupunta ang kaibigan ni Olivia, si Natalie, sa Los Angeles. Nandoon ang mga kapatid niya, kaya may sulat siya para sa kanila.
Olivia's friend, Natalie, will go to Los Angeles. Olivia's siblings are there so she has a letter for them.

OLIVIA : **Baka maabala ka! Sigurado ka ba?**
It may be an inconvenience to you! Are you sure?

NATALIE : **Hindi problema. Malapit ang bahay ng mga kapatid mo sa hotel ko.**
It's not a problem. Your siblings' house is near my hotel.

OLIVIA : **Kung ganoon, <u>pakidala</u> ang sulat ko sa kanila. May mga litrato sa sobre.**
If that's the case, please bring my letter to them. The envelope has some pictures.

NATALIE : **Papasyal din ako sa mga shopping outlet. Anong pasalubong ang gusto mo?**
I would also visit the shopping outlets. What gift would you like?

OLIVIA : **Ayos na. <u>Pinabili ko</u> ng bagong sapatos ang mga kapatid ko.**
All good. I already requested my siblings to buy new shoes.

NATALIE : **<u>Pakisabi</u> sa kanila na tatawag ako sa kanila.**
Please tell them that I will call them.

OLIVIA : **Oo naman. Salamat ulit ha.**
Yes of course. Thank you again.

Vocabulary List

kunin = get
maaari = possible
pakikuha = (please) get
pinakikisakay = (please) give a ride
pakibasa = (please) read
pakidala = (please) bring
maabala = be inconvenienced

sigurado = sure/certain
problema = problem
papasyal = will visit
pinabili = requested to buy
pakisabi = please say
tatawag = will call

Saying *please* in Tagalog requires the use of the prefixes **paki-** and **maki-**, which when added to action roots form derivative verbs that are used for requests.

A **paki-** verb is passive like an **-in-** verb and needs a doer of the action in the possessive form such as **niya** and **mo**.

On the other hand, a **maki-** verb is active like an **-um-** verb and needs a doer in the nominative form such as **si Nestor, ako, siya, and ikaw**.

These verbs have tenses but the imperative form is mostly used. And as Tagalogs prefer to speak in the passive, **paki-** verbs are more widely used in making requests.

Forming **Paki-** and **Maki-** Derivatives

Example: **kuha**	to get
Infinitive: **makikuha**	(**maki-** + root) to please get
Imperative: **makikuha**	(**maki-** + root)
Past: **nakikuha**	(**naki-** + root)
Present: **nakikikuha**	(**nakiki-** + root)
Future: **makikikuha**	(**makiki-** + root)

Example: **kuha**	to get
Infinitive: **pakikuha**	(**paki-** + root) to please get
Imperative: **pakikuha**	(**paki-** + root)
Past: **pinakikuha**	(**pinaki-** + root)
Present: **pinakikikuha**	(**pinakiki-** + root)
Future: **pakikikuha**	(**pakiki-** + root)

Sample Sentences

Pakikuha mo ang aking baro.	(You) Please get my dress.
Pakibasa mo sa akin ang kuwento.	(You) Please read to me the story.
Pakisulat mo ang iyong pangalan.	(You) Please write your name.
Pakidala mo ang aking sulat sa koreo.	(You) Please take my letter to the post office.
Makiluto ka ng adobong manok.	(You) Please cook the chicken *adobo* (a Filipino dish).
Makitawag ka ng doktor para sa akin.	(You) Please call a doctor for me.
Pinakitawag ko ang doktor sa kanya.	I requested him/her to call the doctor for me.

Makikidala ako ng balutan sa iyo.	I shall request you to carry a package for me.
Pakikikuha ko sa katulong ang aking sapatos.	I shall request the housemaid to get the shoes for me.
Pinakikisakay niya ang bata sa aming kotse.	She requests us to give the child a ride in our car.

Using either **nga** or **naman** signals a request and softens an order even without the **paki-** or **maki-** verbs. **Nga** means *truly* or *indeed* and indicates affirmation (**Oo nga.** *Yes indeed/of course.*) or emphasis (see imperative sentences below).

Pakikuha mo <u>nga</u> ang aking baro.	(You) Please get my dress.
Kunin mo <u>nga</u> ang aking baro.	

Naman means a lot of things, including *also*, *too* and *instead*. When used in imperative sentences, it does not specifically translate into any word but it softens requests and expresses emphasis—even without the **paki-** or **maki-** verbs.

Pakikuha mo naman ang aking baro.	(You) Please get my dress.
Kunin mo naman ang aking baro.	

A way of expressing a request in question form is by using **maaari** followed by **ba** with the ligature **-ng** properly attached.

Maaari bang kunin mo ang aking damit?	May you get my dress?
Maaari bang basahin mo ang kuwento?	May you read the story?
Maaari bang bumili ka ng tsokolate para sa akin?	May you buy a chocolate for me?

A positive answer to these requests is **Opo, maaari** (which is demanded in the polite Filipino society) or **Oo, maaari.**

Take note, however, that using **nga** and **naman** when talking to elders and the authorities without the **paki-** and **maki-** verbs is considered impolite. Requests should always be made with all the necessary polite appendages mentioned in Lesson Three such as **po** and the plural forms of pronouns like **sila** and **kayo.**

EXERCISE

Practice making requests with your conversation partner. Use **maki**, **paki** and **maaari** forms at least once each.

This dialogue contains grammar concepts covered in Lessons 25 and 26.

Janice, nasaan ka? Nasa labas kami ng bahay mo.
Janice, where are you? We're outside your house.

Narito ako. Pumasok kayo sa loob ng bahay.
I'm here. Come inside the house.

Nag-text siya. Nasa Baguio siya.
She sent a text. She's in Baguio.

Nasaan si Chris? Hindi niya sinasagot ang tawag namin.
Where's Chris? She's not answering our call.

Nagsasalita si Chris sa isang kumperensiya.
Chris is talking at a conference.

Pupunta ka ba sa kanya?
Will you go to her?

Hanggang sa Lunes si Chris sa Baguio.
Chris is in Baguio until Monday.

Saan kayo nagpunta kanina?
Where did you go earlier?

Mula sa Maynila, tatlong oras ang biyahe doon. Medyo malayo.
From Manila, the trip there takes three hours. It's a bit far.

Mula sa Martes, nandito na siya.
From Tuesday, she'll be here.

Galing kami sa isang basketball game.
We came from a basketball game.

LESSON TWENTY-FIVE

Saan and Nasaan (*Where*)

Nasorpresa si Janice dahil dumating sina Robert at Miguel, pero kulang ang bark-ada nila dahil wala sa Chris.

Janice was surprised that Robert and Miguel came, but their group is incomplete since Chris wasn't there.

ROBERT : **(sa telepono) Janice, <u>nasaan</u> ka? <u>Nasa labas</u> kami ng bahay mo.**
Janice, where are you? We're outside your house.

JANICE : **<u>Narito</u> ako. Pumasok kayo <u>sa loob</u> ng bahay.**
I'm here. Come inside the house.

MIGUEL : **<u>Nasaan</u> si Chris? Hindi niya sinasagot ang tawag namin.**
Where's Chris? She's not answering our call.

JANICE : **Nagsasalita si Chris sa isang kumperensiya.**
Chris is talking at a conference.

MIGUEL : **Nag-text siya. <u>Nasa Baguio</u> siya.**
She sent a text. She's in Baguio.

JANICE : **Pupunta ka ba <u>sa kanya</u>?**
Will you go to her?

MIGUEL : **<u>Mula sa Maynila</u>, tatlong oras ang biyahe <u>doon</u>. Medyo malayo.**
From Manila, the trip there takes three hours. It's a bit far.

JANICE : **<u>Hanggang sa</u> Lunes si Chris sa Baguio.**
Chris is in Baguio until Monday.

ROBERT : **<u>Mula sa</u> Martes, nandito na siya.**
From Tuesday, she'll be here.

JANICE : **<u>Saan kayo nagpunta</u> kanina?**
Where did you go earlier?

MIGUEL : **<u>Galing kami sa</u> isang basketball game.**
We came from a basketball game.

Vocabulary List

dito = here, place is near the
   person speaking
diyan = there, place is near the
   person spoken to
doon = there, place is far from
   both speaker and listener
nasaan = where

silid = room
nagsasalita = is talking
medyo = a little bit... (far, long, etc.)
kanina = earlier
nagpunta = went
saan = where
magsasalita = will talk

Lesson Nine mentions **saan** and **nasaan** as two of the 14 question words. Both Tagalog words mean *where* but each requires different and specific answers.

I. USING **SAAN** 🔊

The question word **saan** is used when asking for the location of an action. It is followed by a verb (see underlined words in sample sentences) in any of the three tenses—past, present and future. A pronoun such as **tayo** or **sila** may be placed between **saan** and the verb. An answer to a question that starts with **saan** is answerable by the following phrase:

sa + name of place

The answer indicates the place where an act was, is, or will be performed. A **saan** question may also be answered by:

dito (or *here*, place is near the person speaking)
diyan (or *there*, place is near the person spoken to)
doon (or *there*, place is far from both)

QUESTIONS	ANSWERS
Saan pumunta si Peter?	**Pumunta si Peter sa Baguio.**
Where did Peter go?	Peter went to Baguio.
Saan magsasalita si Dr. Smith?	**Magsasalita si Dr. Smith sa ospital.**
Where will Dr. Smith speak?	Dr. Smith will speak in the hospital.
Saan tayo kakain?	**Dito tayo kakain.**
Where shall we eat?	We shall eat here.
Saan sila magbabasa?	**Doon sila magbabasa.**
Where will they read?	They will read there.
Saan kayo nagpasko?	**Sa Tagaytay kami nagpasko.**
Where did you spend Christmas?	We spent Christmas in Tagaytay.

II. USING **NASAAN** 🔊

The question word **nasaan** is used when asking for the location of a person or thing. **Nasaan** is always followed by either a noun or a pronoun that is introduced by either a **si** or **ang** article (**sina** or **ang mga** is used when the noun or pronoun is plural). A question that starts with **nasaan** requires a response using the following phrase:

nasa + name of place

The answer indicates the place where a person or a thing is. A **nasaan** question may also be answered by the following single-word responses:

narito (or *here*, place is near the person speaking)
nariyan (or *there*, place is near the person spoken to)
naroon (or *there*, place is far from both)

QUESTIONS	ANSWERS
Nasaan ang bata?	**Nasa paaralan ang bata.**
Where is the child?	The child is in school.
Nasaan ang aking sapatos?	**Nasa silid ang iyong sapatos.**
Where are my shoes?	Your shoes are in the room.
Nasaan ang bahay ninyo?	**Nasa Fairview ang bahay namin.**
Where is your house?	Our house is in Fairview.
Nasaan si Mary?	**Nasa bahay si Mary.**
Where is Mary?	Mary is in the house.
Nasaan sila?	**Nasa paaralan sila.**
Where are they?	They are in school.

EXERCISES

Answer the following questions orally

1. **Nasaan ang iyong lapis?**
2. **Saan nagpunta ang kaibigan mo?**
3. **Saan nakatira ang iyong mga magulang?**
4. **Saan siya galing?**
5. **Nasaan ang batang nag-aaral?**
6. **Saan kayo kumain kanina?**
7. **Saan pumunta ang mga bata?**
8. **Saan kayo nag-aaral ng Tagalog?**
9. **Nasaan ang paaralan ninyo?**
10. **Nasaan ang inyong guro?**

Write ten sentences about your city or hometown using **sa** and **nasa**.

The Preposition **Sa**

Prepositions indicate a relationship between words in a sentence by linking a phrase to the rest of the sentence. While there are *in, to, from, into, on, for, through, at,* and still many others, there is only the versatile Tagalog word **sa** that does most of the jobs of these various English prepositions.

I. MAIN USES OF **SA**

1. As *in*

   Nag-aaral kami sa silid-aralan.   We are studying in the classroom.
   Aawit siya sa aming palatuntunan.   She will sing in our program.

2. As *to*

   Pupunta kami sa Tagaytay bukas.   We shall go to Tagaytay tomorrow.
   Ibibigay ko ito sa kanya.   I shall give this to her.

3. As *from*

   Galing kami sa Baguio.   We came from Baguio.
   Sa nabasa ko, hindi totoo iyan.   From what I read, that is not true.

4. As *for*, when paired with "**para**," i.e. "**para sa**"

   Nagbigay ako ng salu-salo para sa   I gave a party for my friend.
   aking kaibigan.
   Ang damit na ito ay para sa kanya.   This dress is for her.

5. As *on*

   Ang aklat sa mesa ay bago.   The book on the table is new.
   Nakatira ako sa Taft Avenue.   I live on Taft Avenue.

Vocabulary List

silid-aralan = classroom   **palatuntunan** = program
hindi totoo = not true   **salu-salo** = party
tumalon = jumped   **bintana** = window
dyip = jeepney (a mass transport) **umakyat** = climbed

6. As *into*
   Tumalon ang aso sa ilog.   The dog jumped into the river.
   Itinapon ko ang basura sa lata.   I dumped the garbage into the can.

7. As *over*
   Aawit siya sa radyo.   She will sing over the radio.

8. As *through*
   Siya ang pangulo namin sa taong ito.   She is our president through this year.
   Nagdaan siya sa bintana.   He passed through the window.

9. As *at*
   Nililinis niya ang mga bintana sa paaralan.   She cleans the windows at school.
   Nagsusulat ako sa gabi.   I usually write at night.

The universal use of **sa** in Tagalog and other Philippine languages could be the reason why Filipinos find it difficult to learn the different meanings and uses of the various English prepositions.

II. OTHER USES OF **SA**

1. To indicate location

a. In the following phrases and sample sentences, **sa** is followed by a noun that expresses position or location to indicate the direction or location of a person or a thing.

sa loob = *inside*
    Pumasok ang ina sa loob ng bahay.   The mother went inside the house.

sa labas = *outside*
    Kumain kami sa labas ng bahay.   We ate outside the house.

sa harap = *in front*
    Sila ay nakatira sa harap ng aming   They live in front of our school.
       paaralan.

sa tabi = *beside*
    Umupo ka sa tabi ko.   Sit beside me.

sa itaas = *above, up*
    Umakyat (*climb* or *go up*) **siya sa itaas.**   He/She went up.

sa gitna = *in the middle*
  Umupo ang bata sa gitna.   The child sat in the middle.

sa pagitan = *between*
  Tayo ay nasa pagitan ng langit at lupa.   We are between heaven and earth.

sa likuran = *behind*
  Lumakad sa likuran ng dyip ang tao.   The person walked behind the jeepney.

sa ibaba = *below / downstairs*
  Nagpunta sa ibaba ang lalaki.   The man went downstairs.

The article **sa** may be changed to **nasa** to indicate the location of a person or thing such as **nasa loob** or **nasa likuran** in response to a question that starts with **nasaan** (see also Lesson Thirty-Three).

Similarly, **sa** + **may** is used to mean *near* or *about*. Use the phrase to express your doubt as to where the location of someone or something is.

  Siya ay nakatira sa may Roxas Boulevard.   She lives near Roxas Boulevard.

b. To indicate where a person has been, it is clearer to use any of the phrases **galing sa**, **mula sa** or **buhat sa**—which are all equivalent to the English preposition *from* rather than **sa** alone. In fact, the combination of these words literally translates to *from from* as **galing**, **mula** and **buhat** basically mean *from* also. To indicate location, the **sa** phrase is then followed by a name of a place (see Lesson Twenty-Five).

  Galing sa Baguio ang mga bagong kasal.   The newlyweds came from Baguio.

  Mula sa Maynila ang aking sapatos.   My shoes are from Manila.

  Buhat sa Tagaytay, nagbus kami.   From Tagaytay, we rode on a bus.

If a speaker wishes to point out a subject's hometown, only **mula sa** and **buhat sa** may be used to mean *a native of* or *belonging to a place*.

  Siya ay mula sa aming nayon.   He/She is from our town.

  Ang aking ina ay buhat sa Maynila.
  Taga-Maynila ang aking ina.   My mother is from Manila.

2. To indicate periods of time

Similar to the previous subsection on the use of **galing sa**, **mula sa** or **buhat sa**, the prolific word **sa** may also be used to indicate a period of time (see also related uses in Lesson Twenty-Eight).

However, only **mula** and **buhat** are applicable. A third word is **hanggang** (or *until*). These three are partnered with **noon** (literally means *then*), **sa**, **ngayon** and hours or dates. Some combinations are as follows:

> **mula noon hanggang sa ngayon** (*since then until now*)
> **mula sa / buhat sa** + time, date or period (*from + time, date or period*)
> **hanggang sa ngayon** (*until now*)
> **hanggang sa** + time, date or period (*until + time, date or period*)

Non-Tagalog speakers may notice that most of the times, native speakers omit **sa** from phrases that indicate time. The result though is still widely understood.

Mula sa Lunes, sa umaga na ang klase namin.
Mula Lunes, umaga na ang klase namin.
From Monday, our classes will be in the morning.

Buhat sa isang linggo, magkasama na kami.
From next week, we will be together.

Mula sa Lunes hanggang Biyernes, wala kaming klase.
Mula Lunes hanggang Biyernes, wala kaming klase.
From Monday to Friday, we will not have classes.

Buhat sa Oktubre hanggang Pebrero, magiging malamig na.
From October to February, it will be cool.

EXERCISES

Translate the following account of a visitor to the cool and scenic Tagaytay City into Tagalog. Refer to the vocabulary list after the account for the meaning of words. Afterwards, underline all phrases in the translation with **sa**.

We went to Tagaytay for a picnic. Travel (**biyahe**) from Manila to Tagaytay was 45 minutes (**minuto**) by car. There were many fruits (**prutas**) that could be bought along the road. When we reached Tagaytay, we bought pineapples (**pinya**), bananas (**saging**) and oranges (**dalandan**) at a store. The scenery (**tanawin**) was very beautiful. We walked near the lake and took many pictures (**larawan**).

We had some pictures (**larawan**) with the children of the place. They were selling oranges. We wanted to swim but the water was dirty. We returned to the picnic place and ate our lunch. We were all hungry. Afterwards, some played ball while the others just sat on the grass (**damo**). From the picnic site, we could see the whole Taal Lake down below. We left the picnic site at three in the afternoon (**hapon**). We went to Taal Vista Lodge, a nice hotel in Tagaytay, and drank delicious juice (**tubig ng niyog**) from young coconuts (**buko**). We went home to Manila at four in the afternoon, tired but very happy.

Vocabulary List

minuto = minute

pinya = pineapple

saging = banana

dalandan = orange

lawa = lake

buko = young coconut

larawan = pictures

usok = smoke

prutas = fruit

bundok = mountain

hapon = afternoon

masarap = delicious

tuktok; itaas = top

daan = road

The Prepositions **Para Sa** and **Para Kay**

<u>Para kay</u> Olivia ang sapatos.
The shoes are for Olivia.

Dinala ni Natalie ang sulat ni Olivia kay Cheryl, ang pinsan nito.
Natalie brought Olivia's letter to Cheryl, her cousin.

NATALIE : **May sulat at mga litratro si Olivia <u>para sa inyo</u>.**
Olivia has a letter and pictures for you.

CHERYL : **Maalahanin talaga ang pinsan ko.**
My cousin is really thoughtful.

NATALIE : **Sumulat din siya <u>sa mga dating kaklase</u> niya dito.**
She also wrote to her former classmates here.

CHERYL : **Ganoon ba? Ako na ang magpapadala <u>para sa kanya</u>.**
Is that so? Then I'll mail them for her.

NATALIE : **Gusto ko sana bumili ng regalo <u>para sa pamangkin ko</u>.**
I was hoping to buy a gift for my niece.

CHERYL : **Malapit kami sa Disney Store.**
We're near Disney Store.

NATALIE : **Talaga? Sige, pupunta ako doon mamaya.**
Really? Great, I'll go there later.

NATALIE : **Oo nga pala, may regalo ako <u>para sa pamilya mo</u>.**
Oh before I forget, I have a gift for your family.

Vocabulary List

regalo = gift
kapatid na babae = sister
magbayad = to pay
pahayagan = newspaper
litrato = photos
maaalahanin = thoughtful

sumulat = wrote
dati = former/before
magpapadala = will send
pamangkin = niece or nephew
malapit = near

An indirect object is either a noun or pronoun. In an English sentence, an indirect object answers any of the questions *to whom, to what, for whom,* or *for what.* However, an indirect object in a Tagalog sentence is easy to spot as it is introduced by the prepositions **para kay, para sa, kay** and **sa**. The prepositions **para kay** and **para sa** both mean *for* while **sa** and **kay** both mean *to.* The use of **sa** and **kay** is not interchangeable as the following formulas show:

para sa / sa + possessive pronoun (+ ligature **-g** + noun, optional)
para kay / kay ı proper name of a person

Sample Sentences

Bumili siya ng aklat <u>para sa akin</u>.	He/She bought a book for me.
Bumili siya ng aklat <u>para sa aking ina</u>.	He/She bought a book for my mother.
Sumulat ako ng kuwento <u>para sa mga bata</u>.	I wrote a story for the children.
Bumili siya ng aklat <u>para kay Mary</u>.	He/She bought a book for Mary.
Magbayad kayo ng utang <u>sa kanya</u>.	Pay your debt to him.
Bumasa siya <u>sa akin</u> ng isang kuwento.	He/She read to me a story.
Binasa niya ang pahayagan <u>sa kanyang ama</u>.	He/She read the newspaper to his father.
Dinala ko ang aklat <u>sa guro</u>.	I brought the book to the teacher.
Sumulat siya <u>kay Bob</u> kahapon.	He wrote to Bob yesterday.

In contrast to an English sentence, a Tagalog sentence with an indirect object need not have a verb. In many cases, the action is implied as in the sample sentences below with the demonstrative pronouns **ito** and **iyan**. In either word order, the meanings of the sentences below do not change and verbs are still absent.

Ito ay regalo ko <u>para sa iyo</u>.	This is my gift for you.
Regalo ko ito para sa iyo.	
Iyan ay <u>para sa kanila</u>.	That is for them.
Para sa kanila iyan.	
Ito ay regalo ko <u>kay Helen</u>.	This is my gift to Helen.
Regalo ko ito kay Helen.	

When an indirect object introduced by the preposition is plural, some changes also take place (refer to the plurality rule introduced in Lesson Four). Instead of **para kay** or **kay**, **para kina** is used. On the other hand, there are no changes in sentences with **para sa** or **sa** as pronouns have plural forms (such as **para sa kanila** or **sa amin**).

Magbayad kayo <u>kina G. at Gng. Smith</u>.   You pay to Mr. and Mrs. Smith.

Bumasa siya <u>kina Peter at Johnny</u>.   He read to Peter and Johnny.

In an informal situation, one may hear Filipinos use **sa kay**, **para sa kay**, **sa kina**, and **para sa kina**. However, it is acceptable to omit **sa** in the two sample sentences below.

Magbayad ka <u>sa kina G. at Gng. Smith</u>.   You pay to Mr. and Mrs. Smith.
Magbayad ka <u>kina G. at Gng. Smith</u>.

Bumasa siya <u>sa kina Peter at Johnny</u>.   He read to Peter and Johnny.
Bumasa siya <u>kina Peter at Johnny</u>.

EXERCISES

Identify the complete prepositional phrases in the following sentences. Afterwards, translate the sentences into Tagalog.

1. _____ He wrote to me.

2. _____ She cooked for us.

3. _____ He sold the shoes of John.

4. _____ The mother cooks the food for her children.

5. _____ She went with Charles to the Post Office.

6. _____ The boy brought the book to his mother.

7. _____ These flowers are for Annie.

8. _____ You sing for us.

9. _____ I shall sing for Mr. and Mrs. Brown.

Write ten sentences with pronouns as indirect objects and change the pronouns to names of persons.

Telling Time

Anong oras ang alis ng eroplano?
What time is the flight?

Bakasyon na ni Anna at David. Pupunta sila sa paliparan. Dapat umalis sila nang maaga dahil matrapik sa Maynila.
Finally, it's Anna and David's vacation. They will go to the airport. They need to leave early because Manila has lots of traffic.

ANNA : **<u>Anong oras na</u>? Baka mahuli tayo!**
What time is it? We might be late!

DAVID : **<u>A las siyete ng umaga</u>. Maaga pa.**
It's 7 a.m. It's still early.

ANNA : **<u>A las dose</u> ang alis ng eroplano.**
The flight is at 12 p.m.

DAVID : **<u>Kailan</u> tayo pupunta sa airport?**
When will we go to the airport?

ANNA : **<u>Anong araw</u> ba ngayon? Naku, Biyernes. Baka matrapik.**
What day is today? Oh, it's Friday. There may be traffic.

DAVID : **Tatawag na ako ng taxi.**
I'll call a taxi now.

ANNA : **<u>Bukas</u>, nasa Paris na tayo!**
By tomorrow, we'll be in Paris!

Vocabulary List

umaga = morning
madaling-araw = dawn
samakalawa = day after tomorrow
oras = hour
noong Martes = last Tuesday
sa isang buwan = next month

baka = maybe/might
paliparan = airport
maaga = early
matrapik = full of traffic
tatawag = will call

Tagalogs love to ask the time. **Anong oras na?** *What time is it?*, they ask strangers. A learner may thus do well to know how to tell time in Tagalog so as to be able to respond properly in the language of the one who asks.

The following vocabulary words and phrases are fundamental in telling time; please memorize them.

umaga	morning	**tanghali**	noon (basically 11 a.m to 1 p.m.)
hapon	afternoon	**gabi**	night
hatinggabi	midnight	**oras**	hour
kalahati	half	**minuto**	minute
beses	frequency	**ilang beses**	few times
hanggang	until	**madaling-araw**	dawn
sandali	second, moment (as a response, it means *for a while*)		

mula sa umaga hanggang gabi
(use in sentences to indicate present or future activities)
from morning until evening

mula noong Enero hanggang ngayon
(use in sentences to indicate past activities)
from last January until now

To express time in Tagalog, the prefix **ika-** is placed before cardinal numbers. The Spanish equivalent (in Tagalog orthography) of time is included in this lesson as it still has a wider use among Tagalogs and non-Tagalogs.

ENGLISH	TAGALOG	SPANISH
1:00 a.m.	**unang oras ng umaga**	a la una ng umaga
2:00 a.m.	**ikalawa ng umaga**	a las dos ng umaga
3:00 a.m.	**ikatlo ng umaga**	a las tres ng umaga
4:00 a.m.	**ika-apat ng umaga**	a las kuwatro ng umaga
5:00 a.m.	**ikalima ng umaga**	a las sinko ng umaga
6:00 a.m.	**ikaanim ng umaga**	a las seis ng umaga
7:00 a.m.	**ikapito ng umaga**	a las siyete ng umaga
8:00 a.m.	**ikawalo ng umaga**	a las otso ng umaga
9:00 a.m.	**ikasiyam ng umaga**	a las nuwebe ng umaga
10:00 a.m.	**ikasampu ng umaga**	a las diyes ng umaga
11:00 a.m.	**ikalabing-isa ng umaga**	a las onse ng umaga
12:00 noon	**ikalabindalawa ng tanghali**	a las dose ng tanghali
1:00 p.m.	**unang oras ng hapon**	a la una ng hapon
2:00 p.m.	**ikalawa ng hapon**	a las dos ng hapon
3:30 p.m.	**ikatlo at kalahati ng hapon**	a las tres y medya ng hapon
4:00 a.m.	**ika-apat ng hapon**	a las kuwatro ng hapon
5:15 p.m.	**ikalima at labinlimang minuto ng hapon**	a las sinko y kuwarto ng hapon
6:40 p.m.	**ikaanim at apatnapung minuto ng gabi**	a las seis kuwarenta ng gabi

ENGLISH	TAGALOG	SPANISH
7:00 p.m.	**ikapito ng gabi**	a las siyete ng gabi
8:00 p.m.	**ikawalo ng gabi**	a las otso ng gabi
9:10 p.m.	**ikasiyam at sampung minuto ng gabi**	a las nuwebe diyes ng gabi
10:00 p.m.	**ikasampu ng gabi**	a las diyes ng gabi
11:00 p.m.	**ikalabing-isa ng gabi**	a las onse ng gabi
12:00 midnight	**ikalabindalawa ng hatinggabi**	a las dose ng hatinggabi

The shortened forms of time, most common in writing, are:

n.u. = **ng umaga**, a.m.   **n.h.** = **ng hapon**, p.m.

n.t. = **ng tanghali**, noon   **n.g.** = **ng gabi**, evening

Lesson Nine mentions **kailan** (or *when*) as one of the question words. **Kailan** questions are used to ask what time an act happened, happens or will happen or what time someone did, does or will do something. Such questions starting with **kailan** may be answered by using any of the phrases below. Note that each grouping (past, present and future) uses specific words to express time. These words and phrases—**ngayon**, **noong** (**noon** + ligature **-g**), **kaninang** (**kanina** + ligature **-ng**), **sa** or **sa isang** (**isa** + ligature **-ng**), and **sa susunod na**—may be attached to dates to indicate a specific time.

Present:	**ngayon**	now
	ngayong araw	today
	ngayong umaga	this morning (assume that it is still morning)
Past:	**kanina**	a moment ago
	kahapon	yesterday
	kagabi	last night
	kamakalawa	day before yesterday
	noong araw	in the olden times
	noong unang panahon	a long time ago
	noong Linggo	last Sunday
	noong Martes	last Tuesday
	noong isang linggo	last week (as opposed to **Linggo** or *Sunday*)
	noong isang buwan	last month
	noong isang taon	last year
	noong Enero	last January
	kaninang umaga	this morning (assume that it is now afternoon)

Noon(g) cannot be paired with the more recent **kahapon** nor **kagabi**. However, **noong isang hapon** and **noong isang gabi** are acceptable.

Future:	mamaya	later within the day
	mamayang hapon	later this afternoon
	mamayang gabi	later this evening
	bukas	tomorrow
	samakalawa	day after tomorrow
	sa Linggo	next Sunday
	sa Martes	next Tuesday
	sa isang linggo	next week
	sa isang buwan	next month
	sa isang taon	next year
	sa Enero	next January
	sa susunod na Lunes	next Monday
	sa susunod na buwan	next month

Sa bukas is an exception as **bukas** is enough.

Sample Sentences

Anong oras na?
What time is it?

Ngayon ay ika-apat ng hapon.
It is four p.m.

Anong araw at oras ka ba aalis?
What day and time are you leaving?

Aalis ka ba mamaya?
Will you leave later (within the day)?

Oo, mamayang ikalima ng hapon.
Yes, later at five in the afternoon.

Pupunta kami sa kapilya bukas sa ikapito ng umaga.
We will go to the chapel tomorrow at seven in the morning.

Dadalaw kami sa aming kaibigan sa ikalima ng hapon.
We shall visit our friend at five in the afternoon.

Ang mga bata ay aawit sa Luneta bukas ng hapon.
The children will sing at the Luneta tomorrow afternoon.

Tutugtog ang banda (musical band) **sa gabi.**
The band will play in the evening.

Sa isang linggo, kami ay pupunta sa Tagaytay.
Next week, we shall go to Tagaytay.

Noong isang buwan, pumunta kami sa Baguio.
Last month, we went to Baguio.

EXERCISES

Tell the following times in Tagalog. Give the Spanish equivalents.

1. 8:00 p.m. _____

2. 10:00 a.m. _____

3. 5:30 p.m. _____

4. 6:00 a.m. _____

5. 1:00 p.m. _____

6. 6:15 a.m. _____

7. 3:00 p.m. _____

8. 6:30 p.m. _____

9. 7:45 p.m. _____

10. 12:00 a.m. _____

Answer the following questions in complete Tagalog sentences.

1. **Anong oras ka ba aalis bukas?**
2. **Ano bang araw ngayon?**
3. **Anong araw bukas?**
4. **Anong oras ka ba pupunta sa ospital?**
5. **Anong oras ka ba pupunta sa kapilya?**
6. **Ilang oras ang inyong pag-aaral sa Tagalog?**
7. **Anong oras kayo nag-aaral?**
8. **Ilang beses** (*how many times*) **ang inyong pag-aaral sa isang linggo?**
9. **Ilang oras ang inyong pag-aaral araw-araw?**
10. **Ilang oras ang inyong pag-aaral sa isang linggo?**

Read the following aloud:

1. **ika-6:00 n.h.**
2. **ika-2:30 n.u.**
3. **ika-12:00 n.t.**
4. **ika-8:15 n.u.**
5. **ika-7:00 n.g.**
6. **ika-6:45 n.g.**
7. **ika-2:15 n.g.**
8. **ika-10:00 n.u.**

The Word *When* in Tagalog

Pupunta tayo kung saan mo gusto.
We will go where you like.

Hinahanap nina Anna at David ang Luxembourg gardens sa Paris. Pagod na si Anna, pero nawawala sila.
Anna and David are searching for the Luxembourg gardens in Paris. Anna is already tired, but they're lost.

ANNA : **Gusto kong bumalik sa hotel.**
I'd like to go back to the hotel.

DAVID : **Magtatampo ako <u>pag</u> aalis ka.**
I'll feel hurt if you leave.

ANNA : **Alam mo ba <u>kung paano</u> pumunta sa hardin na ito?**
Do you know how to get to this garden?

DAVID : **Ewan ko, pero magtatanong ako.**
I don't know, but I'll ask.

ANNA : **Sumakay na tayo sa metro.**
Let's just go ride the metro.

DAVID : **Tama ka. Kumain muna tayo <u>kung gusto mo</u>.**
You're right. Let's eat first if you like.

ANNA : **Sige. Mas maganda <u>kung</u> busog tayo.**
Sure. It's better if we're full.

Vocabulary List

kailan = when	**kung kailan** = as to when
naghihilik = snores	**Hindi ko alam.** = I do not know.
magtatampo = will be displeased	**bumalik** = to return
babalik = will return	**hardin** = garden
sabihin = say	**magtatanong** = will ask
kung sino = as to who	**sumakay** = to ride

The word *when* can be translated in various ways in Tagalog. It can be a question using the word **kailan**; or the conjunctions **nang** or **noon** to express an action in the past; or the words **kung** or **kapag** to express a present or future action similar to the English word *if*.

I. KAILAN

When is translated using **kailan** when used in a question (see Lesson Nine).

Kailan ka aalis?	When will you leave?
Kailan ka dumating?	When did you arrive?

II. NANG OR NOON

When is translated using either **nang** or **noong** (**noon** + ligature **-g**) to indicate an action that occurred in the indefinite or vague past.

Nang / Noong ako'y maliit, ako'y may aso.	When I was small, I had a dog.
Nakita ko siya nang / noong ako ay nasa Estados Unidos.	I saw him when I was in the United States.

III. KUNG OR KAPAG

When is translated using **kung** or **kapag** (shortened form is **pag**) to indicate an action that is happening in the present or will still happen in the future. In this sense, the English word *if shares* a similar meaning.

Kung aalis ka, sasama ako sa iyo.	When you leave, I shall go with you. If you leave, I shall go with you.
Naghihilik siya kapag natutulog.	He snores when he is sleeping.
Magtatampo ako pag aalis ka.	I will be displeased if you leave.

In addition to expressing action in a certain time frame, **kung** may also be paired with question words to create phrases that start with *as to*. When translated into English, *as to* may be omitted.

1. **kung sino** = *as to who*
   Ewan ko kung sino siya.   I do not know who he/she is.

2. **kung ano** = *as to what*
   Sabihin mo kung ano ang iyong gusto. Say what you like.

3. **kung saan** = *as to where*
   Pupunta tayo kung saan mo gusto.   We shall go to where you like.

4. **kung alin** = *as to which*
   Hindi ko alam kung alin ang pipiliin ko.   I do not know which to choose.

5. **kung kailan** = *as to when*
   Alam mo ba kung kailan siya babalik?   Do you know when he will return?

6. **kung paano** = *as to how*
   Hindi ko alam kung paano magsayaw ng Tinikling (a Philippine folk dance).
   I do not know how to dance the *Tinikling*.

7. **kung kanino** = *as to whom*
   Sasabihin ko kung kanino iyon.   I shall tell to whom that belongs.

EXERCISES

Translate the following sentences into Tagalog.

1. We shall study Tagalog if you like.
2. We shall study Tagalog when you like to.
3. Are you coming with us if we go to Tagaytay?
4. I asked him (as to) who his father is.
5. We eat when we are hungry.
6. I know when he will speak.
7. She cries when she is angry.
8. If you eat much you will be sick.
9. We were friends when we were young.
10. I shall eat if she eats.

Create sentences using the following meanings of *when*:

1. *When* as **kailan**
2. *When* as **nang**
3. *When* as **noon**
4. *When* as **kung**
5. *When* as **pag** or **kapag**
6. **Kung** with all the interrogatives

This dialogue contains grammar concepts covered in Lessons 30 and 31.

LESSON THIRTY

Verb Roots

Sa kumperensya, nag-uusap si Chris at ang kanyang kaibigang guro habang may break.

At the conference, Chris is talking with her teacher-friend while there was a break.

CHRIS   : **Binasa mo ba <u>ang sinulat</u> ko?**
          Did you read what I wrote?

CELESTE : **Oo. At nakinig ako <u>sa mga sinabi</u> mo.**
          Yes. And I listened to what you said.

CHRIS   : **"Mas matagumpay <u>ang mga masipag</u>."**
          "Those who are diligent are more successful."

CELESTE : **Tama ka. Ayaw ko rin <u>ng mga matalino</u> pero tamad.**
          You're right. I also dislike those who are smart but lazy.

CHRIS   : **Tara na. Makinig tayo <u>sa nagsasalita</u>.**
          Let's go back. Let's listen to the one speaking.

CELESTE : **Nakita ko <u>ang sasabihin</u> niya. Maganda rin.**
          I saw what he will say. It's also good.

CIIRIS   : **Kilala mo ba siya?**
          Do you know him?

CELESTE : **Ang kapatid niya <u>ang kilala</u> ko.**
          It's his sister whom I know.

CHRIS   : **Pangalan lang niya <u>ang alam</u> ko.**
          I only know his name.

CELESTE : **Tingnan mo, nagtatanong ang mga bata sa harap.**
          Look, the children in front are asking questions.

CHRIS   : **Mahirap sagutin <u>ang tanong</u> ng mga bata.**
          Children's questions are hard to answer.

Vocabulary List

tanong = question	**katamtaman** = average
mabagal = slow	**binasa** = read (past)
mas matimbang = has more weight	**nakinig** = listened
mahirap sagutin = difficult to answer	**matagumpay** = successful
sagot = answer	**matalino** = smart

A verb root is the basic form of a verb such as **aral**. When an affix is added, the root takes on different tenses (**nag-aral** is in past tense while **mag-aaral** is in the future tense) or becomes an adjective (**aral na tao**, *educated person*; **kilalang guro**, *well-known teacher*). Observe the examples of verb roots below, the derived verb forms and their meanings in English.

VERB ROOTS	DERIVATIVES	MEANING
aral	mag-aral	to study, to learn
sabi	sabihin	to say
alam	malaman	to know (things)
kilala	makilala	to know (persons)
dala	dalhin	to bring or carry
tanong	tanungin	to ask
sagot	sagutin	to answer
laki	lumaki	to grow
ibig	ibigin	to love or like
galing	manggaling	to come from
ayaw	umayaw	to decline or dislike
	or ayawan	to be declined or disliked
lakad	lumakad	to walk

However, when preceded by the article **ang** or its plural form **ang mga**, the verb root becomes a noun (see underlined words below) and may be used as a subject in the sentence.

Mabagal <u>ang aral</u> niya.	His/Her study is slow.
<u>Ang sagot</u> ko ay tama.	My answer is right.
<u>Ang sabi niy</u>a ang mas matimbang sa sinabi mo.	His/Her statement has more weight than yours.
<u>Ang alam</u> ko lamang ay ang pangalan niya.	All I know is his name.
Ang kanyang ama <u>ang kilala</u> ko.	I know his father.
<u>Ang ayaw</u> ng guro ay tamad na estudyante.	What is disliked by the teacher is a lazy student. (literal)

Bola ng kanyang kuya <u>ang dala</u> ni Peter.   Peter is carrying his brother's ball.

Mahirap sagutin <u>ang tanong</u> ng bata.   The question of the child is difficult to answer.

Katamtaman lamang <u>ang laki</u> ng bahay ko.   The size of my house is average only.

**Ibig ng lalaki na makuha <u>ang</u>   The desire of the man is to get the love
  <u>pagmamahal</u> ng babae.**   of the woman.

EXERCISES

Write down the verb root in each sentence. Afterwards, translate the sentences into Tagalog.

1. _____   I know that he is good.

2. _____   What was said by you?

3. _____   Is he liked by the woman?

4. _____   He does not like the life in the province
                                   (lalawigan).

5. _____ Our walk last Saturday was fun.

6. _____ This gift came from my sister.

7. _____ Let us listen to his complaint.

8. _____ The judgement (**hatol**) has been handed down.

9. _____ The guard has left.

10. _____ The hold of the child to his/her mother is tight.

When the roots are preceded by the article **ang** or its plural form **ang mga**, they are used as subjects in the sentence. Write five sentences using verb roots as subjects.

Ex.: **Ang aral sa unibersidad ay mahirap.**
   A university education (or study) is difficult.

Forming Nouns

In the Tagalog language, a verb or an adjective is turned into a noun simply by placing the articles **ang** or **ng** or the preposition **sa** before the verb or adjective. If the noun is plural, this should be reflected in **ang**, **ng** and **sa** as well, which become **ang mga**, **ng mga** and **sa mga** (see Lesson Four). The verb may be in any of its tenses—past, present or future.

With **ang**, **ng** and **sa**, the new noun expresses any of the following:

— the one who
— the thing that
— the one which
— what is

The person or thing being talked about in the resulting sentence may either be stated or implied.

Observe the two sentences below:

Si Jose <u>ang kumain</u> ng mangga.
The one who ate the mango is Jose.

Si Jose <u>ang batang kumain</u> ng mangga.
The child who ate the mango is Jose.

Both sentences are correct but the first one is more widely used for its brevity. The first sentence is shorter and thus easy to articulate whereas the second one is redundant with the mention of **bata**, which is understood to be Jose.

Vocabulary List

pangulo = president
sipag = diligence
igalang = to respect

naaawa = to pity
nagagalit = is angry
masipag = hardworking

Sample Sentences

Binabasa mo ba <u>ang sinulat</u> ko?
Are you reading what was written by me? (literal)

<u>Ang nagsasalita</u> ay ang pangulo.
The one who is speaking is the president.

Parang anghel <u>ang natutulog</u>.
The one sleeping is like an angel.

Masarap <u>ang mga lulutuin</u> ko para sa iyo.
Delicious, what I shall cook for you. (literal)
I shall cook a delicious meal for you.

<u>Ang mga sinasabi</u> niya ay hindi totoo.
What are said by him/her are not true. (literal)
What he is saying is not true.

Nakita ko <u>ang binabasa</u> niya.
I saw what she was reading.

Maraming kaibigan <u>ang mabait</u>.
The one who is good has many friends.

<u>Ang mga mahlhlrap</u> ay walang maraming kagamitan.
The poor people do not have many possessions.

Dapat nating igalang <u>ang matatanda</u>.
We should respect the elders.

Hindi magugutom <u>ang masipag</u>.
Will not go hungry, the hardworking. (literal)
The hardworking will not go hungry.

Humihingi siya <u>ng kinakain</u> ko.
He is asking for what I am eating.

Naaawa ako <u>sa mga humihingi</u> ng pera.
I pity those who are asking for money.

Nagagalit ang guro <u>sa mga tamad</u>.
The teacher is angry with the lazy ones.

<u>Sa nag-aaral</u>, kailangan <u>ang sipag.</u>
To one who is studying, diligence is necessary.

Note that there are two nouns in the last sentence, the noun **sa nag-aaral** (*one who is studying*) formed from a verb and a true noun **sipag** (*diligence*).

EXERCISES

Look for the nouns in the following sentences. Afterwards, translate the sentences into Tagalog.

1. _____ What he writes is good.

2. _____ The one who arrived was my father.

3. _____ This will be for the poor.

4. _____ The one she loves is an intelligent man.

5. _____ I shall give this to the one who is leaving.

6. _____ The one which he read was Rizal.

7. _____ The thing she ate was not good.

8. _____ The one which is good is the thing I bought.

9. _____ The expensive one should not be bought.

10._____ The fat are happy.

Construct sentences using the following phrases as subjects, predicates, or objects.

1. **ang mayaman**
2. **ang nag-aaral**
3. **sa nagluluto**
4. **sa mga magaganda**
5. **ang naglilinis**

6. **ang umalis**
7. **sa dumating**
8. **ang natutulog**
9. **ang mga masarap**
10. **ang magagalit**

I- Verb Forms

Isama natin si Lola Belen.

Let's bring Grandma Belen with us.

Dumalaw ang pamilya ni Ricky sa lola niya. Gustong manood ni Mr. Alvarez ng sine pagkatapos.

Ricky's family visited his grandmother. Mr. Alvarez would like to watch a movie afterwards.

LOLA BELEN	:	**Ricky, ibigay mo sa akin ang pahayagan.** Ricky, give me the newspaper.
RICKY	:	**Ito po, lola.** Here you go, grandma.
RICKY	:	**Tatay, isama natin si lola sa sinehan.** Dad, let's bring grandma with us to the cinema.
LOLA BELEN	:	**Naku, Ricky, ayaw ko ng maingay at masikip.** Oh, Ricky, I don't like noisy and crowded places.
MR. ALVAREZ	:	**Ibalita mo na lang sa lola mo ang kwento.** Just tell your grandmother about the story.
LOLA BELEN	:	**Habang nasa sine kayo, iluluto ko para sa inyo ang sinigang.** While you're at the cinema, I'll cook the *sinigang* for you.
RICKY	:	**Sige po lola, ibibili naman kita ng bulaklak!** Great, grandma, and I will buy flowers for you!
LOLA BELEN	:	**Napakabait ng aking apo.** My grandson is very kind.

Vocabulary List

ihanap (ng) = to have someone look for something
ihulog (ang) = to let something fall
idagdag (ang) = to add
ihiram (ng) = to borrow for someone else
ilagay (ang) = to place in or on

ibigay = to give
isama = to accompany/ to bring someone
ibalita = to narrate
sine = cinema
bulaklak = flower

The prefix **i-** is added to words to form passive verbs indicating that something is used to do something. For example, it may be added to the noun **sulat** (*letter*) to form the verb **isulat** (*to write down something*). When the prefix **i-** is added to a verb, it also indicates that something is done for someone else (**isulat mo ako**, *you write for me*) as well as performing the act expressed by the root word on or for the subject (**ihulog ang sulat**, *post the mail for someone*). Generally, the meaning of the **i-** verb is *to do something for another person.*

The **i-** form of a verb is used only when an active **-um-** or **mag-** verb has a direct object (the noun or pronoun that receives the action of the verb). To find out if there is a direct object in an **-um-** or **mag-** sentence, do the following steps: isolate the verb; place *whom* (or **sino**) or *what* (or **ano**) after the verb; and make it into a question. For example, **Bumili ng isda ang babae para sa kanyang ina. Bumili** *what?* The answer (**isda**) is the direct object (**ang babae** is the subject and **para sa kanyang ina** is the indirect object).

Usually, the **i-** verb is the passive form of a **mag-** verb and seldom of an **-um-** verb. Sometimes, instead of the **i-** verb, a **mag-** verb takes the variant form of **ipag-** that expresses doing something for another (see formation of derivatives in following page) and normally follows the first sentence pattern.

Forming **I-** Verb Forms

I. For verb roots beginning with consonants, the prefix **i-** (or its variant **ipag-**) is attached to all forms and tenses while the infix **-in-** is attached to past and present tenses

Example: **sulat**	letter
Infinitive: **isulat**	(**i-** + root word) to write for another
Imperative: **isulat**	(**i-** + root word) write for another
Past: **isinulat**	(**i-** + infix **-in-** after first letter of root word) wrote for another
Present: **isinusulat**	(**i-** + infix **-in-** between first syllable + root word) writes for another
Future: **isusulat**	(**i-** + duplicated first syllable + root word) will write for another

Example: **sama**	accompany
Infinitive: **isama**	(**i-** + root word) to take someone along
Imperative: **isama**	(**i-** + root word) take someone along
Past: **isinama**	(**i-** + infix **-in-** after first letter of root word) took someone along
Present: **isinasama**	(**i-** + infix **-in-** between first syllable + root word) takes someone along
Future: **isasama**	(**i-** + duplicated first syllable + root word) will take someone along

Example: **sulat**   write

Infinitive: **ipagsulat**   (**ipag-** + root word) to write for another

Imperative: **ipagsulat**   (**ipag-** + root word) write for another

Past: **ipinagsulat**   (infix **-in-** after first two letters of prefix **ipag-** + root word) wrote for another

Present: **ipinagsusulat**   (infix **-in-** after first two letters of prefix **ipag-** + duplicate first syllable + root word) writes for another

Future: **ipagsusulat**   (**ipag-** + duplicate first syllable + root word) will write for another

II. For verb roots beginning with vowels and the consonants **h, l, y** and **w**, the prefix **i-** is attached to all forms and tenses, and the infix **-in-** becomes infix **-ni-** that is attached to the past and present tenses

Example: **hanap**   search

Infinitive: **ihanap**   (**i-** + root word) to have someone look for something

Imperative: **ihanap**   (**i-** + root word) have someone look for something

Past: **inihanap**   (**i-** + infix **-ni-** + root word) had someone look for something

Present: **inihahanap**   (**i-** + infix **-ni-** + duplicate first syllable + root word) having someone look for something

Future: **ihahanap**   (**i-** + duplicate first syllable + root word) will have someone look for something

Example: **luto**   cook

Infinitive: **iluto**   (**i-** + root word) to cook something

Imperative: **iluto**   (**i-** + root word) cook something

Past: **iniluto**   (**i-** + infix **-ni-** + root word) cooked something

Present: **iniluluto**   (**i-** + infix **-ni-** + duplicate first syllable + root word) is cooking something

Future: **iluluto**   (**i-** + duplicate first syllable + root word) will cook something

Sentence Patterns for **I-** Verbs

An **i-** verb is used only when an active **-um-** or **mag-** verb has a direct object in a sentence. This rule in turn dictates which of the direct or indirect object in the **-um-** or **mag-** sentence becomes the subject in the **i-** sentence. Refer to the following sentence patterns of **i-** verbs.

I. FIRST SENTENCE PATTERN

When the **i-** verb has its active form in **-um-**, the indirect object (underlined in the following examples and introduced by the prepositions **sa**, **para sa**, **kay** and **para kay**) becomes the subject (see Lesson Twenty-Seven on these prepositions and indirect objects).

Note that the article **ang** shifted its place from **ang anak** in the first sentence to **ang ina** in the second sentence and made **ang ina** the subject in the passive **i-** sentence. Remember that the article **ang**—along with **si**—introduces the noun that is used as the subject in a sentence (see Lesson Four on these articles).

1. **Bumili ng isda ang babae <u>para sa</u>**   The woman bought fish for her
      <u>kanyang ina</u>.   mother.
      Ibinili ng babae ng isda <u>ang kanyang ina</u>.

2. **Bumasa ng aklat ang guro <u>para kay Joe</u>.**   The teacher read the book to Joe.
      Ibinasa ng guro ng aklat <u>si Joe</u>.

Because Joe is a name of a person, **si** is used instead of **ang** since **ang** introduces names of places and things.

II. SECOND SENTENCE PATTERN

When the **i-** verb has its active form in **mag-** (or in its variant form **nag-** in the past tense), the direct object (underlined in the following examples) becomes the subject, appropriately introduced by either **si** or **ang**, in the passive **i-** sentence.

1. **Nagluto siya <u>ng pagkain</u> para sa anak.**   She/He cooked the food for
      Iniluto niya <u>ang pagkain</u> para sa anak.   her/his child.

2. **Nag-ayos <u>ng silid</u> si Benjamin.**   Benjamin arranged the room.
      Iniayos ni Benjamin <u>ang silid</u>.

Note that when a personal pronoun (such as **siya**) or a name of a person (**si Benjamin**) is used in the **mag-** sentence, the article before the pronoun changes into a possessive pronoun (such as **niya**) or a possessive pronoun (such as **ni Benjamin**) in the **i-** sentence.

III. THIRD SENTENCE PATTERN

When the **-um-** and **mag-** verbs have similar meanings (refer to Lesson Fourteen on the **-um-** and **mag-** verbs), the **i-** verb follows the first sentence pattern.

Bumasa ng aklat ang guro <u>para sa bata.</u>	The teacher read the book to the
Nagbasa ng aklat ang guro <u>para sa bata</u>.	child.
Ibinasa ng aklat ng guro <u>ang bata</u>.	

EXAMPLES OF **I-** VERBS

In the list of **i-** verbs below, the articles in the parentheses should be used to introduce the receiver of the action in the **i-** sentence. The first four **i-** verbs require a subject introduced by **si** or **ang** whereas the remaining **i-** verbs require a subject introduced by **ni** or **ng**.

ihanap	**(ng)**	to have someone look for something
ibili	**(ng)**	to have someone buy something
ibasa	**(ng)**	to read for another
ihiram	**(ng)**	to borrow for someone else
isulat	**(ng)**	to write for another
iluto	**(ang)**	to cook
ituro	**(ang)**	to teach
ihulog	**(ang)**	to let something fall
itapon	**(ang)**	to throw away
ibigay	**(ang)**	to give something to someone
iwala	**(ang)**	to lose
idagdag	**(ang)**	to add
ibalita	**(ang)**	to give information
ilagay	**(ang)**	to place
ibilad	**(ang)**	to place under the sun

Sample Sentences

Ihahanap ko siya ng bagong aklat.	I shall look for a new book for him/her.
Iluto mo ang isda ngayong gabi.	You cook the fish tonight.
Ibigay mo sa akin ang pahayagan.	Give me the newspaper.
Iniwala ni Peter ang aking bola.	Was lost by Peter my ball. (literal)
	Peter lost my ball.
Ihuhulog ko ang sulat sa koreo.	I will drop the letter at the Post Office.
Itinuturo niya sa amin ang	She/He is teaching us the Tagalog
wikang Tagalog.	language.

Ibinili ako ng baro ng aking ina.	Bought for me a dress by my mother. (literal)
	My mother bought a dress for me.
Ibibilad ko ang sapatos.	Will put under the sun by me the shoes. (literal)
	I shall put the shoes under the sun.
Itatanim ng aming katulong ang saging.	Will be planted by our helper the banana tree. (literal)
	Our helper will plant the banana.
Itinapon niya ang lumang tinapay.	Thrown away by him/her the stale bread. (literal)
	He threw away the stale bread.

COMMON ERRORS WITH I- VERBS
Note the following non-existent words in the Tagalog vocabulary and their correct derivatives:

balitain	from **balita**	but there is **ibalita**	= to relay or give out news
hulugin	from **hulog**	but there is **ihulog**	= to let something fall or drop
tanimin	from **tanim**	but there is **itanim**	= to plant
punasin	from **punas**	but there is **ipunas**	= to use something to wipe with
turuin	from **turo**	but there is **ituro**	= to teach
tapunin	from **tapon**	but there is **itapon**	= to throw away
walain	from **wala**	but there is **iwala**	= to lose
balikin	from **balik**	but there is **ibalik**	= to return
bukasin	from **bukas**	but there is **ibukas**	= to cause to open
sarahin	from **sara**	but there is **isara**	= to shut

Thus, the past forms of the verbs above

are:	and not:
ibinalita	**binalita**
inihulog	**hinulog**
itinanim	**tinanim**
ipinunas	**pinunas**
ituro	**tinuro**
itinapon	**tinapon**
iniwala	**niwala**
ibinalik	**binalik**
ibinukas	**binukas**
isinara	**sinara**

EXERCISES

Pick out the **i-** verb forms from the following sentences and translate the sentences into Tagalog.

1. _____   Peter lost his ball.

2. _____   Cook the meat for us.

3. _____   He returned the book to the library.

4. _____   Open the door.

5. _____   He closed the windows.

6. _____   She taught me Tagalog at the Philippine Women's University.

7. _____   I shall buy a dress for my child.

8. _____   He gave me a pretty flower.

9. _____   Get some food for the old man.

10. _____   The woman planted the tree in the garden.

Create your own sentences using the other **i-** verbs in the previous page.

Change the **i-** sentences above into their active forms using **mag-** or **-um-** verbs based on the three sentence patterns. The subjects of the **i-** sentences will now become the direct or indirect objects of the **mag-** or **-um-** sentences.

Try to repeat orally the different tense forms of as many **i-** verbs as possible.

LESSON THIRTY-THREE
-An Verb Forms

<u>Binasahan</u> ni Chris ang mga bata.
Chris read to the kids.

Sa klase, tinatawanan ng mga bata ang kwento tungkol sa pagong at matsing. Kinukwentuhan sila ni Chris.
In class, the students are laughing at the story about the turtle and the monkey. Chris was telling them the story.

CHRIS : **<u>Buksan</u> ninyo ang aklat sa pahina 20.**
Open your book to page 20.

ANTONIO : **<u>Hiningan</u> ng pagong ang matsing ng saging.**
The turtle asked the monkey for some bananas.

CHRIS : **Nagbigay ba ng saging ang matsing?**
Did the monkey give any bananas?

MARTA : **Hindi <u>binigyan</u> ng matsing ang pagong.**
The monkey did not give any to the turtle.

ANTONIO : **Kaya nagalit ang pagong.**
Thus the turtle got angry.

CHRIS : **At <u>nilagyan</u> ng pagong ng tinik ang puno ng saging.**
And the turtle put thorns on the banana tree.

MARTA : **<u>Binantayan</u> niya ang matsing hanggang bumaba ito.**
He watched until the monkey came down.

ANTONIO : **Matalino pa rin ang pagong kahit mabagal!**
The turtle is still smart even though he's slow.

Vocabulary List

kuwento = story
anyayahan = to invite
hingan = to ask
pakinggan = to listen
halikan = to kiss
hugasan = to wash
tawanan = to laugh at
mukha = face

buksan = to open
matsing = monkey
pagong = turtle
tinik = thorn
binantayan = watched/guarded
matalino = smart
mabagal = slow

When the suffix **-an** is attached to a word, the **-an** word that is created then represents a place associated with the root word such as **aklatan** (root word is **aklat** or *book*, thus **aklatan** is a *library*) or **gupitan** (**gupit** is *to cut*, **gupitan** is *a place where they cut* or a *barber shop* or *beauty salon*).

The **-an** word forms may also express action in the passive form similar to the **-in** verb (**sulatan** is *to write* or the *act of writing* from the root **sulat** or *writing*). It is also used to indicate a description of size (**damihan** is *to increase the number* from the root **dami** or *many*) and quality (**putikan** is *muddy* from the root **putik** or *mud*).

Note that this lesson will focus on the formation of **-an** words rather than on the context of the words in the **-an** sentences.

Forming **-An** Words

The suffix **-an** is attached to roots ending in consonants as well as roots that end in vowels and pronounced with a glottal catch (such as **hingi** or *to request*). On the other hand, its variant form **-han** is attached as a suffix to roots that end in vowels and pronounced without a glottal catch (such as **sama** or *to accompany*). Derivatives of **-an** verbs are formed in the following manner:

I. FOR VERB ROOTS ENDING IN CONSONANTS

Example: **alis**	remove
Infinitive: **alisan**	(root word + **-an**) to remove something from someone
Imperative: **alisan**	(root word + **-an**) remove something from someone
Past: **inalisan**	(prefix **in-** + root word + **-an**) was/were removed
Present: **inaalisan**	(prefix **in-** + duplicate first syllable + root word + **-an**) is/are being removed
Future: **aalisan**	(duplicate first syllable + root word + **-an**) will be removed

II. FOR VERB ROOTS ENDING IN VOWELS

Example: **basa**	read
Infinitive: **basahan**	(root word + **-han**) to read to someone
Imperative: **basahan**	(root word + **-han**) read to someone
Past: **binasahan**	(infix **-in-** after first letter of first syllable + **-han**) was/were read to someone
Present: **binabasahan**	(infix **-in-** after first letter of first syllable + root word + **-han**) is/are being read to someone
Future: **babasahan**	(duplicate first syllable + root word + **-han**) will be read to someone

III. FOR IRREGULAR VERB ROOTS

Example: **lagay**	put
Infinitive: **lagyan**	(root word without the last vowel + **-an**) to put in something
Imperative: **lagyan**	(root word without the last vowel + **-an**) put in something
Past: **nilagyan**	(**ni-** + root word without the last vowel + **-an**) (Note that with the consonants **l**, **w** and **y**, the infix **-in-** becomes the prefix **ni-**, see irregular verb formations using **in-** in Lesson Fifteen) was/were put in
Present: **nilalagyan**	(**ni-** + duplicate first syllable + root word without the last vowel + **-an**) is/are being put in
Future: **lalagyan**	(duplicate first syllable + root word without the last vowel + **-an**) will be put in

EXAMPLES OF REGULAR **-AN** VERBS

bawasan	to diminish or reduce	**anyayahan**	to invite someone
butasan	to bore a hole	**ayawan**	to be refused
bantayan	to watch	**upahan**	to rent
halikan	to kiss	**sulatan**	to write to
damitan	to dress up someone	**upuan**	to seat on
bayaran	to pay	**bihisan**	to change someone's dress
sabugan	to scatter		
abutan	to hand someone something	**samahan**	to accompany
alagaan	to care for	**hugasan**	to wash (not referring to clothes)

EXAMPLES OF IRREGULAR **-AN** VERBS

In forming the derivatives of irregular **an-** verbs, the second vowel of the root word is dropped. What should have been the regular derivatives of the verbs are enclosed in parentheses below. There are also other changes in forming the derivatives of irregular verbs as seen in the last example (**hipan**) where the second syllable (**hi**) is deleted altogether.

labhan	(labahan)	to wash (clothes)
lagyan	(lagayan)	to put in something
sundan	(sunuran)	to follow someone
lakhan	(lakihan)	to enlarge something
bigyan	(bigayan)	to give someone something
tamnan	(taniman)	to have a place planted with
takpan	(takipan)	to cover
hingan	(hingian)	to ask someone for something
asnan	(asinan)	to mix with salt
tirhan	(tirahan)	to leave remains for someone

tingnan	(tinginan)	to look at
higan	(higaan)	to lie down on something
sakyan	(sakayan)	to go aboard
saktan	(sakitan)	to hurt
buksan	(bukasan)	to open
tawanan	(tawahan)	to laugh at
kunan	(kuhanan)	to take from
dalhan	(dalahan)	to bring someone something
bilhan	(bilihan)	to buy from
hipan	(hihipan)	to blow into or on something (from the root **hihip**, which means *blow*)

Sentence Patterns for **-An** Verbs

To change **-um-** or **mag-** sentences into **-an** sentences, take note of the following guidelines:

I. WITHOUT A DIRECT OBJECT

For an **-um-** or **mag-** sentence without a direct object, the indirect object introduced by the any of the prepositions **para kay**, **kay**, **para sa** and **sa** or the place introduced by **sa** becomes the subject in the **-an** sentence. The doer of the act, on the other hand, is then preceded by a possessive article (either **ni** or **ng**) in the **-an** sentence.

1. **Su̲mulat**   ang bata   <u>sa aklat</u>.
                   (doer)   (place)

   Sinula̲tan   ng bata   <u>ang aklat</u>.
                   (doer)   (subject)

   The child wrote on the book.

2. **Magbasa**   ka   sa akin.
                   (doer)   (indirect object)

   Basahan   mo   ako.
                   (doer)   (subject)

   You read to me.

Note that the indirect object **sa akin** in the **mag-** sentence above becomes the subject **ako** in the **-an** sentence (see Lesson Six on personal and demonstrative pronouns).

II. WITH A DIRECT OBJECT

In an **-um-** or **mag-** sentence with a direct object (the noun or pronoun that receives the action of the **-um-** or **mag-** verb), the object shall be preceded by the possessive article **ng** in the **-an** sentence.

As to the indirect object and the doer of the act in the **-um-** or **mag-** sentence, apply the preceding rule.

1. **Sumulat**   **ang bata**   <u>**ng pangalan**</u> **niya**   **sa aklat.**
             (doer)   (direct object)   (place)

   Sinulat<u>an</u>   **ng bata**   **ng pangalan niya**   **ang aklat.**
             (doer)   (direct object)   (subject)

   The child wrote his name on the book.

2. <u>**Magbasa**</u>   **ka**   <u>**ng kuwento**</u>   **sa akin.**
             (doer)   (direct object)   (indirect object)

   Basa<u>han</u>   **mo**   **ako**   <u>**ng kuwento**</u>**.**
             (doer)   (subject)   (direct object)

   You read to me a story.

III. WITHOUT **-IN-** VERBS

When an **-um-** or **mag-** verb has no **-in-** form, the direct object becomes the subject in the **-an** sentence.

Magbukas   **ka**   **ng pinto.**
          (doer)   (direct object)

Buks<u>an</u>   **mo**   **ang pinto.**
          (doer)   (subject)

Open the door.

Sample Sentences

Lagyan mo ng alak ang baso.	Fill the glass with wine.
Sundan ninyo ang itinuturo ko.	Follow what I am teaching.
Pakinggan ninyo ako. (a **pa-** + **-an** verb)	Listen to me.
Buksan mo ang bintana.	Open the window.
Susulatan ko ang aking ina.	I will write to my mother.
Bayaran mo ang iyong utang sa akin.	Pay your debt to me.

Inalisan ng babae ng pagkain ang anak.
Removed by the woman the food from her child. (literal)
The woman removed the food from her child.

Hinalikan ng bata ang kamay ng kanyang lola.
Was kissed by the child the hand of her grandmother. (literal)
The child kissed the hand of her grandmother.

Babasahan ko ng magandang kuwento ang aking ama.
Will be read by me a nice story for my father. (literal)
I will read a nice story to my father.

Nilabhan ng katulong ko ang aming damit.
Were washed by my helper our clothes. (literal)
My helper washed our clothes.

EXERCISES

Identify the subjects in the ten passive sample sentences in the previous page: is the subject an indirect object or a place? Then change the sentences into their active forms.

Example:

Passive	**Inalisan ng babae ng pagkain ang anak.**
Subject	**anak** (indirect object)
Active	**Nag-alis ang babae ng pagkain sa anak.**

Form the derivatives of all regular and irregular **-an** verbs in this lesson.

Change the following active sentences into passive sentences using both **i-** and **-an** verbs.

1. **Bumasa ang bata ng pahayagan sa kanyang lola.**
   The child read the newspaper to her grandmother.

2. **Nagluto ang babae ng isda sa kawali.**
   The woman cooked the fish in the pan.

3. **Nagbayad siya ng dalawang libong piso sa akin para sa sapatos.**
   He paid me two thousand pesos for the shoes.

4. **Maglalagay siya ng tubig sa mga baso.**
   She/He will put water into the glasses.

5. **Magtakip ka ng panyo sa mukha.**
   Cover your face with a handkerchief.

Adverbs

Nagmamaneho si Robert at Miguel nang nagka-aksidente sa daan. Huminto sila para tumulong.
Robert and Miguel were driving when an accident happened on the road. They stopped to help.

ROBERT : **Ano ang nangyari?**
What happened?

CYCLIST : **Nagbibisikleta ako <u>nang mabilis</u>...**
I was biking fast...

CYCLIST : **...<u>at</u> hindi huminto ang kotse.**
...and the car did not stop.

MIGUEL : **May mga nakakita ba ng plaka ng kotse?**
Did anyone see the license plate?

CYCLIST : **Wala. <u>Pero agad</u> na tumawag ng ambulansya ang mga tao.**
No. But people called an ambulance right away.

ROBERT : **Huwag kang gumalaw <u>habang</u> naghihintay tayo.**
Don't move while we're waiting.

MIGUEL : **<u>Dahil</u> baka nabalian ka.**
Because you may have broken something.

ROBERT : **<u>Sa wakas</u>, dumating na rin ang ambulansya.**
Finally, the ambulance is here.

MEDIC : **Paano siya tumama sa poste?**
How did he hit the light post?

ROBERT : **<u>Ganito</u> siya bumagsak mula sa bisikleta.**
He fell from his bike like this.

MEDIC : **Itataas ko ang braso mo <u>nang dahan-dahan</u>.**
I will slowly lift up your arm.

CYCLIST : **<u>Aray! Sobrang sakit!</u> Bali yata.**
Ouch! It's very painful. It's probably broken.

MEDIC : **Kung ganoon, <u>pahiga</u> ka namin dadalhin sa ospital.**
If so, we'll carry you to the hospital lying down.

Vocabulary List

magpakain = to feed someone	**kotse** = car
magpabasa = to order someone to read	**tumawag** = called
mahihirap na tao = poor people	**ambulansya** = ambulance
buhok = hair	**naghihintay** = waiting
nangyari = happened	**braso** = arm
nagbibisikleta = was biking	**dahan-dahan** = gently/slowly
huminto = stopped	**dadalhin** = will bring

Some words depict actions: **tumalon, gumulong, lumuha** (*jump, roll, cry*). Other words describe how the action was done: **tumalon nang mataas, gumulong nang pababa, lumuha nang malakas** (*jumps high, rolled down, cried loudly*). In this lesson, one will learn about adverbs, which modify action words by describing how, where and when an action has happened, happens or will happen.

I. ADVERBS OF MANNER

An adverb modifies how an action occurred, occurs or will occur. Generally, the article **nang** introduces this kind of adverb that is formed by attaching the prefix **pa-** to a verb root.

When translated into English, the combination of "**nang** + **pa-** + verb root" produces *-ing* verbs that resemble a participle such as the words *sitting* and *standing*. However, a **pa**-prefixed Tagalog word modifies verbs whereas a participle modifies nouns or pronouns.

Examples of adverbs of manner are the following:

1. **paupo** = *sitting down*
   patayo = *standing*
   pahiga = *lying down*

Nagbasa ang bata nang paupo.	The child read sitting down.
Nagbasa ang bata nang patayo.	The child read standing.
Nagbasa ang bata nang pahiga.	The child read lying down.

2. **ganito** = *like this* (near the speaker)
   ganyan = *like that* (near the one spoken to)
   ganoon = *like that* (far from both)

   Ganito siya kung lumakad.
   She is like this when she walks. (literal)
   She walks like this.

3. **mabilis** = *fast*
   Kumakain nang mabilis si Peter.   Peter is eating fast.

4. **dahan-dahan** = *slowly; softly*

Lumalakad siya nang dahan-dahan.	She walks slowly.
Dahan-dahan siyang lumalakad.	She walks slowly.
Dahan-dahan si Dulce na lumalakad.	Dulce walks slowly.

Adverbs of manner may be placed before or after verbs as shown in the examples above. But when the adverb comes before the verb and the subject is a name of a person (see last example), use the ligature **na** (similar examples can be found in Lesson Twenty-Three) after the subject Dulce. As for the second example, use the ligature **-ng** after the subject **siya**. However, **nang** is lost in the second structure where the adverb is placed before the verb.

5. **bigla, agad** = *suddenly; at once*

 Tumayo siya nang bigla.
 Tumayo siyang bigla. (or **biglang tumayo**)

 Siya ay agad na tumayo. (or **agad tumayo**)   He/She stood up suddenly.
 Siya ay tumayo agad.

The sequence "verb + **nang** + adverb" **(tumayo nang bigla)** may be appropriately replaced with the sequence "verb + ligature **-ng**, **-g** or **na** + adverb" **(tumayong bigla)** or the sequence "adverb + ligature **-ng**, **-g** or **na** + verb" **(biglang tumayo)** as the arrangement will not affect the meaning of the sentence. Similarly, in the case of the second set of sentences above where the ligature **na** is deleted, the meaning of the statement does not change.

II. ADVERBS OF PLACE

Similarly, adverbs describe where an action took place, is taking place or will take place. Note that all phrases with the preposition **sa** before a name of a place, either specific or general, are adverbs of place. Examples are **sa baryo** (*in the barrio or village*), **sa kusina** (*in the kitchen*), and **sa eskuwelahan** (*in school*).

Other adverbs of place include the following:

1. **dito** = *here* (near the speaker)
 diyan = *there* (near the listener)
 doon = *there* (far from both speaker and listener)

 Naglalaro ang aking kapatid na lalaki dito.   My brother plays here.

2. **saanman** = *wherever*
 Saanman siya pumunta, sasama ako.   Wherever she goes, I shall go with her.
 Saan ka man pumunta, sasama ako.   Wherever you go, I shall go with you.

The adverb **saanman** is only broken up when the shortened pronoun **ka** (the singular *you*) is the subject in the sentence. All other pronouns in the Tagalog language come after **saanman**.

3. **sa loob** = *inside*
   sa labas = *outside*

   Naglalaro ang mga bata sa loob.
   The children are playing inside (the home).

4. **buhat** = *from*
   maghuhat = *from*
   mula = *from*
   buhat sa ... hanggang = *from ... to*

Kami ay lumakad buhat (mula) sa baryo.
Lumakad kami buhat (mula) sa baryo.
We walked from the barrio.

Kami ay lumakad buhat sa baryo hanggang sa lungsod.
Lumakad kami buhat sa baryo hanggang sa lungsod.
We walked from the barrio to the city.

III.   ADVERBS OF TIME

There is a considerable number of adverbs of time which Tagalogs use. Some are monosyllabic words (introduced in Lesson Ten) while others are phrases.

Because the preposition **sa** is such a versatile word (see Lesson Twenty-Six), it is also used to indicate adverbs of time when it is placed before hours, days, months and years such as **sa Lunes** (*on Monday*), **sa hapon** (*in the afternoon*) and **sa Marso** (*in March*).

Other adverbs of time include the following:

1. **na** = *already*
   Siya ay umalis na.   He left already.

2. **pa** = *yet, more*
   Hindi pa ako kumakain.   I have not eaten yet.
   Gusto ko pa ng matamis.   I like more sweets.

3. **nang, noong** = *when*
   Nagalit siya nang umalis ako.   He/She got angry when I left.

Noong followed by date (hours, days, months or years) also means *last*. Thus, **noong Lunes** means *last Monday*.

   Natapos niya ang kolehiyo noong Marso.   He/She finished college last March.

4. **sandali** = *for a while*
   Halika sandali.   Come here for a while.

5. **pagkatapos** (+ infinitive verb) = *after*
   Matulog tayo pagkatapos kumain.   Let us sleep after eating.

6. **bago** (+ infinitive verb) = *before*
   Kumain siya bago umalis.   He/She ate before he/she left.

7. **pirmi, parati, lagi** = *always*
   Parating nag-aaral si Peter.   Peter always studies.

8. **tuwi** (+ ligature **-ng** + date) = *every*
   Tuwing Lunes, siya ay tinatamad.   Every Monday, she feels lazy.

9. **saka na** = *later*
   Saka na tayo mag-usap.   Let us talk later.

10. **buhat noon...hanggang** = *from...until; since*
    Buhat noong Lunes hanggang ngayon ay wala pa siya.
    From Monday until now he has not been here.
    Since Monday, he has not been here.

11. **kung minsan** = *sometimes* (use with the present tense of verbs)
    Kung minsan, nagagalit siya.   Sometimes she gets angry.

12. **bihira** = *seldom*
    Bihirang maglaro si Mary.   Mary seldom plays.

13. **samantala, habang** = *meanwhile, while* (use with the present tense of verbs)
    Samantala, tama na ang isang libong piso para sa iyo.
    Meanwhile, a thousand pesos is enough for you.

    Samantalang / habang nagsasalita siya, ako'y nakikinig.
    While he is talking, I am listening.

14. **habang-panahon** = *forever*
    Magiging magkaibigan sila habang-panahon.
    They will be friends forever.

15. **sa tanang buhay ko** = *in my whole life*
    Hindi pa ako naglalakbay sa tanang buhay ko.
    I have never travelled in my whole life.

16. **sa ibang araw; sa ibang oras** = *some other day, some other time*
    Sa ibang araw na kami dadalaw sa iyo.
    We shall visit you some other day.

IV. ADVERBS OF QUANTITY

Adverbs can also describe the scale of an action. Some examples of these adverbs are:

1. **marami** = *many; much*
   Maraming kinain si Tom.   Tom eats much.
   Malakas kumain si Tom. (colloquial)

2. **kaunti** (shortened to **konti**) = *little*
   Kaunti lamang ang sinabi niya.   He just said a little.

   Nagbigay ng konting pagkain ang batang maramot.
   The stingy child gave a little amount of food.

3. **wala** = *none; nothing*
   Walang kinakain ang sanggol na may sakit.   The sick infant eats nothing.
   Wala akong gusto.   I like nothing.

EXERCISES

Complete the sentences below by adding five possible adverbs of manner, then translate the sentences into English.

1. **Kumakain ang bata nang**   _____.

       _____.

       _____.

       _____.

       _____.

2. **Lumalakad ang matandang lalaki nang**   _____.

       _____.

       _____.

       _____.

       _____.

3. **Umawit si Mary nang**   _____.

       _____.

       _____.

       _____.

       _____.

Write sentences using these words and others of their kind.

Write a composition describing a party, a picnic or a trip you had in the past. Put a modifier to all the action words you use. Underline the modifiers.

Conjunctions and Interjections

Conjunctions and interjections are very important. Conjunctions join together two clauses, phrases or words to show a relationship between them whereas interjections are added to a sentence to express a particular emotion.

I. CONJUNCTIONS

Conjunctions join individual words, phrases and clauses, and show the relationship between them by pointing out that a thought—expressed in the word, phrase or clause—is less important than or as important as the other one. The most common example of a Tagalog conjunction is the word **at** which means *and* in English. Following are the meanings and examples of **at** and other Tagalog conjunctions:

1. **at** = *and* (may be shortened to **'t** when the first word ends in a vowel)

   Nagsusulat siya, gabi at araw.   He writes night and day.
   Nagsusulat siya, gabi't araw.

2. **o** = *or*

   Ako ba o siya ang ibig mo?   Do you like me or him/her?

3. **pero, nguni't, datapuwa't, subali't** (last two conjunctions are not to be used in ordinary conversation) = *but*

   Ibig kong umalis pero umuulan.   I like to leave but it is raining.
   Ako'y mataba nguni't siya'y payat.   I am fat but he/she is thin.

Vocabulary List

naghihintay = waiting   **pagdiriwang** = celebration
sayang = what a pity   **bunga** = fruit

4. **kung** = *if* (synonymous to **pag**)

Aalis ako kung sasama ka.   I will leave, if you are coming along.
Kung umulan, hindi ako lalakad.   If it rains, I shall not go.
Pag umulan, hindi ako lalakad.

5. **samantala, habang** = *meanwhile, while* (use with the present tense of verbs)

Tayo ay umawit samantalang naghihintay sa kanila.
Let us sing while waiting for them.
Samantalang natutulog ang sanggol, ako'y maglalaba.
While the baby sleeps, I shall do the laundry.

6. **nang** = *in order that, so that, so*

Huwag kang maingay nang ako'y   Do not be noisy so I can sleep.
    makatulog.
Kumain ka nang hindi ka magutom.   You eat so that you'll not go hungry.

7. **kung hindi** (shortened to **kundi**) = *except, but* (literally, *if not*)

Walang naparito kundi si Mary.   Nobody came except Mary.
Sino ang tutulong sa akin kundi ikaw?   Who will help me but you?

8. **dahil sa** = *because of*

Dahil sa iyo, dadalo ako sa pagdiriwang. Because of you, I shall attend the
                                         celebration.
Umiyak siya dahil sa akin.   He cried because of me.

9. **sapagka't, mangyari** = *because* (used to answer the question **bakit** or *why*)

> **Bakit ka ba malungkot?**   Why are you sad?
> **Mangyari ako'y may sakit.**   Because I am sick.
> **Sapagka't ako'y may sakit.**

10. **samakatuwid / samakatwid** = *therefore*

> **Hindi ka mabait, samakatuwid, ayoko sa iyo.**   You are not nice, therefore, I do not like you.
>
> **Samakatwid, ayaw mong mag-aral?**   Therefore, you do not like to study?

11. **kung ano ... siya rin** = *as ... so is ...; like ... like ...*

> **Kung ano ang ama ay siya ring anak.**   Like father, like son.
> **Kung ano ang puno ay siya ring bunga.**   As the tree is, so is the fruit.

12. **at sa wakas** = *finally, at last*

> **At sa wakas, pagpalain kayo ng Diyos.**   Finally, may God bless you.

II. INTERJECTIONS

Emotions are expressed in Tagalog sentences by using an interjection such as **naku** followed by an exclamation mark. A shortened term for **Inay ko po!** (*Oh my mother!*), **naku** expresses surprise, amazement or disbelief. There are other Tagalog interjections of this type, two of which reflect the Tagalog's Spanish heritage of faith such as **Susmaryosep!** (shortened form of the names Jesus, Maria y Jose or *Jesus, Mary* and *Joseph*) and **Sus!** (shortened form of *Jesus*).

An interjection is not related to or dependent on any other part of the sentence. It can stand alone or may be added to a sentence. It is common in conversations but not in formal writing.

Some common examples of Tagalog interjections, including **naku**, are the following. Note where they are usually placed:

1. **Ay!**   = expresses despair   **Ay! Ang hirap ng buhay.**
   What a hard life!

2. **Aba!**   = expresses surprise   **Aba! Kailan ka dumating?**
   When did you arrive?

3. **Aray!**   = expresses pain   **Aray! Masakit ang ulo ko.**
My head is aching!

4. **Naku!**   = expresses surprise   **Naku! Ang ganda ng bahay mo!**
Your house is beautiful!

= expresses disbelief   **Naku! Totoo ba?**
Is it true?

5. **Sayang!**   = expresses pity   **Nawala ang pera ko. Sayang!**
Sayang! Nawala ang pera ko.
My money was lost. What a pity!

6. **Mabuhay!**   = expresses welcome   **Mabuhay!**
(a welcome greeting to foreign visitors)

= expresses adoration   **Mabuhay si Pacquiao** (a Filipino boxing champion)**!**
Long live Pacquiao!

Magpa- and Pa- + -In Verb Forms

Sa isang salon sa Maynila
In a salon in Manila

Gustong <u>magpagupit</u> ng buhok si Janice. Magpapamasahe naman si Chris.
Janice would like to get a haircut. Chris on the other hand would like to get a massage.

MANEDYER : **Sino ho ang <u>magpapagupit</u>?**
Who would like to get a haircut?

JANICE : **Ako. At <u>magpapamasahe</u> ang kaibigan ko.**
I do. And my friend is getting a massage.

MANEDYER : **Baka gusto ninyong <u>magpa-manicure</u> rin?**
Perhaps you'd also like to get a manicure?

CHRIS : **Sige, <u>magpapalinis</u> rin ako ng kuko.**
Sure, I'll also get my fingernails cleaned and filed.

MANEDYER : **<u>Pinatawag</u> ko ho ang manikurista.**
I've had the manicurist called.

JANICE : **Chris, mamaya <u>magpasundo</u> tayo kay Robert.**
Chris, later let's have Robert pick us up.

Vocabulary List

magpakain = to feed someone
magpabasa = to order someone to read
mahihirap na tao = poor people
buhok = hair

magpapagupit = will get a haircut
magpapamasahe = will get a massage
magpasundo = ask to be picked up

The affixes **magpa-** and **pa-** + **-in** are used to form verbs that express an order to be done to the subject of the verb (such as **magpapakain sa mga bisita**, which means *will feed (food to) visitors* or **pinakain ang mga bisita** which means *visitors were fed*). While **magpa-** verbs are active, **pa-** + **-in** and its variant **pa-** + **-an** verbs are passive. Both of these verbs differ from the passive **i-** verbs which express actions done for someone. **Magpa-** and **pa-** + **-in** verbs suggest that someone is giving orders to have something done to another.

Forming **Magpa-** and **Pa-** + **-In** Derivatives

The derivatives of **magpa-** and **pa-** + **-in** verbs are formed differently. In addition, **pa-** + **-in** verbs make use of the **-hin** suffix when the roots end in vowels.

I. FOR VERB ROOTS ENDING IN CONSONANTS

1. Active **magpa-** verbs

Example: **kain**	eat
Infinitive: **magpakain**	(**magpa-** + root word) to feed someone
Imperative: **magpakain**	(**magpa-** + root word) feed someone.
Past: **nagpakain**	(**magpa-** becomes **nagpa-** + root word) fed someone
Present: **nagpapakain**	(**magpa-** becomes **nagpa-** + duplicated second syllable of prefix + root word) feeds someone
Future: **magpapakain**	(**magpa-** + duplicated second syllable of prefix + root word) will feed someone
Verbal Noun: **pagpapakain**	(**magpa-** becomes **pagpa-** + duplicated second syllable of prefix + root word) feeding someone

Lesson Thirty-One discusses the forming of nouns by adding appropriate articles before the verbs and adjectives. The same may be done on both **magpa-** and **pa-** + **-in** derivatives whose verbal nouns become quite similar to the English gerund phrase wherein the verb ends in an *-ing* (for example, _Feeding someone makes him happy_).

2. Passive **pa-** + **-in** verbs

Example: **kain**	eat
Infinitive: **pakainin**	(prefix **pa-** + root word + suffix **-in**) to feed someone
Imperative: **pakainin**	(prefix **pa-** + root word + suffix **-in**) feed someone.
Past: **pinakain**	(infix **-in-** between first and second letters of prefix **pa-** + root word) was/were fed
Present: **pinakakain**	(infix **-in-** between first and second letters of prefix **pa-** + duplicated first syllable of root word + root word) is/are fed
Future: **pakakainin**	(prefix **pa-** + duplicated first syllable of root word + root word + suffix **-in**) will be fed

Verbal Noun: **pagpapakain** (prefix **pa-** becomes **pagpa-** + duplicated second syllable of prefix + root word)
feeding someone

II. FOR VERB ROOTS ENDING IN VOWELS

1. Active **magpa-** verbs

Example: **basa**	read
Infinitive: **magpabasa**	(**magpa-** + root word) to have someone read
Imperative: **magpabasa**	(**magpa-** + root word) have someone read
Past: **nagpabasa**	(**magpa-** becomes **nagpa-** + root word) had someone read
Present: **nagpapabasa**	(**magpa-** becomes **nagpa-** + duplicated second syllable of prefix + root word) have someone read
Future: **magpapabasa**	(**magpa-** + duplicated second syllable of prefix + root word) will have someone read
Verbal Noun: **pagpapabasa**	(**magpa-** becomes **pagpa-** + duplicated second syllable of prefix + root word) having someone read

2. Passive **pa-** + **-in** verbs

Example: **basa**	read
Infinitive: **pabasahin**	(prefix **pa-** + root word + suffix **-hin**) to order someone to read
Imperative: **pabasahin**	(prefix **pa-** + root word + suffix **-hin**) order someone to read
Past: **pinabasa**	(infix **-in-** between first and second letters of prefix **pa-** + root word) made someone read
Present: **pinababasa**	(infix **-in-** between first and second letters of prefix **pa-** + duplicated first syllable of root word + root word) making someone read
Future: **pababasahin**	(prefix **pa-** + duplicated first syllable of root word + root word + suffix **-hin**) will make someone read
Verbal Noun: **pagpapabasa**	(prefix **pagpa-** + duplicated second syllable of prefix + root word) having someone read

Sample Sentences 🔊

Nagpapabasa sila sa mga paaralan ng mga aklat ni Rizal.
They order to be read in schools the books of Rizal. (literal)
They order the books of Rizal read in schools.

Pinababasa sa mga paaralan ang mga aklat ni Rizal.
Are ordered read in schools the books of Rizal. (literal)
The books of Rizal are ordered read in schools.

Nagpakain kami ng mahihirap na tao.
Were fed by us the poor people. (literal)
We fed the poor.

Pinakain namin ang mahihirap na tao.
Gave food by us the poor people. (literal)
The poor people were fed by us.

Although the translation of the above sentences are similar, the first sentence emphasizes the giving of food by the subject (**namin**) while the second sentence emphasizes the receiver (**mahihirap na tao**) of the action.

Nagpagupit siya ng (kanyang) buhok.
He/She ordered his/her hair cut. (literal)
He/She had a haircut.

Pinagupit niya ang kanyang buhok.
Had cut his/her hair. (literal)
He/She had a haircut.

EXERCISES

Change the following into passive sentences then translate into English.

1. **Ang aking katulong ay nagpakain ng bata.**
2. **Nagpapabasa ang aming guro ng pahayagan araw-araw.**
3. **Nagpalinis ako ng silid sa paaralan sa mga bata.**
4. **Nagpapagamot ng sakit ang matandang babae sa doktor.**
5. **Nagpaalis ng mga bata sa kanyang hardin ang matandang lalaki.**

Change the following into active sentences then translate into English.

1. **Pinakuha ko ang aklat sa bata sa aklatan.**
2. **Pasusulatin ng ina ang kanyang anak.**
3. **Pinaayos ko ang aking silid sa aming katulong.**
4. **Pakukunin ko ng pera sa bangko ang aking asawa.**
5. **Pinakain ko ang bata.**

Give ten other **magpa-** and **pa-** + **-in** verbs and use them in sentences.

Expressing Disagreement, Agreement or Doubt

Sa sakayan ng bus at dyipni
In a bus and jeepney station

Pupunta sa Daranak Falls sina Chris and Miguel. Naghahanap sila ng pinakamabilis na ruta mula sa Maynila.
Chris and Miguel are going to Daranak Falls. They're looking for the fastest route from Manila.

MIGUEL	:	**Huwag** tayong sumakay sa dyip. Hindi pa ito aalis.
		Let's not ride the jeepney. It will not leave yet.
CHRIS	:	**Sang-ayon** ako. **Ayokong** abutan ng dilim.
		I agree. I don't want to be out until dark.
MIGUEL	:	**Siyanga. Tila** uulan pa.
		It's true. It might even rain.
BUS DRIVER	:	**Totoo. Mag-bus na lang kayo. Mas mabilis ito.**
		Indeed. Just take the bus. It's faster.
MIGUEL	:	**Siguro** darating tayo doon nang alas dose, hindi ba?
		Maybe we'll get there at 12 p.m., right?
BUS DRIVER	:	**Hindi ako sigurado. Depende iyan sa trapiko.**
		I'm not sure. That depends on the traffic.

Vocabulary List

madalas = often
magpasyal = to take a walk
dilim = dark
totoo = true
dyip = jeepney

dilim = darkness
abutan = to reach
uulan = will rain
depende = depends (on something)

As one person differs from another in terms of his or her beliefs and orientation, expressing disagreement and agreement on the convictions or statements of one another—as well as casting doubt on another's abilities or statements—is an important part of his human nature. To convey such differences or similarities in opinions using the Tagalog language, one must learn how to use the following words. Observe that most of these words can stand alone as a response or expression.

I. EXPRESSING DISAGREEMENT

1. **Hindi** (shortened to '**di**) = *no*

The word **hindi** is the most common negative answer to a question except one that starts with **may** or **mayroon**. The negative answer to questions like **May aklat ba kayo?** (*Do you have a book?*) or **Mayroon ba siyang asawa?** (*Does he have a wife?*) is **wala** (or *none*) and not **hindi** (see Lesson Twelve). The following questions though may be answered by **hindi**:

Aalis ba tayo?	Are we leaving?
Hindi tayo aalis. (or **Hindi.**)	No, we are not leaving. (No.)
Ikaw ba si Jane?	Are you Jane?
Hindi, ako si Barbara. (or **Hindi.**)	No, I am Barbara. (No.)

The word **hindi** may be paired with monosyllabic words such as **pa** or **na** (for emphasis) or may be included in a sentence.

On the other hand, a word may be expressed in the negative or may take on a meaning contrary to its original definition in two ways. One is to simply place **hindi** before the word, which may be a verb, an adverb, a pronoun, a noun or a substantive (the technical term for a word or group of words that acts as a noun). The other is to affix the shortened form of **di** or **di-** as a prefix. Observe the following sentences:

Hindi mabait ang bata.	The child is not good.
Di mabait ang bata.	(with an end glottal catch on **di** and an end stress on **mabait**)
Di-mabait ang bata.	(hyphen between **di** and **mabait,** and with an end stress on **mabait** only)

2. **Huwag** = *do not, not to, not*

The word **huwag** simply means *Don't!* In other cases, it may mean *Stop!* It can be said at any time when one wants to put a stop to something one dislikes or to warn others not to do something.

Gusto mong paluin kita?	Do you want me to beat you?
Huwag!	Don't!

Huwag may either stand alone as a negative response or be a part of a sentence. When a sentence containing **huwag** uses an active verb (such as an **-um-**, **mag-**, **ma-** and **magpa-** derivative), a personal pronoun like **ka**, **kayo** or **tayo** is required. On the other hand, when the sentence uses a passive verb (such as an **-in**, **i-** or **-an** derivative), it needs a possessive pronoun like **mo** or **natin**.

ACTIVE

Huwag kang umalis.	Don't leave.
Huwag kayong bumasa sa dilim.	Don't read in the dark.
Huwag tayong matulog.	Let us not sleep.
Huwag kang magpaulan.	Don't get caught in the rain.

PASSIVE

Huwag mong kanin iyan.	Don't eat that.
Huwag mong basahan ng sulat si Ate.	Don't read my letter to Ate.
Huwag natin ibili ng kendi si Jun.	Let us not buy candy for Jun.

Huwag also goes with the infinitive form or the future tense of a verb in a sentence that expresses a command or request.

Huwag kang maligo ngayon. (command, infinitive)
Do not take a bath now.

Huwag mong babasahan ang bata bukas. (command, future)
Do not read to the child tomorrow.

Huwag kayong makikain nang madalas. (request, infinitive)
Don't eat often.

Huwag tayong makikigaya sa kanila. (request, future)
Let us not imitate them.

3. **Ayaw** = *to dislike, do not like*

The opposite of the pseudo-verb **gusto** (*to like*) or **ibig** (*to like*) is **ayaw**, which is a verb root and expresses dislike of someone or something.

It may either be active as in **umayaw** or passive as in **ayawan**. Thus, similar to **huwag**, **ayaw** in its active form needs a personal pronoun and, in its passive form, needs a possessive pronoun. **Ayaw** also goes with the infinitive form of a verb.

ACTIVE

Ayokong (ayaw ako) kumain.	I don't like to eat.
Ayaw siyang magsalita.	He does not like to talk.
Ayaw silang lumakad.	They do not like to go.
Ayaw ba kayong magpasyal?	Don't you like to take a walk?

PASSIVE

Ayaw kong kumain.	I don't like to eat.
Ayaw niyang magsalita.	He does not like to talk.
Ayaw nilang lumakad.	They do not like to go.
Ayaw ba ninyong magpasyal?	Don't you like to take a walk?

II. EXPRESSING AGREEMENT

1. **Oo** = *yes* (**opo/oho** is a polite *yes*, equivalent to *yes, sir/ma'am*)

As discussed in Lesson Three, **opo** and **oho** (*yes, sir/ma'am*) should pepper the sentences and questions of younger people to express respect for older people or persons with honorific titles or authority (regardless of age). The words reflect the speaker's good manners and his respect to the one spoken to.

Reserve **oo** as a response to people within one's age and status.

2. **Siyanga** = *that is right, that is true*

Siyanga is an idiomatic expression. Do not confuse with **siyanga** nor with the personal pronoun **siya** (*he/she*). Otherwise, this would give an altogether different meaning of *It is him/her indeed*.

Use **siyanga** when you are in total agreement with another person's statement or when you want someone to confirm an information you heard from another source.

Siyanga, mabait siya.	That's right, he/she is good.
Siyanga ba? Aalis kayo?	Is it true? Are you leaving?

3. **Totoo** = *true, indeed, truly*

The word **totoo**, as a one-word affirmative response, confirms an information. It may be the answer to either a **totoo** or **siyanga** question (**Totoo? Siyanga?**) and may even take the place of **oo** in some instances.

Totoo, hindi na siya babalik.	Truly, he/she is not coming back anymore.
Totoong-totoo.	It is very true.
Totoo ba ang balita? Totoo.	Is the news true? True.

4. **Talaga** = *yes, indeed; really*

Use **talaga** to emphasize the nature of the subject, as expressed by an adjective, or to affirm the truth in a sentence. Like other affirmative words, it can be a stand-alone response. It should be placed at the start of the sentence or near the adjective or adverb.

Mabuting tao talaga si G. Santos.
Talagang mabuting tao si G. Santos.
Mr. Santos is a really good man.

Talaga, papunta kami sa Estados Unidos.
Yes, indeed, we are going to the United States.

A colloquial and negative definition of this expression is *Really?* that is spoken with raised eyebrows and raised intonation that connotes disbelief.

III. EXPRESSING DOUBT

1. **Marahil** = *maybe*

Marahil, which is also a one-word response, is placed either at the beginning of the sentence or near the subject, even at the end of the sentence.

Marahil siya ay darating bukas.
Maybe he is arriving tomorrow.

Si Pepe na marahil ang pinakamasuwerteng tao sa buong mundo.
Ang pinakamasuwerteng tao sa buong mundo ay si Pepe na marahil.
Pepe maybe the luckiest person in the whole world.

2. **Tila** = *it seems*

A **tila** sentence expresses a speaker's view of things. The word **tila** is placed at the start of a sentence or whenever another person's statement or view is included in the speaker's sentence (see Lesson Twenty-One).

Tila uulan ngayon.	It seems it will rain today.

3. **Siguro** = *maybe* or *definitely*

As discussed in Lesson Three, the meaning of **siguro** depends on the response to the question being asked. For example, there may be three responses to the question **Siguro ka?** or *Are you sure?*:

Oo, siguro ako.	Yes, I am sure (or *Yes, definitely*).
Hindi ako siguro (or **sigurado**).	I am not sure.
Siguro.	Maybe.
Siguro darating siya bukas.	Maybe he is arriving tomorrow.
Darating siya bukas siguro.	

Observe that **siguro** may be a one-word response and may be placed anywhere in the sentence.

4. **Baka** = *might be*

There is not much difference in the use of **marahil**, **siguro** (as *maybe*) and **baka** when expressing doubt. However, **baka** is the most widely used term because it is the shortest, most contemporary and the most pleasant among the three (see first example) although a speaker's delivery of the sentence or his choice of words may give exactly the opposite.

Baka ka magkasakit.	You might get sick.
Baka ikaw ang mauna.	You might be first.

Be careful in pronouncing the word **baka** and note the glottal catch on the last syllable as the Tagalog word for *cow* is the stressless **baka**.

5. **Maaari** = *it can be* or *possible*

Maaaring totoo means *it can be true*. **Maaaring mali** means *it can be wrong*. Thus, **maaari** functions similarly as **hindi**, which gives the opposite of a word. **Maaari** gives a blanket of doubt over a word. However, **maaari** on its own as a stand-alone response (although **posible** or **puwede** are more popular) means *It is possible*. Note also that **maaari** is used in requests (see Lesson Twenty-Four).

Maaaring totoo na mag-aasawa na siya.
It could be true that he/she is getting married.

Maaaring mali ang hinala natin.
Our suspicions could be wrong.

EXERCISES

What would be the response to each question or situation below? Is it **totoo** or **marahil**? Give all three possible responses.

1. **Kayo na raw ang magkasama sa eskuwelahan ngayon?**
   Is it true you are now a pair in school?

   sang-ayon/agree

   _____

   di sang-ayon/disagree

   _____

   alinlangan/doubt

   _____

2. **Tunay bang mahal ni Nilda si Andrew?**
   Does Nilda truly love Andrew?

   sang-ayon/agree

   _____

   di sang-ayon/disagree

   _____

   alinlangan/doubt

   _____

3. **Gusto mo bang makilaro sa amin?**
   Do you want to play with us?

   sang-ayon/agree

   _____

   di sang-ayon/disagree

   _____

   alinlangan/doubt

   _____

This dialogue contains grammar concepts covered in Lessons 38 and 39.

Forming Nouns from Verbs

Pagbabasa ng mga balita
Reading the news

Nagbabasa ng pahayagan sina Mr. at Mrs. Alvarez at nag-uusap sila tungkol sa mga balita.
Mr. and Mrs. Alvarez are reading the newspaper and talking about the news.

MR. ALVAREZ : **Mahirap ang <u>pagtaas</u> ng presyo ng langis.**
The price increase of gas is difficult.

MRS. ALVAREZ : **Lalo sa <u>kabuhayan</u> ng mga mahirap.**
And especially for the livelihood of the poor.

MR. ALVAREZ : **Sabi rin dito, kulang ang mga <u>mangagamot</u> sa maraming probinsya.**
It also says here, that we're lacking doctors in a lot of provinces.

MRS. ALVAREZ : **Mabuti tumutulong ang mga <u>kabataan</u>.**
It's good that the youth are helping.

MR. ALVAREZ : **Oo, sila ang <u>tagadala</u> ng mga gamit <u>pangmedikal</u> doon.**
Yes, they're the ones who bring the medical supplies there.

MRS. ALVAREZ : **<u>Tagaulat</u> din sila ng mga pangyayari.**
They're also the ones reporting what's happening.

MR. ALVAREZ : **<u>Kaligayahan</u> nila ang tumulong.**
Their happiness is to be of help/service.

MRS. ALVAREZ : **Ano ang pwede natin gawin?**
What can we do?

MR. ALVAREZ : **Sa <u>pasukan</u>, magboboluntaryo ako sa <u>aklatan</u>.**
On school days, I'll volunteer at the library.

MRS. ALVAREZ : **Tama, kailangan ng mga bata ng tulong sa <u>pagbasa</u> at <u>pagsulat</u>.**
Great, the kids need help in reading and writing.

Vocabulary List

pag-alis = departure
takdang-aralin = homework
bakuran = yard
buhay = life
madalas = often
trabaho = job
pagtaas = increase

presyo = price
langis = gas/crude oil
kabuhayan = livelihood
kulang = lacking
kabataan = youth
kaligayahan = happiness/satisfaction
aklatan = library

The English gerund is a verbal noun and is exactly what its name implies: a noun derived from a verb. A gerund or a verbal noun in English usually ends in *-ing*, or may also be a phrase with an *-ing* verb, and functions as a noun in a sentence. For example, in the sentence *Writing calms my mind*, the word *writing* is a gerund or a verbal noun. A pronoun may replace *writing* in a succeeding sentence (*It calms my mind*) and confirms that *writing*, as used in the sentence, is indeed a gerund.

In Tagalog, gerunds are formed in several ways as described below. Note that the article **ang** (along with **ng** and **sa**) helps in forming nouns from verbs or adjectives (see Lesson Thirty-One). In this lesson, however, **ang** (or **ang mga** if the verbal noun is plural) alone is needed to form gerunds along with six affixes.

I. FORMING NOUNS FROM **-UM-** VERB FORMS

formula: prefix **pag-** + root

Examples:			
	umalis	= **pag-alis**	= leaving
	lumakad	= **paglakad**	= walking
	umibig	= **pag-ibig**	= love

Umalis siya patungong Estados Unidos. (verb)
He left for the United States.

Ang kanyang pag-alis ay ikinalungkot ko. (gerund)
His departure made me sad.

II. FORMING NOUNS FROM **MAG-** VERB FORMS

prefix **pag-** + duplicated first syllable + root

Examples:			
	maglaro	= **paglalaro**	= playing
	magtanim	= **pagtatanim**	= planting

Gusto kong magtanim ng hasmin sa aming bakuran. (verb)
I like to plant jasmine in our yard.

Mahirap ang pagtatanim ng hasmin. (gerund)
Planting jasmine is difficult.

III. FORMING NOUNS FROM -IN VERB FORMS

pag- + root

Examples: | **basahin** | = **pagbasa** | = reading
| **tawagin** | = **pagtawag** | = [act of] calling

Basahin mo ang buhay ni Rizal. (verb)
I read the life of Rizal.

Hindi nila gusto ang pagbasa ko ng buhay ni Rizal. (gerund)
They did not approve of my reading of Rizal's life.

IV. FORMING NOUNS FROM PAKI- VERB FORMS

paki- + duplicated last syllable of **paki-** + root

Examples: | **pakihiram** | = **pakikihiram** | = borrowing
| **pakisulat** | = **pakikisulat** | = writing

Pinakisulat ko ang aking takdang-aralin sa kanya. (verb)
I requested her to write my homework for me.

Ang pakikisulat ko ng takdang-aralin sa kanya ay di-mabuti. (gerund)
My request that she write my homework is not good.

V. FORMING NOUNS FROM MA- VERB FORMS

pag- + root (for actions)
pagka- + root (for feelings)

Examples: | **maligo** | = **pagligo** | = bathing
| **magalit** | = **pagkagalit** | = being angry; anger

Madalas ang kanyang pagligo. (verb)
His bathing is frequent.

Natakot ako sa kanyang pagkagalit. (gerund)
I was afraid of his being angry.

VI. FORMING NOUNS FROM -AN VERB FORMS

pag- + duplicated first syllable + root

Examples: | **tawanan** | = **pagtatawa** | = laughing
| **hugasan** | = **paghuhugas** | = washing

Hugasan mo ang mga pinggan. (verb)
Wash the dishes.

Mahirap na trabaho ang paghuhugas ng pinggan. (gerund)
Washing dishes is a tough job.

EXERCISES

Give the verbal nouns of the following verbs.

1. _____ **mag-isip** = to think

2. _____ **umiyak** = to cry

3. _____ **buksan** = to open

4. _____ **maglakbay** = to travel

5. _____ **umibig** = to love

6. _____ **tugtugin** = to play an instrument

7. _____ **umawit** = to sing

8. _____ **magsalita** = to speak

9. _____ **mag-alis** = to remove

10. _____ **sakyan** = to ride

Create sentences from the verbal nouns formed above.

Translate the following sentences into Tagalog.

1. His frequent eating will make him fat.
2. I will be sad on the departure of my friend.
3. Traveling is a good education.
4. She is thin because of playing much.
5. Bathing everyday is necessary.
6. He likes writing very much.
7. Selling a house in Manila is difficult.
8. I like his reading of Rizal's "My Last Farewell."
9. Planting during the rainy season is good.
10. His coming is sudden.

LESSON THIRTY-NINE
Noun Affixes

In Lesson Thirty-One, you are introduced to the formation of nouns by placing the articles **ang** or **ng** or the preposition **sa** before a verb or adjective.

In this lesson, you will become acquainted with other affixes that turn a verb or an adjective into a noun, or even change the meaning of one noun into another.

The following are the various affixes that help to create new nouns and the formulas that are used to create these nouns, which are then categorized according to their new meanings.

I. **-AN** OR **-HAN** SUFFIXES

1. (root + **-an**) Refers to *a place where things are stored or placed*

aklat = book	**aklatan** = library
kahoy = wood	**kahuyan** = woodpile
bahay = house	**bahayan** = group of houses
baboy = pig	**babuyan** = piggery

2. (root + **-an**) Refers to *a season*

ani = harvest	**anihan** = harvest time
pasok = enter	**pasukan** = school day
tanim = plant	**taniman** = planting season

3. (root + **-an**) Refers to *an article or instrument*

inom = to drink	**inuman** = something to drink from
sulat = to write, letter	**sulatan** = something to write on
luto = to cook, cooked	**lutuan** = cooking utensils, place for cooking
sakay = to ride	**sasakyan** = something to ride in

Vocabulary List

kabutihan = goodness	**kaligayahan** = happiness
kabataan = youth	**magsasaka** = farmer
pagtatanim = planting	**kartero** = postman
sangkapuluan = archipelago	**panauhin** = visitors

4. (root duplicated and hyphenated + **-an**) Refers to *a miniature version*

bahay = house	**bahay-bahayan** = playhouse
baro = damit	**baru-baruan** = doll clothes

5. (root duplicated and hyphenated + **-an**) Refers to *an imitator or copycat*

ina = mother	**ina-inahan** = pretending to be like a mother
hari = king	**hari-harian** = acting like a king
pari = priest	**pari-parian** = not a real priest

II. KA- + -AN OR KA_HAN

1. (**ka-** + root ι -an) Refers to *an idea or concept*

buti = good	**kabutihan** = goodness
buhay = life	**kabuhayan** = livelihood
ligaya = happy	**kaligayahan** = happiness

2. (**ka-** + root + **-an**) Refers to *a group*

bahay = house	**kabahayan** = place of many houses
bukid = farm	**kabukiran** = farmlands
Tagalog = refers to a language or people	**Katagalugan** = place of the Tagalogs
bata = child	**kabataan** = youth
tanda = age	**katandaan** = elders

Note that for roots ending in **o** such as **luto** and **baro** or with **o** in the last syllable such as **inom** and **pasok**, the vowel **o** is changed to **u** when a suffix is attached. In roots ending in **d** such as **bukid**, **d** becomes **r** when a suffix is attached.

III. MAG-

1. (**mag-** + hyphen for roots that start with a vowel + root) Refers to *a relationship*

ina = mother	**mag-ina** = mother and child
ama = father	**mag-ama** = father and child
asawa = spouse	**mag-asawa** = husband and wife
kapatid = sibling	**magkapatid** = brothers or sisters

2. (**mag-** + duplicated first syllable of root + root) Refers to *a work or profession*

bigas = rice	**magbibigas** = rice merchant
saka = farming	**magsasaka** = farmer

IV. MANG- OR MAN-

1. (**mang-** + duplicated first syllable of root + root) Refers to *a work or profession*

As with other roots that begin with the consonants **d, l, r, s** and **t**, the variant of most prefixes are used, for example, **man-** instead of **mang-** (see Lesson Eleven).

gamot = to cure	**manggagamot** = doctor
langoy = to swim	**manlalangoy** = swimmer
dagat = sea	**mandaragat** = seaman
digma = war	**mandirigma** = warrior
laro = to play, game	**manlalaro** = player

V. PAG-

1. (**pag-** + hyphen if root starts with a vowel + root) Creates gerunds or verbal nouns when affix replaces **-um-**

umalis = left	**pag-alis** = departure
lumakad = walked	**paglakad** = walk
umibig = loved	**pag-ibig** = love

2. (**pag-** + duplicated first syllable + root) Creates gerunds or verbal nouns when affix replaces **mag-**

maglaro = to play	**paglalaro** = act of playing
magsulat = to write	**pagsusulat** = writing
magtanim = to plant	**pagtatanim** = planting

3. (**pag-** + root) Creates gerunds or verbal nouns when affix replaces **-in** or **-hin**

basahin = read	**pagbasa** = reading
tawagin = call	**pagtawag** = calling

VI. SANG-, SAN-, SAM-

1. (**sang-** + **ka-** + root + **-an**) Means *the whole of*
The prefix **sang-** changes to **san-** when attached to roots starting with the consonants **d, l, r, s** and **t**. The prefix changes to **sam-** when the roots start with the consonant **p** (see Lesson Thirteen on Numbers).

pulo = island	**sangkapuluan** = archipelago
langit = heaven	**sangkalangitan** = heaven

2. (**sang-** + root) Means *one*

gabi = night	**sanggabi** = one night
buwan = month	**sambuwan** = one month
laon = year	**santaon** = one year

VII. TAG-

1. (**tag-** + root) Refers to *season or time of*

araw = sun, day	**tag-araw** = dry season
ulan = rain	**tag-ulan** = wet season
lamig = cold	**taglamig** = cold season
gutom = hunger	**taggutom** = famine
ani = harvest	**tag-ani** = harvest time

VIII. TAGA-

1. (**taga-** + name of place) Means *a native or resident of*

Taga-Batangas si Laurel.	Laurel is from Batangas.
Ang mga Muslim ay taga-Mindanao.	Muslims are from Mindanao.

Marunong magtanim ang mga taga-baryo.
Those from the barrio know how to plant.

2. (**taga-** + root) Refers to *one who frequently acts out the root*

dala = bring	**tagadala** = one who brings

Ang kartero (postman) **ay tagadala ng sulat.**
The postman delivers letters.

turo = teach   **tagaturo** = one who teaches
Tagaturo ako ng Tagalog.
I teach Tagalog.

bili = buy   **tagabili** = one who buys
Julia is the one who buys food in the market.

luto = cook   **tagaluto** = one who cooks
My wife is the one who cooks for us.

IX. **TALA-** + **-AN**

1. (**taga-** + root + **-an**) Refers to *a list of things associated with the root word*

tinig = voice   **talatinigan** = dictionary
aklat = books   **talaaklatan** = catalogue of books
araw = day   **talaarawan** = diary or journal
upa = rent   **talaupahan** = payroll

The Plurality Rule

The Tagalog language has a plurality rule (introduced in Lesson Four). Nouns, verbs, articles, prepositions and question words are made plural when the subjects are also plural.

As this discussion focuses on the affixes that turn a verb into a noun or the meaning of a noun into another, it becomes appropriate to further discuss how nouns can be made plural. Following are the means:

1. Use the plural forms of articles: **sina** with proper nouns and **ang mga** with common nouns.

2. Use numbers as well as adjectives such as **ilan** (*a few*) and **marami** (*many*) before a noun.

Sampung tao ang umalis.   Ten men left.
Ilang tao ang umalis.   A few men left.
Maraming tao ang umalis.   Many men left.

3. Use the formula for creating plural adjectives: **ma** + duplicated first syllable + root.

<u>Magaganda</u>ng dalaga ang aming panauhin. (visitors)
Our visitors are pretty ladies.

<u>Mababait</u> na bata ang inyong mga anak.
Your children are good.

Bahay na <u>malalaki</u> ang nakita namin.
We saw big houses.

4. Duplicate the root word.

Pumaroon kami sa mga bahay-bahay sa Lingayen.
We went from house to house in Lingayen.

Bumili kami ng mga bagay-bagay para sa kusina.
We bought several things for the kitchen.

Forming Participles Using **Naka-**

Nakaupo na ba ang mga pasahero?
Are the passengers already sitting down?

Sa eroplano pabalik sa Maynila, humingi ng tulong si Natalie sa flight attendant.
In an airplane back to Manila, Natalie asked for help from the flight attendant.

NATALIE	:	<u>Nakaupo</u> ho kayo sa upuan ko. Seat number 15A. You're sitting on my seat, ma'am. Seat number 15A.
ELDERLY WOMAN	:	Pasensya ka na. Hindi ako <u>nakasalamin</u>. Nagkamali ako. Please excuse me. I'm not wearing glasses. I made a mistake.
NATALIE	:	Ok lang ho. Magpatulong ho tayo sa flight attendant. It's okay, ma'am. Let's ask the flight attendant for help.
FLIGHT ATTENDANT	:	Sa seat number 18A ho kayo. You're on seat number 18A, ma'am.
ELDERLY WOMAN	:	Ganoon ba? May taong <u>nakauniporme</u> doon. Is that so? There's a person in uniform there.
FLIGHT ATTENDANT	:	Kasamahan ko ho siya. Aalis siya pag dating ninyo. She's a co-worker, ma'am. She'll leave once you arrive.
NATALIE	:	Maraming salamat. Thank you very much.
FLIGHT ATTENDANT	:	Walang anuman. Mabuti <u>nakatulong</u> ako. You're welcome. It's good that I was able to help.

Vocabulary List

mataas na silya = high chair	**maingay** = noisy
tamad = lazy	**nakaupo** = sitting down
kagabi = last night	**nakasalamin** = wearing glasses
pinto = door	**nagkamali** = made a mistake
sinehan = movie house	**nakauniporme** = wearing a uniform

The English verbal gerund and participle are both formed from verbs but they function differently. While the gerund functions like a noun, the participle functions like an adjective and modifies a noun or pronoun. An English participle can be either in the present form (ending in *-ing*) or past form (ending in *-ed*, *-n* or *-t*).

In Tagalog, participles are formed by affixing the prefix **naka-** to a root word (**naka-** + root word) that is either a noun or a verb. The **naka-** participle then expresses the state, condition or appearance of a person or thing based on the root. A **naka-** word has no tense forms as it is descriptive just like an adjective.

This prefix should not be confused with the past tense of a **maka-** verb, which indicates capability to do something and such words are purely action words (Lesson Eighteen).

Sample Sentences

Nakaupo ang bata sa mataas na silya.
The child is seated on a high chair.

Nakatayo sa tabi ng pinto ang aking ina.
My mother is standing by the door.

Ang lalaking nakahiga ay tamad.
The man lying down is lazy.

Bulag ang taong nakasalaming iyon.
That man with eyeglasses is blind.

Kailangang nakasapatos ang bata sa paglalaro.
Children need to wear shoes when playing.

Sila ay nakakotse nang dumating.
They were in a car when they arrived.

Nakatulala si Miriam nang dumating ako.
Miriam is in shock when I arrived.

Puwede ka sumama pero dapat nakamaong ka.
You may come along but you should be in jeans.

EXERCISES

Can you tell if the following are **naka-** participles or **naka-** verb forms (past tense of **maka-** verb forms)? Translate the sentences into English and find out.

1. Nakapasok kami sa sinehan kagabi.
2. Nakalakad na ang matandang maysakit.
3. Nakabasa na siya ng mga aklat ni Romulo.
4. Nakatulog din ako kahit na maingay.

Use the following **naka-** participles in sentences.

1. nakasumbrero
2. nakauniporme
3. nakaputi
4. nakakotse
5. nakakabayo
6. nakasigarilyo
7. nakaitim
8. nakabus
9. nakasingsing
10. nakapayong

Formation of Adjectives

Salamat para sa mga pasalubong
Thank you for the gifts

Nakabalik na si Anna mula sa Paris at may pasalubong siya para sa mga pinsan niya.
Anna has come back from Paris and she has gifts for her cousins.

ANNA : <u>**Kayganda**</u> **ng Paris!**
Paris is very beautiful!

ROBERT : <u>**Matao**</u> **ba noong nandoon kayo?**
Was it crowded when you were there?

ANNA : <u>**Maginaw**</u> **noong Pebrero kaya hindi matao.**
February was cold so it was not crowded.

JANICE : **Marami ba tayong** <u>**kababayan**</u> **doon?**
Do we have a lot of fellow Filipinos there?

ANNA : **Siguro. Ito ang mga pasalubong ko para sa inyo!**
Perhaps. These are my gifts for you!

JANICE : <u>**Ang ganda**</u>**! Blusang mabulaklak at makulay.**
How nice! A flowery and colorful blouse!

ROBERT : **At sapatos na** <u>**panlakad**</u> **para sa akin.**
And walking shoes for me.

ANNA : <u>**Makabago**</u> **iyan at** <u>**tamang-tama**</u> **sa tag-ulan!**
These are modern and very good for the rainy season.

Vocabulary List

matamis = sweet
mabunga = with plenty of fruits
pang-umaga = for morning (literal)
makabago = modern
matao = many people
Kaybuti! = How good!

kayganda = very beautiful
matao = crowded
kababayan = fellow countrymen
mabulaklak = flowery
makulay = colorful
tamang-tama = appropriate

There are five affixes which may be used to turn a root word into an adjective. The following are the various affixes that help to create adjectives and the formulas used to create these adjectives. These are then categorized according to their new meanings.

I. MA-

1. (**ma-** + root) Means *having the quality expressed by the root*; use with abstract nouns (refer to page 91, Lesson Twelve)

ganda = beauty	**maganda** = beautiful (**may ganda**)
bait = goodness	**mabait** = good (**may bait**)
tamis = sweetness	**matamis** = sweet (**may tamis**)
dunong = knowledge	**marunong** = learned (**may dunong**)

Observe that with a **ma-** prefix, the initial letter and consonant **d** in a root word change to **r** as in **ma-** + **dunong** becomes **marunong**.

2. (**ma-** + root) Means *having many or much of the feature expressed by the root*; use with concrete nouns

bulaklak = flower	**mabulaklak** = many flowers
tao = person	**matao** = many people
bigas = rice	**mabigas** = plenty of rice
bunga = fruit	**mabunga** = plenty of fruits or fruitful

II. KA-

1. (**ka-** + root) Refers to *a reciprocal relationship*

balat = skin	**kabalat** = of the same skin
sama = to go along	**kasama** = accompanied

III. KAY-

1. (**kay-** + root) An exclamation referring to *the trait of the root word*, **kay-** literally translates to *how*

ganda = beauty	**kayganda** = how beautiful!
aga = early	**kay-aga** = how early!
buti = goodness	**kaybuti** = how good!

IV. MAKA-

1. (**maka-** + root, may be a proper name) Means *in favor of someone over another* or *inclined to believe in someone or something*

Rizal = Philippines' national hero   **maka-Rizal** = in favor of Rizal
bago = new   **makabago** = (in favor of new); modern
luma = old   **makaluma** = (in favor of old); old fashioned

V. PANG-, PAN- OR PAM-

1. (**pang-** + root) Refers to *specific use as expressed by the root*

The prefix **pang-** is used with words that start with the vowels (**a, e, i, o** and **u**) and the consonants **k, g, h, m, n, ng, w, y**. A hyphen separates **pang-** from roots that start with vowels. On the other hand, the alternant prefix **pam-** is used with words that start with **b** and **p** whereas the other alternant prefix **pan-** is used with roots that start with **d, l, r, s** and **t**.

umaga = morning   **pang-umaga** = of the morning
bayad = pay   **pambayad** = for payment
sala = filter   **pansala** = for straining
kayod = scrape   **pangkayod** = for scraping
walis = sweep   **pangwalis** = for sweeping
hila = pull   **panghila** = for pulling
tulog = sleep   **pantulog** = for sleeping
lakad = walk   **panlakad** = for walking
pasok = enter   **pampasok** = uniform (used for going to office or school)

Sira na ang sapatos na _pambahay_.
The shoes _for [use in] the house_ are already worn out.

Pang-umaga ang klase ko.
My class is _in the morning_. (literal)
I have a morning class.

Ang perang ito ay _pambayad_ sa utang.
This money is _for payment_ of debts.

Nawala ang plumang <u>pansulat</u>.
The pen <u>for writing</u> was lost.

Ang <u>pang-ospital</u> na uniporme ay puti.
The <u>hospital uniform</u> is white.

IV. MAPAG- AND PALA-

The prefixes **mapag-** and **pala-**, when attached to a root, describe the habitual and frequent action of the doer as expressed by the root word. The prefixes are interchangeable except when attached to adjectives. The prefix **pala-** only goes with action roots while the prefix **mapag-** may go with both action and describing words. The resulting words are always accented on the last syllables.

1. **tawa** = laugh   **palatawa** or **mapagtawa** = laughs frequently

   Ayaw ang binata sa dalagang palatawa / mapagtawa.
   The young man does not like a girl who laughs frequently.

2. **aral** = study   **palaaral** or **mapag-aral** = studies frequently

   Magiging marunong ang batang palaaral / mapag-aral.
   A child who studies habitually becomes learned.

3. **inom** = drink   **palainom** or **mapag-inom** = drinks frequently

   Palainom / mapag-inom ng tubig si Edwin.
   Edwin is fond of drinking water.

4. **isip** = think   **palaisip** or **mapag-isip** = deep in thought

   Madaling tumanda ang mga taong palaisip / mapag-isip.
   Deep thinkers get old faster.

5. **mahal** = beloved   **mapagmahal** = loving or affectionate

   Gusto ni Claudette ang mapagmahal na si Pepeng.
   Claudette likes the affectionate Pepeng.

EXERCISES

Write five adjectives to describe the following subjects. Use a variety of affixes with the descriptive words.

New York

1. _____
2. _____
3. _____
4. _____
5. _____

guro

1. _____
2. _____
3. _____
4. _____
5. _____

babae

1. _____
2. _____
3. _____
4. _____
5. _____

Use **pang-**, **pam-** or **pan-** with the following roots to form adjectives.

1. _____ **bansa**
2. _____ **gamit**
3. _____ **aral**
4. _____ **basa**
5. _____ **lahat**
6. _____ **langoy**
7. _____ **bata**
8. _____ **kain**
9. _____ **baro**
10. _____ **ilaw**

Plural Forms of Verbs

Nagsisipagsayaw ang mga tao!
The people are dancing!

Dumaan sina Chris and Miguel sa Tanay, Rizal. May pista noon at buhay na buhay ang bayan.
Chris and Miguel passed by Tanay, Rizal. There was a fiesta then and the town was very lively.

MIGUEL : **<u>Nagsisipagsayaw</u> ang mga tao sa daan.**
People are dancing on the streets.

CHRIS : **<u>Pinagbubuksan</u> din nila ang mga bahay nila sa bisita.**
They also opened up their homes to guests.

MIGUEL : **Oo nga. Tanghalian na pala!**
That's true. I didn't realize it's time for lunch.

RESIDENTE : **<u>Magsikain</u> muna kayo dito.**
Come eat here first.

CHRIS : **Maraming salamat ho pero papunta kami sa Daranak Falls.**
Thank you so much but we're on our way to Daranak Falls.

RESIDENTE : **Naku, sige na, minsan lang ito.**
Oh do come in, this doesn't happen often.

MIGUEL : **Oo nga naman, <u>nagsipaghanda</u> ang lahat para sa pista!**
I agree with him, everyone prepared for the fiesta!

Vocabulary List

magsikain = to eat (plural)
hapunan = supper
nagsisipagdasal = are praying
magsialis = to leave (plural)
pagsulatin = to write (plural)
bintana = window
nagsisipagsayaw = dancing (plural)

pinagbubuksan = opened (plural)
tanghalian = lunch
minsan = infrequent
nagsipaghanda = prepared (plural)
pista = fiesta
residente = resident

The grammar book (**Balarila ng Wikang Pambansa**) prepared by Lope K. Santos in 1939 as head of the Institute of National Language states that the use of plural forms of verbs with plural subjects is "not compulsory" and the use of a plural subject with a singular verb "does not make the sentence or the sense wrong." The plurality rule was introduced in this book in Lesson Four then discussed in detail in various pages and finally in Lesson Thirty-Nine. This far, a student should have been familiar with the rule already.

While it is easy for native Tagalog speakers to say **mangagsikain**, **mangagkain**, **magsipagkain**, **mangagsipagkainan** and **mangagkainan**, foreigners and non-Tagalog speakers will find these words very difficult to pronounce. Thus, the discussion on forming the plural derivatives of Tagalog words in this lesson shall be extended to the more simple plural affixes with two each in the active (**magsi-** and **magsipag-**) and passive voices (**pag-** + **-in** and **pag-** + **-an**). These will be enough to arm non-Tagalog speakers with necessary plural verbs to pass an advanced Tagalog conversation.

For Active Forms (**MAGSI-** and **MAGSIPAG-**)

Both **magsi-** and **magsipag-** verb forms are the plural forms of **-um-** and **mag-** (see Lesson Fourteen), which emphasize the doer of the action or the act itself.

I. **MAGSI-** VERB FORMS

The prefix **magsi-** is used to form the plural derivatives of **-um-** verb forms. Following are the formulas for the infinitive and imperative forms as well as the three tenses—past, present and future.

Example: **kain**	eat
Infinitive: **magsikain**	(**magsi-** + root) to eat
Imperative: **magsikain**	(**magsi-** + root) eat
Past: **nagsikain**	(**magsi-** becomes **nagsi-** + root) ate
Present: **nagsisikain**	(**magsi-** becomes **nagsi-** + duplicated second syllable of **magsi-** + root) are eating
Future: **magsisikain**	(**magsi-** + duplicated second syllable of **magsi-** + root) will eat

Example: **alis**	leave
Infinitive: **magsialis**	(**magsi-** + root) to leave
Imperative: **magsialis**	(**magsi-** + root) leave
Past: **nagsialis**	(**magsi-** becomes **nagsi-** + root) left
Present: **nagsisialis**	(**magsi-** becomes **nagsi-** + duplicated second syllable of **magsi-** + root) are leaving
Future: **magsisialis**	(**magsi-** + duplicated second syllable of **magsi-** + root) will leave

Examples of **MAGSI-** Verbs

magsilakad	to go	**magsisulat**	to write
magsibasa	to read		

II. **MAGSIPAG-** VERB FORMS

The prefix **magsipag-** is used to form the plural derivatives of **mag-** verb forms. **Magsipag-** is followed by a hyphen when the verb root after it starts with a vowel such as **aral** (*study*) and **akyat** (*climb*).

Example: **lakad**   walk
Infinitive: **magsipaglakad**   (**magsipag-** + root) to walk
Imperative: **magsipaglakad**   (**magsipag-** + root) walk
Past: **nagsipaglakad**   (**magsipag-** becomes **nagsipag-** + root) walked
Present: **nagsisipaglakad**   (**magsipag-** becomes **nagsipag-** + duplicated second syllable of **magsipag-** + root) are walking
Future: **magsisipaglakad**   (**magsipag-** + duplicated second syllable of **magsipag-** + root) will walk

Example: **dasal**   prayer
Infinitive: **magsipagdasal**   (**magsipag-** + root) to pray
Imperative: **magsipagdasal**   (**magsipag-** + root) pray
Past: **nagsipagdasal**   (**magsipag-** becomes **nagsipag-** + root) prayed
Present: **nagsisipagdasal**   (**magsipag-** becomes **nagsipag-** + duplicated second syllable of **magsipag-** + root) are praying
Future: **magsisipagdasal**   (**magsipag-** + duplicated second syllable of **magsipag-** + root) will pray

Examples of **MAGSIPAG-** Verbs

magsipagbait	to be good	**magsipagpasyal**	to take a walk
magsipag-aral	to study	**magsipag-akyat**	to go up

Sample Sentences

Nagsisibasa ba kayo ng Bibliya?	Do you read the Bible?
Magsilakad na kayo sa paaralan.	You all go now to school.
Nagsisikain na ang mga bata ng hapunan.	The children are eating their supper already.
Nagsisipag-aral nang mabuti ang aking mga anak.	My children study well.
Nagsisipagdasal ang mga babae sa simbahan.	The women pray in church.

For Passive Forms (**Pag-** + **-in** and **Pag-** + **-an**)

Both **pag-** + **-in** and **pag-** + **-an** verb forms are the plural forms of **-in** and **-an** verb forms (see Lessons Fifteen and Thirty-Three), which emphasize the receiver of the action.

I. **PAG-** + **-IN** VERB FORMS

The prefix **pag-** + **-in** or its variant **pag-** + **-hin** is used to form the plural derivatives of a passive **-in** verb.

Example: **luto**	cooking
Infinitive: **paglutuin**	(**pag-** + root + **-in**) to cook
Imperative: **paglutuin**	(**pag-** + root + **-in**) cook
Past: **pinagluto**	(infix **-in-** after first letter of prefix **pag-** + root) were cooked
Present: **pinagluluto**	(infix **-in-** after first letter of prefix **pag-** + duplicated first syllable of root + root) are being cooked
Future: **paglulutuin**	(**pag-** + duplicated second syllable of root + root + **-in**) will be cooked

Example: **sulat**	writing
Infinitive: **pagsulatin**	(**pag-** + root + **-in**) to write
Imperative: **pagsulatin**	(**pag-** + root + **-in**) write
Past: **pinagsulat**	(infix **-in-** after first letter of prefix **pag-** + root) were madc to write
Present: **pinagsusulat**	(infix **-in-** after first letter of prefix **pag-** + duplicated first syllable of root + root) are being made to write
Future: **pagsusulatin**	(**pag-** + duplicated second syllable of root + root + **-in**) will be made to write

Observe that the **o** in **luto** is changed to **u** before the second half of the affix **pag-** + **-in** is attached to the imperative form and the future tense. This change in vowels will be required for similar verbs ending in the vowel **o**.

Refer to Lesson Fifteen for the peculiarities in forming an **-in** verb form that ends in a vowel and with or without an end glottal catch, as well as when to use the variant **-hin**.

Examples of **PAG-** + **-IN** Verbs

pag-alisin	to remove	**paglinisin**	to clean
pagbasahin	to read		

Note that in conversational language, the repetition of the first syllable in all forms and tenses of **pag-** + **-in** or **pag-** + **-an** verbs are allowed. See examples below.

		Conversational
Infinitive and imperative:	**paglutuin**	**paglulutuin**
Past:	**pinagluto**	**pinagluluto**
Present:	**pinagluluto**	**pinaglululuto**
Future:	**paglulutuin**	**paglulululutuin**

II. **PAG-** + **-AN** VERB FORMS

The prefix **pag-** + **-an** or its variant **pag-** + **-han** is used to form the plural derivatives of a passive **-an** verb form.

Example: **hugas**	washing
Infinitive: **paghuhugasan**	(**pag-** + duplicated first syllable of root + root + **-an**) to wash
Imperative: **paghuhugasan**	(**pag-** + duplicated first syllable of root + root + **-an**) wash
Past: **pinaghuhugasan**	(infix **-in-** after first letter of prefix **pag-** + duplicated first syllable of root + root + **-an**) were washed
Present: **pinaghuhuhugasan**	(infix **-in-** after first letter of prefix **pag-** + triplicated first syllable of root + root + **-an**) are being washed
Future: **paghuhuhugasan**	(**pag-** + triplicated first syllable of root + root + **-an**) will be washed

Example: **bukas** (irregular)	open
Infinitive: **pagbubuksan**	(**pag-** + duplicated first syllable of root + root without the last vowel + **-an**) to open
Imperative: **pagbubuksan**	(**pag-** + duplicated first syllable of root + root without the last vowel + **-an**) open
Past: **pinagbubuksan**	(infix **-in-** after first letter of prefix **pag-** + duplicated first syllable of root + root without the last vowel + **-an**) were opened
Present: **pinagbububuksan**	(infix **-in-** after first letter of prefix **pag-** + triplicate first syllable of root + root without the last vowel + **-an**) are being opened
Future: **pagbububuksan**	(**pag-** + triplicate first syllable of root + root + **-an**) will be opened

Examples of **PAG-** + **-AN** Verbs

pag-aayusan	to arrange	**pagpipintahan**	to paint
pagbibihisan	to change clothes		

Many **-an** verb forms are derived from irregular verb roots (see list of some of these roots on page 265). Usually, the second vowel of the root is dropped. In others, the second syllable is deleted. A student should try to memorize these irregular roots.

bukas	**pagbubuksan**	= to open
laba	**paglalabhan**	= to wash clothes
lagay	**paglalagyaan**	= to put something

Sample Sentences

Paghuhugasan na ninyo ang mga pinggan.	You (plural) have the plates washed.
Pinagbubuksan niya ang lahat ng mga bintana.	The windows are being opened by her/him.
Pag-aaayusan namin ng buhok ang mga bata.	We will fix the children's hair.
Pinagpipintahan ng lalaki ang mga paso.	The pots are being painted by the man.

EXERCISES

Change the verbs in the following sentences into their plural forms. Afterwards, transform the sentences into English.

1. Bumasa ang bata ng pahayagan sa kanyang lola.
2. Nagluto ang babae ng isda sa kawali.
3. Nagbayad siya ng dalawang libong piso sa akin para sa sapatos.
4. Maglalagay siya ng tubig sa mga baso.
5. Magtakip ka ng panyo sa mukha.

Contractions

Teka, bibili ako ng sorbetes.
Wait, I'll buy ice cream.

Pagkatapos ng klase, pumunta ang mga magkaibigan sa parke para maglaro.
After class, the friends went to the park to play.

RICKY : **Tena, mag-basketball tayo.**
Let's go play basketball.

MARTA : **Ayoko ng basketball. Volleyball na lang.**
I do not like basketball. Let's play volleyball instead.

ANTONIO : **Kahit ano, okay lang. 'Lika na!**
Whatever, it's fine. Let's get going.

RICKY : **Teka, bibili muna ako ng sorbetes.**
Wait, I'll buy ice cream first.

MARTA : **Sayang, 'la akong pera.**
Too bad, I don't have money.

RICKY : **Penge ho kami ng extra ha.**
Please give us extra okay!

RICKY : **Para sa atin lahat ito, 'di ba?**
This is all for us, right?

Vocabulary List

teka = wait	**ayoko** = do not like
ikamo = you said	**sorbetes** = ice cream
penge = give me	**pera** = money
hamo = let it be	**konti** = a little

When we talk or write to a person with whom we are very familiar, we usually skip over some words or syllables or press them together rather than pronouncing them completely. The economical use of words in speech or writing—or brevity—matters. Contractions allow much to be said or written in a shorter time. It is done by shortening a word, syllable or word group or by omitting some letters to create a new, shorter word.

Contracted English words like *don't* and *let's* follow certain rules. So do *isn't*, *don't*, *we're* and *he's*. However, in Tagalog words, many different letters and syllables might be omitted or changed depending on the speaker. For example, in **hintay ka** (or *wait*), the syllable **hin** is omitted and the syllable **tay** is changed to **te** and attached to **ka**. A simple rule to follow in spotting Tagalog contractions is that these are not regular words with noticeable affixes or root words.

Below is a list of common contractions used in everyday conversation. Once these are memorized, look out for new contractions used by the younger generation that may creep in and be accepted into the language.

1. **teka** (from **hintay ka**) = *Wait!*
   Teka sandali, kakain muna ako.   Wait a moment, I will just eat.

2. **dalika** (from **magmadali ka**) = *Be quick!*
   Dalika, mahuhuli tayo.   Be quick, we will be late.

3. **tena** (from **tayo na**) = *Let's go!*
   Tena, huli na tayo.   Let's go, we are already late.

4. **tamo** (from **nakita mo**) = *You see?* or *See?*
   Tamo, bagay sa iyo iyan!   You see? That suits you!

5. **hamo** (from **hayaan mo**) = *Let her/him/it be.*
   Hamo siya, ayaw siyang makinig.   Let him be, he does not like to listen.

   Hamo, makakalimutan mo rin iyan.   Let it be, you will soon forget it.

6. **ayoko** (from **ayaw ko**) = *I don't like.*
   Ayoko ng biruan.   I do not like jokes.

7. **'lika** (from **hali ka**) = *Come* or *Come here.*
   'Lika, alis na tayo.   Come, we're leaving now.

8. **meron** (from **mayroon**) = *has* or *have*
   Meron akong anak.   I have a child.

9. **'la** (from **wala**) = *nothing* or *None.*
   'La akong pera.   I don't have money.

10. **penge** (from **pahingi**) = *Give me.*
    Penge ng tinapay, gutom ako.   Give me bread, I am hungry.

The first ten contracted words may stand alone as responses to questions or as single-word command sentences (such as **dalika** and **'lika**). Note also that contracted words with missing initial syllables or letters, such as the following words, are very common in the Tagalog language.

11. **'di** (from **hindi**) = *not* or *Right?* (use as a tag question)

'Di siya sasama.	He/She is not coming along.
Akin 'yan, 'di ba?	That is mine, isn't it (right)?

12. **'no** (from **ano**) = *Right?* (use as a tag question)

Tama ito, 'no?	This is correct, right?

13. **ikamo** (from **wika mo**) = *you said*

Ikamo [ay] manonood tayo ng pelikula.	You said we are going to see a movie.

14. **ikako** (from **wika ko**) = *I said*

Ikako ay bukas na tayo aalis.	I said we are going tomorrow.

The contractions **ikamo** and **ikako** (or **kamo** and **kako** in some areas) are more commonly used by older people in the rural areas while **sabi ko** (*I said*) or **sabi nila** (*they said*) is more commonly used by younger people.

15. **eka** (from **pahingi ka**) = *give me*

Eka ng mais.	Give me a cob of corn.

16. **tangko** (from **tingnan ko**) = *let me see* or *let me have a look*

Tangko nga, ngayon ko lang nakita iyan.	Let me have a look, I have not seen that yet.

17. **kana** (from **akin na**) = *give me* (used as a command)

Kana ang aklat ko.	Give me my book.

Colors

Kwentuhan nina Olivia at Natalie
Olivia and Natalie's catch-up

Nag-uusap sina Olivia at Natalie tungkol sa bakasyon ni Natalie sa California.
Olivia and Natalie are talking about Natalie's vacation in California.

OLIVIA : **Kumusta ang bakasyon mo?**
How was your vacation?

NATALIE : **Ang saya-saya. Nagmaneho ako papunta sa San Francisco.**
It was so fun. I drove to San Francisco.

OLIVIA : **<u>Asul na asul</u> ang dagat, ano?**
The ocean is very blue, right?

NATALIE : **Oo, pero <u>kulay abo</u> ang buhangin. Mas pino ang mga tabing-dagat sa Pilipinas.**
Yes, but the sand is ash colored. The beaches in the Philippines are finer.

OLIVIA : **Tama ka. Natandaan ko rin na walang <u>dilaw</u> na mangga doon.**
You're right. I also recall that there's no yellow mango there.

NATALIE : **Meron, pero mas matamis ang mangga dito.**
There is, but the mango here is sweeter.

OLIVIA : **Bumili ka ba ng mga <u>pulang-pulang</u> mansanas?**
Did you buy very red apples?

NATALIE : **Isang beses lang, sa farmer's market.**
Just once, in the farmer's market.

Vocabulary List

kayumanggi = brown (referring to race or color of skin)
berde/luntian = green
kulay kahel = orange
itim = black
asul/bughaw = blue
ube = violet

lila = purple
nagmaneho = drove
kulay abo = gray
pino = fine
tabing-dagat = beach
dilaw = yellow
pulang-pula = very red

The English names for colors in the Tagalog language are quite incomplete. The language, for instance, has no equivalent for brown and its different shades such as golden brown. What is commonly used for golden brown is **pula** (*red*) as in the following direction for cooking:

> **Prituhin mo ang isda hanggang pumula.**
> Fry the fish until it turns golden brown.

However, the Tagalogs use **kayumanggi** when referring to the color of the Filipino race and their skin color (sometimes called **morena**, which is Spanish in origin). This word is specific to the race and skin color, and does not apply to anything that is brown. Descriptive words are used instead to indicate the brownness of a thing or object like **kulay kape** (*coffee-colored*) or **kulay tsokolate** (*chocolate-colored*).

I. BASIC COLORS

The Tagalog term for *black* is **itim** and that for *white* is **puti** while the terms for the primary and secondary colors are:

red	**pula**	green	**berde** or **luntian**
blue	**asul** or **bughaw**	violet	**ube**
yellow	**dilaw**	orange	**kulay kahel**

II. DARK COLORS

When expressing the darker, solid or brilliant shades of colors, duplicate the names of colors by using the ligatures **na** and **-ng**. Refer to the following examples of dark colors.

navy blue	**asul na asul**	dark green	**berdeng-berde**
bright yellow	**dilaw na dilaw**	very black	**itim na itim**

III. LIGHT COLORS

Lighter colors, unless those that have specific Tagalog names, such as pale blue, light green, pale yellow, require the word **mura** (which means *pale* or *light* although **mura** also refers to an *unripe fruit* as well as *something that is cheap or not expensive*) attached either before or after the Tagalog names.

pale blue	**asul na mura**	purple	**lila**
light green	**murang berde**	pink	**rosas**
pale yellow	**dilaw na mura**	gray	**abo** (literally *ash*)

IV. SHADES

To express shades of primary and secondary colors, make use of the prefix **ma-** (following this formula: **ma-** + duplicated root word separated by a hyphen) or the suffix **-an** or **-han** (following this formula: root word + **-an**). Note that **asul** and **itim** use the prefix **mang-** instead of **ma-**.

blue	**mangasul-ngasul** or **asulan** (note that the **-ng** in **mang-** in the first half of the word is repeated in the second half after the hyphen)
green	**maberde-berde** or **luntian**
red	**mapula-pula / mamula-mula** or **pulahan**
white	**maputi-puti / mamuti-muti** or **putian**
yellow	**manilaw-nilaw** or **dilawan**

Note that with a prefix such as **ma-**, the initial **d** in **dilaw** is changed to **n** and the **p** in **pula** and **puti** is changed to **m**. These changes are highlighted in previous lessons.

V. OTHER COLORS

Other color names are more specific and use common materials as a point of reference whose mere mention of their names connotes a specific color, such as those listed below:

apple green	**berdeng mansanas**
moss green	**berdeng lumot**
gold/golden	**ginto / ginintuan**
silver	**pilak / pinilakan**

Sample Sentences

Pulang-pula ang kanyang sapatos.
His/her shoes are bright red.

Malamig sa mata ang mga luntiang dahon.
Green leaves are refreshing to the eyes.

Ang dilaw na mura ay bagay sa maputing balat.
Pale yellow is suited to those who are fair skinned.

Marami akong barong tagalog na kulay-abo.
I have many ash-colored *barong tagalog* (formal wear for men).

Appendices

FOODS

Foreigners in the Philippines who look for certain items in the vegetable, fruit, fish or meat sections in wet markets may find difficulty in communicating with local vendors who do not know the local names of some, if not most, of the products they need. Although most supermarkets may have these products as well as the English names of the products on the packages, wet markets still offer cheaper prices and wider variety of these food items. This is on top of the experience of having to haggle prices with local vendors. Take note though that a number of food items are known by their English names such as carrot, cauliflower, greenshells and yellow fin tuna.

To help you look for what you exactly need, here is a comprehensive list of food items in their English names and their Tagalog equivalents.

Vegetables

Bamboo shoots = **labong**
Banana heart = **puso ng saging**
Bean sprouts = **toge**
Beets = **remolatsa**
Bitter melon = **ampalaya**
Bottle gourd = **upo**
Cabbage = **repolyo**
Cashew nut = **kasuy**
Cassava = **kamoteng kahoy**
Chayote = **sayote**
Chili = **sili**
Chinese bok choi = **petsay**
Chinese celery = **kintsay**
Coconut heart = **ubod**
Coriander leaves = **wansoy**
Corn = **mais**
Cucumber = **pipino**
Daikon radish = **labanos**
Eggplant = **talong**
Garbanzo beans = **garbanzos**
Garlic = **bawang**
Horseradish = **malunggay**
Hyacinth beans = **bataw**
Leeks or chives = **kutsay**
Lettuce = **letsugas**
Lime = **dayap**
Long beans = **sitaw**
Malabar nightshade or Malabar spinach = **alugbati**
Mung bean = **mongo**

Mushroom = **kabute**
Mustard = **mustasa**
Native onions = **sibuyas Tagalog**
Onion = **sibuyas**
Peanuts = **mani**
Potato = **patatas**
Red yam = **ube**
Snowpeas = **sitsaro**
Soybeans = **utaw**
Spinach = **kulitis**
Sponge gourd = **patola**
Spring onions/shallots = **sibuyas na mura; sibuyas dahon**
String beans = **abitswelas**
Sweet potato = **kamote**
Tomato = **kamatis**
Turnip or jicama = **singkamas**
Water chestnut = **apulid**
Water spinach = **kangkong**
Wax gourd = **kundol**
Winged beans = **sigarilyas**
Yellow squash = **kalabasa**

Fish and Shellfish

Anchovy = **dilis**
Blue sturgeon = **labahita**
Catfish (freshwater) = **hito**
Catfish (saltwater) = **kanduli**
Cavalla = **talakitok**
Clam = **halaan**
Crab = **alimasag**

Dried shrimp = **hibi**
Goby = **biya**
Golden caesio (or yellow tail fusilier) = **dalagang bukid**
Grouper = **lapu-lapu**
Herring = **tamban**
Lobster = **banagan**
Mackerel = **hasa-hasa**
Milkfish = **bangus**
Mud crab = **alimango**
Mud fish = **dalag**
Mullet = **banak**
Mussel = **tahong**
Oyster = **talaba**
Pompano = **pompano; maratini**
Prawn = **sugpo**
Red snapper = **maya-maya**
River shrimps = **ulang**
Salt cod (dried) = **bacalao**
Seabass = **apahap**
Small shrimps = **alamang**
Snail = **kuhol**
Sole = **dapa**
Spanish mackerel = **tanigue**
Squid = **pusit**
Striped mackerel = **alumahan**
Tilapia = **tilapia**

Noodles

Fine wheat noodles = **miswa**
Glass or cellophane noodles = **sotanghon**
Rice vermicelli = **bihon**
Wheat noodles with egg = **miki**
Yellow egg noodles = **canton**

Meats

Beef = **karne ng baka**
Beef shank = **biyas ng baka**
Brisket = **punta y pecho**
Deer = **usa**
Gizzard = **balun-balunan**
Goat or lamb = **kambing**
Ground beef = **giniling na karne ng baka**
Ground pork = **giniling na karne ng baboy**
Ham = **hamon; pigi**
Liver = **atay**
Meat = **karne**
Ox tongue = **dila; lengua**

Pork = **karne ng baboy**
Pork belly = **liyempo**
Rabbit = **kuneho**
Sheep = **tupa**
Spare ribs = **tadyang**
Water buffalo or carabao = **kalabaw**
Wild boar = **baboyramo**

Poultry

Chicken = **manok**
Duck = **pato**
Egg = **itlog**
Eggwhite = **puti ng itlog**
Egg yolk = **pula ng itlog**
Quail = **pugo**
Quail egg = **itlog ng pugo**
Turkey = **pabo**

Spices and Condiments

Anise wine = **anisado; anis**
Annatto seeds = **atswete**
Bay leaf = **laurel**
Black wood ear mushrooms = **tenga ng daga**
Cinnamon = **kanela**
Clove = **clavio de comer**
Dry mustard = **pulbos ng mustasa**
Fermented soybeans = **tausi**
Fish paste = **bagoong isda**
Fish sauce = **patis**
Garlic = **bawang**
Green or red pepper = **siling berde; siling pula**
Lemongrass = **tanglad**
Lye = **lihiya**
Monosodium glutamate = **vetsin**
Nutmeg = **anis maskado**
Oregano = **oregano**
Paprika = **paminton**
Pepper = **paminta**
Peppercorn = **pamintang buo**
Saffron = **kasubha**
Saltpeter = **salitre**
Sesame seeds = **linga**
Soybean paste = **miso**
Soy sauce = **toyo**
Turmeric = **luyang dilaw**
Vinegar = **suka**

COOKING TERMS

Filipino cuisine has been influenced and inspired by various eastern and western cuisines from which it has adopted various culinary procedures, imported ingredients and foreign dishes that were assimilated to fit local culture. Filipinos adopted culinary influences from China, Spain, Mexico and the United States and each of the various regions in the Philippines then provided their own local taste to these foods.

According to the late teacher and food critic Doreen Fernandez, what makes up the Filipino kitchen are the "history and society that introduced and adapted them; the people who turned them to their tastes and accepted them into their homes and restaurants, and especially the harmonizing culture that combined them into contemporary Filipino fare." Thus, Filipino food today is a gastronomic presentation of Philippine history.

The previous lesson introduced you to the Tagalog names of food items. In the following two lessons, you will be treated to cooking terms and culinary dishes that reflect this fusion of foreign inputs and local taste. For the meantime, reflect on these terms before moving on to the next lesson.

1. Bake = **ihurno; lutuin sa hurno** (oven)
   Nagluto ako ng pasta sa hurno.
   I baked a pasta (dish) in the oven.

2. Baste = **pahiran ng mantika** (cooking oil) **o ng sarsa** (sauce)
   Pahiran mo ng mantika ang balat ng baboy para hindi matuyo.
   Baste the pork skin to prevent drying.

3. Beat = **batihin**
   Batihin mo ang anim na itlog para sa torta.
   Beat six eggs for the omelet.

4. Blanch = **banlian**
   Binanlian ko ang mga pili para maalis ang balat.
   I blanched the pili nuts to remove the skin.

5. Blend = **haluin**
   Haluin mo ang mga sangkap nang mabuti.
   Blend the ingredients very well.

6. Boil = **pakuluin**
   Pakuluin mo ang tubig sa kaldero.
   Boil the water in the kettle.

7. Broil = **ihawin**
   Inihaw ko ang daing sa baga.
   I broiled the dried fish on live coals.

8. Cut = **hiwain** (with knife); **gupitin** (with scissors)
   Hiwain ninyo ang tinapay sa gitna.
   Cut the bread in the middle.

   Gupitin ninyo ang tali ng supot.
   Cut the string of the bag.

9. Chop = **tadtarin**
   Tadtarin mo ang baboy para sa torta.
   Chop the pork for the omelet.

10. Drain = **patuluin**
    Pinatulo niya muna ang langis mula sa baboy bago niya ito hinango sa kawali.
    She drained the oil from the pork before he/she removed it from the pan.

11. Fry = **prituhin**
    Pinirito ng aming katulong ang bangus.
    Our helper fried the milkfish.

12. Marinate = **ibabad sa suka** (vinegar), **toyo** (soy sauce) **at kalamansi** (native lemon)
    Ibababad ko ang liempo sa suka, toyo at kalamansi.
    I will marinate the pork belly in vinegar, soy sauce and kalamansi.

13. Melt = **tunawin**
    Tinunaw ni Ana ang mantikilya sa kawali.
    Ana melted the butter in the pan.

14. Mince = **dikdikin sa maliliit na piraso** (small pieces)
    Dikdikin mo ang bawang para sa adobo.
    Mince the garlic for the *adobo* (see next page for description).

15. Peel = **talupan**
    Talupan mo ang mga mansanas para sa salad.
    Peel the apples for the salad.

16. Pit = **alisan ng buto** (seeds)
    Alisan ninyo ng buto ang mga bayabas bago matamisin.
    Pit the guavas before preserving them.

17. Saute = **igisa**
    Igisa mo ang giniling na karne sa bawang, sibuyas at kamatis.
    Saute the ground beef in garlic, onions and tomatoes.

18. Soak = **ibabad**
    Ibinabad ni Ana ang mongo sa tubig.
    Ana soaked the mung beans in water.

19. Steam = **pasingawan**
    Pinasingawan niya ang puto.
    She steamed the rice cake.

20. Toast = **tustahin**
    Masarap tustahin ang tinapay para sa agahan.
    It is nice to toast some bread for breakfast.

POPULAR FILIPINO DISHES AND DELICACIES

Filipinos love food. It plays an important role in the culture and contributes to myriad anecdotes regarding Filipino hospitality. Generally, foreign guests complain of overeating and being overfed when visiting Filipino homes. This is apparent because Filipinos eat three full meals, one morning snack and one afternoon snack each day. Cooked rice is essential in these meals plus a dish of meat and/or vegetables. Snacks are called **merienda** where, more often than not, rice in its sweet and glutinous form is also served.

Filipino dishes seem to retain that unique local touch whether prepared in simple roadside eateries called **karinderia** or **turo-turo** (so called because customers point to, or **turo**, the food they want to order) or in restaurants or homes. Basically, some dishes transcend regional or social border and grace every Filipino table. These dishes are enumerated below.

Adobo is regarded by many Filipinos as the official national dish. It uses either pork or poultry, or both. It is cooked in vinegar with garlic, peppercorns, soy sauce and bayleaf.

Arroz caldo is a rice-based gruel with bits of chicken and ginger. It is a favorite merienda dish and is best taken while steaming hot.

Balut, a street food delicacy, is actually a steamed fertilized 17-day old duck embryo. Inside the egg is the hardened yellow yolk, the harder egg white, some tasty broth and the embryo. It is eaten with either salt or vinegar.

Bibingka is a glutinous rice cake with toppings such as cheese, salted egg or grated coconut and sugar. A small plain rice cake with just cheese or no topping at all is called **puto**. Similar preparations from cassava (**kamoteng kahoy**) and glutinous rice with coconut milk (**gata**) are called **kakanin**.

Dinuguan is pig's blood stew with cut-ups of pork and pig organs. The dark broth is made up of vinegar and pig's blood. **Dinuguan** is paired with **puto**.

Ginataan is a traditional merienda fare consisting of sweet potato, **nangka**, **saba**, glutinous rice balls and tapioca pearls (**sago**) cooked in a slightly thick coconut milk.

Halo-halo literally means *mix-mix*. It is a cool salad-like preparation consisting of sweetened root tubers and fruits like sweet potato, **saba** (a variety of banana used for cooking), **nangka** (jackfruit), garbanzos, ube, yam, red beans, and topped with shaved ice and evaporated milk.

Kare-kare or oxtail stew uses pork or calf leg and oxtail, vegetables like egg plant, banana heart, string beans and **pechay** (or bok choi) cooked in peanut sauce with a dash of **bagoong** (shrimp paste).

Lechon (from Spanish **leche** or milk) or **litson** is basically roasted suckling pig cooked over low charcoal fire for a day. The slow roasting produces crisp red skin and succulent meat. A **lechon** from the Luzon island is usually served with liver sauce while that from the Visayas and Mindanao islands is prepared with stuffings made of spices, wines and even **paella** (a Spanish dish of meat and seafood) and needs no sauce.

Lumpia has two varieties. One is the fried spring roll made of sauteed vegetables and ground meat rolled up in a thin egg or flour wrapper. It is topped with peanut sauce and crisp ginger bits. The other spring roll is **sariwang lumpia** (fresh **lumpia**) without the wrapper.

Menudo is a dish made of diced pork and liver cooked with potato, garbanzos and tomato sauce or fresh tomatoes.

Paksiw is a fish or meat dish cooked with enough vinegar, ginger and other spices, usually bayleaf and pepper.

Pinakbet is a combination of sauteed native vegetables with **bagoong** or strips of dried fish.

Sinigang is a sour broth of shrimp, fish or pork, and vegetables (**okra**, **kangkong** and string beans). The broth is made sour by tamarind or **kamias** (green sour fruit).

TAGALOG IDIOMS

An idiom is made up of words that, when taken together, means something other than the meaning of the individual words. Idioms carry a regional story or a logic behind them as well as lend color, grace and precision to speech and writing.

Every language has its own set of idioms, nonnative speakers of the language are challenged and experience difficulty in learning the cultural meaning of such phrases. They are sometimes hesitant to use idioms in conversation for fear of being misunderstood; but they just need confidence and practice to be able to use these expressions correctly.

Filipinos have thousands of idioms. The best way to get acquainted with them is by listening to Filipinos conversing in their own language, reading Filipino comic strips in leading newspapers (some have been made into comic books like Pol Medina Jr.'s depiction of Filipino life and society in his **Pugad Baboy**, literally *Pig's Nest*), watching Filipino TV variety shows and Tagalog dramas, listening to radio talk shows and listing down unfamiliar words or phrases. Below are some Filipino idiomatic expressions that make conversations in Filipino alive.

Anak-pawis (literally, child of perspiration) = *poor people, laboring class*
Ang mga anak-pawis ay mahal ng Diyos.
Poor people are loved by God.

Basa ang papel (literally, the paper is wet) = *cannot be trusted, no longer credible*
Basa na ang papel niya sa akin.
He/She cannot be trusted.
He/She is no longer credible.

Bukas ang palad (literally, with open palm of hand) = *generous with money*
Ang aking ama ay bukas ang palad sa mahihirap.
My father is generous with the poor.

Buto't balat (literally, skin and bones) = *very thin, emaciated*
Buto't balat na si Pedro nang lumabas sa ospital.
Pedro was very thin when he checked out of the hospital.

Di-mahulugang karayom (literally, no needle may be dropped) = *too crowded*
Di-mahulugang karayom sa dami ng tao ang Rizal Park.
Rizal Park is too crowded.

Hating-kapatid (literally, divide among siblings) = *divide or allocate equally, equal share*
Dapat hating-kapatid ang pagbibigay ng kendi sa mga bata.
The candies should be divided equally among the children.

Hulog ng langit (literally, dropped from Heaven) = *blessing from God, good fortune*
Ang batang iyan ay hulog ng langit sa aming pamilya.
That child is a blessing from God to our family.

Kanang-kamay (literally, right hand) = *efficient helper, assistant*
Siya ang kanang kamay ko sa tanggapan.
He/She is my efficient helper in the office.

Kumukulo ang dugo (literally, the blood is boiling) = *very angry*
Kumukulo ang dugo ko sa taong iyon.
I am very angry with that person.

Mababa ang luha (literally, shallow tears) = *cries easily*
Ang aking ina ay mababa ang luha.
My mother cries easily.

Mabigat ang bibig (literally, heavy mouth) = *rude, uncouth, insulting, uncivil*
Walang maraming kaibigan ang taong mabigat ang bibig.
Rude people do not have many friends.

Mabilis pa sa alas kuwatro (literally, faster than four o'clock) = *acts swiftly, very fast*
Mabilis pa sa alas kuwatro kung siya'y maligo.
He/She takes a bath very fast.

Magbanat ng buto (literally, stretch the bone) = *to work very hard*
Kailangang magbanat ng buto upang mabuhay.
We must work hard to survive.

Magsunog ng kilay (literally, to burn eyebrows) = *to study hard*
Magsunog ka ng kilay para sa iyong kinabukasan.
Study hard for your future.

Mahaba ang dila (literally, long tongue) = *gossiper, gossip monger*
Maraming babae ang mahaba ang dila.
Many women are gossipers.

Mahaba ang buntot (literally, long tailed) = *spoiled*
Huwag mong pagbigyan ang lahat ng gusto ng bata, baka humaba ang buntot niya.
Don't give in to everything the child wants lest he/she gets spoiled.

Mahabang dulang (literally, long low table) = *wedding, get married*
Kailan ka ba magmamahabang-dulang?
When are you getting married?

Mahangin (literally, windy) = *boastful*
Umiwas ka sa taong mahangin.
Avoid boastful people.

Mahirap pa sa daga (literally, poorer than a rat) = *extremely poor*
Ang mag-anak na iyon ay mahirap pa sa daga.
That family is extremely poor.

Maitim ang buto (literally, black bones) = *evil*
Huwag kang makisama sa taong iyan. Maitim ang kanyang buto.
Don't get involved with that person. He/She is evil.

Makitid ang noo (literally, narrow forehead) = *dumb*
Makitid ang noo ng kanyang kaklase.
His/Her classmate is dumb.

Malikot ang kamay (literally, restless hands) = *pickpocket, a person who steals from pockets or bags*
> **Ang taong malikot ang kamay ay nahuli.**
> The pickpocket was arrested.

Matigas ang mukha (literally, hard face) = *stern-faced*
> **Ayoko sa babaeng matigas ang mukha.**
> I don't like a stern-faced woman.

Mukhang Biyernes Santo (literally, a Holy Friday face) = *sad or gloomy face*
> **Siya ay mukhang Biyernes Santo.**
> She looks very sad.

Pagputi ng uwak (literally, when the raven turns white) = *never, infinitely*
> **Makababayad siya ng utang pagputi ng uwak.**
> He/She can never pay his/her debts.

Parang palengke (literally, like a market) = *noisy*
> **Parang palengke ang silid ng mga bata.**
> The children's room is noisy.

Saling-pusa (literally, join-cat) = *not really part of the group*
> **Saling-pusa lamang si Raissa sa laro.**
> Raissa is not part of the game.

Sira-ulo (literally, broken head) = *crazy*
> **Huwag mong pansinin ang sira-*ulong* iyan.**
> Don't mind that crazy person.

Tuta (literally, puppy) = *one who blindly follows someone*
> **Siya ay tuta ng isang pulitiko.**
> He is a blind follower of a politician.

Usad-pagong (literally, moves like a turtle) = *very slow*
> **Ang kanyang pag-unlad ay usad-pagong.**
> His progress is very slow.

EVERYDAY TAGALOG EXPRESSIONS

In Lesson Three, an adequate number of everyday expressions—in addition to local versions of *Good day*, *How are you* and *Excuse me* as well as an introduction to **po**, which is the Tagalog term for respect—were laid down as groundwork for succeeding lessons.

Listed in this lesson are more standard and common expressions in specific locations such as market and kitchen as well as instructions to children that would be more useful in interacting with native Tagalog speakers.

I. LOCATIONS AND DIRECTIONS

May I ask something?	**Puwedeng magtanong?**
Where can I find a good restaurant?	**Saan ako makakakita ng isang magaling na restawran?**

Where can I find a Protestant church?	**Saan ako makakakita ng simbahang Protestante?**
Where can I find a doctor?	**Saan may doktor?**
What is the name of this street?	**Ano ang pangalan ng kalsadang ito?**
Where does Mr. Cruz live?	**Saan nakatira si Ginoong Cruz?**
[Please] stop (at the corner)!	**Para po (sa kanto)!**
Turn right/left.	**Kanan/Kaliwa.**
Straight ahead.	**Diretso lang.**
Does a bus stop here?	**Tumitigil ba ang bus dito?**
How long before the (next) bus comes?	**Gaano katagal ang dating ng (susunod na) bus?**
Where is this bus going?	**Saan paparoon ang bus na ito?**
What time does this bus arrive in Manila?	**Anong oras ang dating nitong bus sa Maynila?**
How do I get to Ortigas Avenue from here?	**Paano pumunta sa Ortigas Avenue mula dito?**
What is the name of this barrio?	**Ano ang ngalan ng baryong ito?**
Is this water safe to drink?	**Puwede bang inumin ang tubig na ito?**
Where can we buy food?	**Saan makakabili ng pagkain?**
Please show me the way.	**Pakituro sa akin ang daan.**
Let us take a taxi.	**Mag-taksi tayo.**
Wait here.	**Maghintay ka rito.**

II. INSTRUCTIONS FOR CHILDREN

Come here.	**Halika.**
Wash your hands and face.	**Maghugas ka ng kamay at mukha.**
Put on your shoes and clothes.	**Isuot mo ang iyong sapatos at damit.**
Sit down and rest.	**Maupo ka at magpahinga.**
Go to sleep.	**Matulog ka na.**
Pick up your toy.	**Kunin mo ang iyong laruan.**
Put away your toys.	**Iligpit mo ang iyong mga laruan.**
Do not cry.	**Huwag kang umiyak.**
Don't quarrel.	**Huwag kayong mag-away.**
Go out and play.	**Lumabas kayo at maglaro.**
Do not wake up the baby.	**Huwag mong gisingin ang sanggol.**
Be a good boy (or girl).	**Magpakabait ka.**

III. TIME

What time is it?	**Anong oras na?**
Today is Sunday.	**Linggo ngayon.**
Tomorrow is Monday.	**Lunes bukas.**
Yesterday was Saturday.	**Sabado kahapon.**
It is now Holy Week.	**Mahal na Araw ngayon.**
This month is January.	**Ang buwang ito ay Enero.**
The date is April 20.	**Ang petsa ay ika-20 (or a bente) ng Abril.**
The year is 2007.	**Ang taon ay dalawang libo at pito.**

IV. SPEAKING IN TAGALOG

I am learning to speak Tagalog.	**Nag-aaral akong magsalita ng Tagalog.**
I speak only little Tagalog.	**Nagsasalita ako ng kaunti lamang.**
Please talk to me in Tagalog.	**Kausapin mo ako sa Tagalog.**
How do you say ... in Tagalog?	**Paano sinasabi sa Tagalog ang ...?**
Please correct my pronunciation.	**Iwasto mo ang aking pagbigkas.**
We are studying your language.	**Nag-aaral kami ng inyong wika.**
Do you speak Tagalog?	**Nagsasalita ka ba ng Tagalog?**
I do not understand.	**Hindi ko maintindihan.**
Please repeat.	**Paki-ulit nga.**
What did you say?	**Anong sinabi mo?**

V. MAKING INTRODUCTIONS

My name is Jonathan.	**Jonathan ang pangalan ko.**
What is your name?	**Ano ang pangalan mo?**
Who are you?	**Sino ka/kayo?**
Where do you live?	**Saan ka nakatira?**
This is my friend Paolo.	**Ito ang kaibigan kong si Paolo.**
I am pleased to meet you.	**Ikinagagalak kong makilala kayo.**
Please come and visit us.	**Dumalaw kayo sa amin.**
I am Jolina's friend.	**Kaibigan ako ni Jolina.**
Who are your companions?	**Sino ang mga kasama mo?**
Are you my sister's friend?	**Ikaw ba ang kaibigan ng kapatid kong babae?**
Do I know you?	**Kilala ba kita?**
I know you.	**Kilala kita.**
I do not know you.	**Hindi kita kilala.**

VI. DRESSING UP

What will you wear?	**Ano ang iyong isusuot?**
I do not know. I don't have a new dress.	**Ewan ko. Wala akong bagong damit.**
That is an old one.	**Luma na iyan.**
I have nothing to wear.	**Wala akong maisuot.**
I will wear my Barong Tagalog.	**Isusuot ko ang aking Barong Tagalog.**
I like the Barong Tagalog.	**Gusto ko ang Barong Tagalog.**

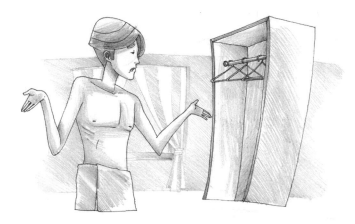

| It is cool. | Ito ay malamig isuot. |
| A coat is warm. | **Mainit ang amerikana** (refers to the formal coat and tie introduced by the Americans). |

VII. AT A PARTY

The food is ready. Let's eat.	**Handa na ang pagkain. Kumain na tayo.**
Eat well.	**Kumain kayong mabuti.**
Do you like more rice?	**Gusto mo pa ng kanin?**
Please get some more.	**Kumuha pa kayo.**
Don't be shy.	**Huwag kayong mahiya.** (This is a very common expression of hosts when they offer food to their guests and want to make the guests feel more welcome to their homes.)
Thank you. I am already full.	**Salamat. Busog na ako.** (or **Huwag na. Salamat.**)

VIII. GOODBYES

It is late (at night). Let's go home.	**Gabi na. Umuwi na tayo.**
Thank you for coming.	**Salamat sa inyong pagparito.**
We enjoyed the party.	**Nasiyahan kami sa inyong handa.**
Please come again.	**Pumarito kayo uli.**
We will return.	**Babalik kami.**
Goodbye. Thank you very much.	**Paalam. Maraming salamat.**
Goodbye, until next time.	**Paalam, hanggang sa muli.**

IX. IN THE MARKET

Is the meat fresh?	**Sariwa ba ang karne?**
How much is this?	**Magkano ito?**
How much is a kilo of pork?	**Magkano ang isang kilo ng baboy?**
Give me one kilo of beef.	**Bigyan mo ako ng isang kilo ng baka.**
This is expensive.	**Ang mahal naman nito.**
Do you have other things?	**Meron pa ba kayong iba?**

Is this made in the Philippines?	Gawa ba ito sa Pilipinas?
Where can I buy souvenirs?	Saan ako makakabili ng mga subenir?
The price is fair.	Magandang presyo (or Sulit ang presyo).
This is not the correct change.	Hindi tama ang sukli.
Please wrap this item.	Pakibalot nga ninyo ito.

X. IN THE KITCHEN

The stove is hot.	Mainit ang pugon.
The pot is full.	Puno ang kaserola.
The knife is sharp.	Matalas ang kutsilyo.
The pantry is empty.	Walang laman ang paminggalan.
The dishes are clean.	Malilinis ang mga pinggan.
The floor is dirty.	Marumi ang sahig.
Let us cook the food.	Lutuin natin ang pagkain.
Wash the vegetables thoroughly.	Hugasan nang mabuti ang mga gulay.
Keep the cabinets in order.	Iayos mo ang mga kabinet.

XI. IN THE DINING ROOM

It is time to eat.	Oras na para kumain (or Kainan na).
What's for breakfast (or lunch or dinner)?	Ano ang ulam? (Ulam or viand goes with rice very meal time.)
Let us say our graces.	Magpasalamat tayo [sa ating pagkain].
Will you have meat?	Gusto mo ng karne?
Please pass the rice.	Pakiabot ng kanin.
Do you have tea?	Meron bang tsa?
I would like more tea.	Gusto ko pa ng tsa.
Please bring the bread.	Pakidala ng tinapay.
We are through eating.	Tapos na kaming kumain.
A glass of water please.	Isang basong tubig nga.
Please clear the table.	Pakiligpit ang mesa.
That was a good meal!	Ang sarap ng pagkain!

XII. IN THE LIVING ROOM

Please come in and sit down.	Tuloy kayo. Maupo kayo.
We are happy that you came.	Natutuwa kami sa pagparito ninyo.
This chair is comfortable.	Komportable ang upuang ito.
Do you wish to listen to some music?	Ibig ba ninyong makinig ng tugtog?
Would you like to read the newspaper?	Ibig ba ninyong magbasa ng diyaryo?
Would you like some cold water?	Ibig ba ninyo ng malamig na tubig?
How long have you been living here?	Gaano katagal na kayong nakatira rito?
We enjoy living here.	Nasisiyahan kaming tumira rito.
The people here are friendly and helpful.	Ang mga tao dito ay mabubuti at matutulungin.

MORE EXAMPLES OF CONVERSATIONS IN TAGALOG

Below are given several more examples of Tagalog conversations immediately followed by their English translations (enclosed in brackets). A vocabulary list as well as some cultural notes provide definitions and descriptions of words that have not been used or introduced in the previous lessons. **Note that these sentence examples are more of an intermediate level than the introductory dialogues in the lessons.**

Pagtatagpo at Pagpapakilala

Meeting Someone and Making Introductions

Dumating si Peter Smith galing sa Hong Kong. Sinalubong siya ni Linda Reyes, tag-apamahala ng mga benta ng kanilang kompanya. (Peter Smith arrived from Hong Kong. He was met by Linda Reyes, sales director of their company.)

LINDA : **Maligayang pagdating, Ginoong Smith.** (Welcome, Mr. Smith.)

PETER : **Salamat, kumusta ka Martin?** (Thank you. How are you, Linda?)

LINDA : **Mabuti po naman. Kayo? Kumusta ang inyong biyahe?** (I am fine. And you? How was your trip?)

PETER : **Mabuti naman. Maayos ang lahat.** (It was all right. Everything was fine.)

LINDA : **May reserbasyon kayo sa Manila Peninsula. Narito na ang sundo ninyo na magdadala sa inyo sa otel. Magkita po tayo mamaya doon sa otel para sa pulong.** (You have a reservation at the Manila Peninsula. Here's the person who will drive you to the hotel. I'll see you later at the hotel for the meeting.)

PETER : **Maraming salamat.** (Thank you.)

Pinulong ni Peter Smith ang mga kawani ng kanilang kompanya sa otel. (Peter Smith met the personnel of the company in the hotel.)

LINDA : **Ikinararangal kong ipakilala sa inyo ang ating pangulo, Si Ginoong Peter Smith.** (I have the honor to introduce to you our president, Mr. Peter Smith.)

PETER : **Maraming salamat, Martin. Magandang umaga sa inyong lahat. Natutuwa ako sa muli nating pagkikita sa simula ng bagong taong ito. Binabati ko rin kayong lahat sa inyong magandang benta noong nakaraang taon.** (Thank you very much, Linda. Good morning to you all. I am happy to see you again at the start of this new year. I also congratulate you for the good sales last year.)

LINDA : **Maraming salamat po. Talaga pong nagsikap ang lahat para maabot at malagpasan ang ating kota. Ginoong Smith, bago po tayo mag-umpisa ng miting, maari po bang ipakilala ko ang mga bago nating direktor?** (Thank you very much, sir. Everybody really tried hard to reach and go beyond our quota. Mr. Smith, before we start the meeting, may I introduce our new directors?)

PETER : **Sige, ipagpatuloy mo.** (By all means, continue.)

LINDA : **Ginoong Smith, si Ricardo Sandoval ang ating Katulong na Direktor sa Pagbebenta.** (Mr. Smith, this is Ricardo Sandoval, Assistant Director for Sales.)

PETER   : **Ikinagagalak kitang makilala, Ricardo.** (I am pleased to meet you, Ricardo.)
RICARDO   : **Maraming salamat po.** (Thank you, sir.)
LINDA   : **At ito po naman si Binibining Delia Orosa, ang bago nating Direktor sa Pananaliksik.** (And this is Miss Delia Orosa, our new Director for Research.)
PETER   : **Ikinalulugod kong mapabilang ka sa ating pangkat, Delia.** (I am happy to have you in our group, Delia.)
DELIA   : **Salamat po.** (Thank you, sir.)

Vocabulary List

sundo = somebody who fetches
pagbebenta = sales
pagpapakilala = introduce
pananaliksik = research
pangkat = group

pangulo = president
paliparan = airport
pulong = meeting
magsikap = to work hard
ipagpatuloy = continue

Pagtatanong Ng Direksiyon
Asking Directions

Bagong dating ang mag-inang Aling Ana at Sally sa Quezon City. Galing sila sa lalawigan at bumaba sila sa estasyon ng bus sa Cubao. Pupunta sila sa Makati upang dalawin ang kapatid ni Aling Ana. Nagtanong sila sa isang lalaking dumaraan. (Aling Ana and her daughter Sally had just arrived in Quezon City. They came from the province and got down at the bus station in Cubao. They are going to Makati to visit Aling Ana's sister. They asked a man who was passing by.)

ALING ANA : **Mawalang-galang na po. Saan ba ang sakayan patungong Makati?** (Excuse me, sir. Where can we get a ride to Makati?)
LALAKI   : **Dumiretso kayo riyan, tumawid sa Edsa at sumakay sa bus na may karatulang Ayala.** (Go straight ahead, cross Edsa and board the bus with the signboard Ayala.)
ALING ANA : **Tanghali na kami. Marahil mas mabilis ang taksi.** (We're already late. Perhaps a taxi will be faster.)
SALLY   : **Nay, bakit hindi natin subukan ang MRT?** (Mother, why don't we try the MRT?)
LALAKI   : **Mas mabilis ang MRT. Madali kayong makararating sa Makati. Ang estasyon ng MRT Cubao ay nasa Farmers' Plaza. Bumili kayo ng tiket para sa Buendia Station. Pagdating ninyo roon, marami na kayong masasakyang jeepney o FX.** (MRT is faster. You will reach Makati easily. The Cubao MRT station is in Farmers' Plaza. Buy a ticket for Buendia Station. When you get there, you can take a jeepney or FX.)
ALING ANA : **Maraming salamat po sa inyong tulong.** (Thank you for your assistance, sir.)
LALAKI   : **Walang anuman po.** (You're welcome, madam.)

ALING ANA : **Ibang-iba na ang Maynila ngayon. May MRT at FX na. Sa ating probinsi-ya ay marami pa ring karetela at traysikel.** (Manila is very different now. They already have the MRT and FX. In the province, we still have a lot of carriages and tricycles.)

Vocabulary List and Notes

bumaba = to go down
diretso = straight ahead
dumalaw = to visit
lalawigan = province
malapit = near

malapit-lapit = nearer; a bit near
malayo = far
malayo-layo = farther; a bit far
tumawid = to cross
MRT = Metro Rail Transit

FX = an air-conditioned vehicle that can accommodate nine passengers. FX fare is more expensive than a jeepney's.
EDSA = Epifanio de los Santos Avenue, a major thoroughfare crossing several cities in Metro Manila.

Sa Bangko
At the Bank

Kagagaling lamang ni Nestor sa Saudi Arabia. Kailangan niyang magpapalit ng dolyar. Nagpasama siya kay Juan sa bangko. (Nestor has just arrived from Saudi Arabia. He needs to change his dollars into pesos.)

NESTOR : **Magandang umaga. Maari bang magpapalit ng limang daang dolyar sa piso? Magkano ang palitan ngayon?** (Good morning. May I have my $500 changed into peso? What is the current exchange rate?)

TELLER : **Kuwarenta y nuwebe po sa dolyar. Pakipunan po ninyo ang aplikasyon na ito.** (Forty-nine pesos to a dollar. Please fill up this application form.)

NESTOR : **Salamat. Kung nais kong maglagak sa inyong bangko, magkano ang paunang deposito?** (Thank you. If I wish to deposit in your bank, how much is the initial deposit?)

TELLER : **Sampung libong piso po ang unang deposito.** (The initial deposit is P10,000, sir.)

NESTOR : **Ano naman ang mga kailangan para magbukas ng account?** (What are needed to open an account?)

TELLER : **Kailangan ng dalawang ID tulad ng lisensiya ng drayber, pasaporte o SSS.** (Two IDs are needed like a driver's license, passport or SSS.)

NESTOR : **Kailangan rin ba ng litrato?** (Is a photo needed?)
TELLER : **Opo, puwede po kahit ano ang sukat.** (Yes, sir. Any size will do.)
NESTOR : **Maraming salamat. Babalik na lamang ako sa ibang araw.** (Thank you, I'll come back some other day.)

Vocabulary List

lisensiya = license
litrato = photo
magbukas = to open
maglagak = to deposit

magpalit ng pera = to change currency
pakipunan = please fill up
sukat = size

Sa Isang Pulong

In a Meeting

Ang pulong ng samahan ni Tessie ay tuwing ikalawang Martes ng buwan. Ito ay gina- ganap sa isang restoran sa Malate. Ang layunin ng kanilang samahan ay tumulong sa mga maralitang kababaihan at kabataan sa Barangay 83 ng Sta. Ana. Noong Martes na iyon, pagkatapos ang pag-awit ng Pambansang Awit at ang panalanging pambungad, tinawag ng kalihim ang mga pangalan ng dumalo sa miting. (Tessie's club meets every second Tuesday of the month. It is held in a restaurant in Malate. The purpose of their club is to help the poor women and children of Barangay 83 of Sta. Ana. That particular Tuesday, after the singing of the National Anthem and the opening prayer, the secretary called the names of those who attended the meeting.)

TESSIE : **Magandang hapon sa inyong lahat. Kalihim Elsa, ilang kasapi ang dum- alo sa pulong na ito?** (Good afternoon, everyone. Secretary Elsa, how many members are present in this meeting?)

ELSA : **May labinlimang kasapi ang naririto ngayon maliban kina Mary at Kris.** (There are 15 members present now excluding Mary and Kris.)

TESSIE : **Basahin natin ngayon ang mga tala ng nakaraang miting.** (Let's now read the minutes of the past meeting.)

TESSIE : **Salamat, Kalihim Elsa. Tatalakayin naman natin ang ating pang- kabuhayang proyekto sa Tondo. May ulat ang tagapangulo ng lupon, si Pacita.** (Thank you, Secretary Elsa. We will now discuss our livelihood project in Tondo. Pacita, the chairperson of the committee will report.)

PACITA : **Sa ika-8 ng Pebrero, gaganapin ang ating proyekto na magtuturo sa mga kababaihan ng barangay ng iba't ibang paggawa ng longganisa.** (On February 8, we will conduct our project to teach the women of the barangay the different ways of making sausages.)

TESSIE : **Salamat, Pacita. At tungkol naman sa mga bata, ano ang ulat mo, Carol?** (Thank you, Pacita, Regarding the children, what is your report, Carol?)

CAROL : **Sa ika-16 ng Marso, dadalhin natin ang mga bata sa Museo Pambata sa Roxas Boulevard kung saan matututo sila ng maraming kaalaman tung- kol sa kanilang paligid. Pagkatapos ay ipapasyal sila sa Rizal Park.** (On March 16, we will take the children to the Children's Museum on Roxas Blvd where they will learn a lot about their surroundings. Then we are taking them to Rizal Park.)

TESSIE : **Paano ang pagkain ng mga bata?** (What about the children's food?)

CAROL : **Isang kompanya ng gatas ang umako sa kanilang pagkain pati na ng kanilang transportasyon.** (A milk company will take care of their food as well as their transportation.)

TESSIE : **Binabati ko kayo, Pacita at Carol sa inyong magandang pamumuno. May iba pa bang bagay tayong tatalakayin? Kung wala na, tinatapos ko na ang miting na ito. Maraming salamat sa inyong pagdalo.** (Congratulations, Pacita and Carol for your fine leadership. Are there other matters to dis- cuss? If none, the meeting is adjourned. Thank you very much for coming.)

Sa Palengke at Tindahan

At the Market and in a Store

Si Ginang Jones at ang kusinera niyang si Ada ay nagpunta sa palengke. Magkakaroon ng munting salu-salo si Ginang Jones para sa mag-asawang Thomas na galing sa Bangkok. Nais ni Ginang Jones na bumili ng mga sariwang prutas at gulay sa palengke. Pumunta sila sa puwesto ng mga prutas kung saan nakakita sila ng mga mangga, saging, dalandan, papaya, tsiko at lansones. (Mrs. Jones and her cook Ada went to the market. Mrs. Jones will have a small party for the Thomas couple who arrived from Bangkok. Mrs. Jones wants to buy fresh fruits and vegetables in the market. They went to the fruit stand first where they saw mangoes, bananas, oranges, papaya, chico and lanzones.)

GNG. JONES	:	**Magkano ang mangga?** (How much are the mangoes?)
MALE VENDOR	:	**Sisenta po ang isang kilo.** (Sixty pesos per kilo.)
ADA	:	**Saan ba galing ang mga iyan?** (Where do they come from?)
MALE VENDOR	:	**Sa Pangasinan. Matatamis ang mga mangga na galing doon.** (From Pangasinan. Mangoes from that place are very sweet.)
GNG. JONES	:	**Bigyan mo ako ng dalawang kilo. Gusto ko rin ng saging na lacatan at isang piña.** (Give me two kilos. I also like lacatan and pineapple.)
ADA	:	**Bibili rin po ba kayo ng pakwan, madam?** (Are you also buying watermelon, madam?)
GNG. JONES	:	**Oo, gustong-gusto ni Ginoong Jones ang pakwan.** (Yes, Mr. Jones likes watermelon very much.)
MALE VENDOR	:	**Narito na lahat ng inyong pinamili.** (Here are all the things you have bought.)
GNG. JONES	:	**Salamat. Pakikuwenta lahat.** (Thank you. Please add up everything.)

Pagkatapos sa prutasan, nagtungo naman sila sa sa gulayan. (From the fruitstand, they went to the vegetable section.)

GNG. JONES	:	**Bumili tayo ng letsugas, kamatis at sibuyas para sa salad.** (Let's buy lettuce, tomatoes and onions for the salad.)
ADA	:	**Nais ba ninyong gumawa ako ng lumpiang sariwa?** (Do you want me to prepare fresh vegetable spring roll?)
GNG. JONES	:	**Oo, gusto ko iyon. Sarapan mo ang salsa.** (Yes, I like that. Make the sauce delicious.)
ADA	:	**Bibili ako ng petsay, karot, repolyo, abitsuelas at patatas. Hahaluan ko rin ng singkamas ang lumpia.** (I will buy Chinese cabbage, carrot, cabbage, beans and potatoes. I'll also mix turnips in the spring roll.)
GNG. JONES	:	**Sige, ikaw ang bahala. Pihadong magugustuhan ng ating mga panauhin ang lumpiang Pilipino.** (Okay, it's up to you. For sure, our visitors will like Filipino spring roll.)

Mula sa palengke, nagtungo si Ginang Jones at si Ada sa supermarket na malapit sa kanilang bahay sa Makati. Di kalakihan ang pamilihan pero maraming mga paninda, lokal man o galing sa ibang bansa. Pumunta si Ginang Jones at si Ada sa karnihan. Bumili sila ng lomo, giniling na karneng-baboy, lengua at manok. Nagtungo rin sila sa isdaan. (From the market, Mrs. Jones and Ada went to the supermarket near their house. The supermarket is not very big but it sells a lot of goods, both local and imported. Mrs. Jones and Ada went to the meat section where they bought sirloin, ground pork, ox tongue and chicken. They also went to the fish section.)

GNG. JONES : **Maganda at sariwa ang mga lapu-lapu dito. Pumili ka ng ilang piraso. Pumili ka na rin ng kaunting halaan at sugpo. Ayan, palagay ko nabili na natin ang lahat ng kailangan. Umuwi na tayo.** (The grouper here is good and fresh. Choose a few pieces. Also choose some clams and prawns. There, I guess we have all that we need. Let's go home.)

Sa Mall
At the Mall

Isa sa mga libangan ng mga Pilipino sa lungsod ay ang pagtungo sa mall tuwing Sabado at Linggo. Isang Sabado, ang mag-asawang Fidel at Dolor at ang kanilang mga anak na sina Boyet at Helen, ay nagpunta sa isang mall sa Quezon City. (One of the recreational activities of Filipinos in the city is going to the mall on weekends. One Saturday, the couple Fidel and Dolor and their children, Boyet and Helen, went to a mall in Quezon City.)

DOLOR　　: **Tumingin-tingin muna tayo sa mga tindahan bago manood ng sine.** (Let's take a look around at the stores first before we watch a movie.)

HELEN　　: **Pumunta tayo sa tindahan ng mga plaka. May bagong labas ngayon ang bandang Hale.** (Let's go to the record store. The band Hale has a new release.)

BOYET　　: **Sa tindahan ng mga kompyuter ang gusto ko. May mga bagong labas na mga laro.** (I like to go to computer stores. There are new games.)

DOLOR　　: **Pumunta rin tayo sa loob ng department store. Bagsak-presyo sila sa maraming bagay. Baka makabili ako ng sapatos.** (Let's go inside the department store. They have slashed prices on many items. I might be able to buy a pair of shoes.)

FIDEL　　: **Ay naku, lumalaki ang gastos!** (My! It's getting more expensive!)

HELEN　　: **Daddy, tignan mo. Napakaraming kainan dito. Parang masarap lahat.** (Look Daddy, there are many restaurants here. They all seem good.

FIDEL　　: **Oo nga, pero mahal lamang ng kaunti.** (Yes, it's true, but it's a bit more expensive.)

DOLOR　　: **Fidel, bakit hindi ka bumili ng bagong pantalon? Luma na ang damit pampasok mo sa opisina.** (Fidel, why don't you buy a new pair of pants? Your office clothes are already worn-out.)

FIDEL　　: **Tignan natin.** (Let's see.)

BOYET　　: **Daddy, Mommy, may palabas pala ang mga artista dito. Manood tayo.** (Daddy, Mommy, there's a show by artists here. Let's have a look.)

DOLOR　　: **Baka tayo gabihin.** (It might be late by then.)

BOYET　　: **Sandali lamang po. Wala namang pasok bukas.** (It won't take long. Anyway, there are no classes tomorrow.)

DOLOR　　: **Siya, siya, sige na nga.** (All right, all right, let's go.)

Notes

It is never sufficient to translate the word *mall* into **tindahan** (or *store*) in Tagalog. The malls in the Philippines are multistory shopping centers that offer everything from food to entertainment to books and clothes. Also, the word *mall* has been adapted into the language of Filipinos, probably since the early 1990s. The word is also quite synonymous to a department store although it may be also found inside a mall.

Sa Oras ng Pagkain

At Mealtime

A. ALMUSAL (Breakfast)

Magkasabay nag-agahan ang pamilyang Aquino nang umagang iyon. Gaya ng dati, naghanda ng sinangag na kain si Aling Betty para sa pamilya. Nagprito rin siya ng tuyo at nagbati ng itlog. (The Aquino family had breakfast together that morning. As usual, Aling Betty prepared fried rice for her family. She also fried dried fish and scrambled eggs.)

ALING BETY   : **Kumain kayo habang mainit pa ang sinangag.** (You better eat now while the fried rice is still hot.)
MANG JOSE   : **Magdasal muna tayo bago kumain.** (Let's pray first before eating.)
DAUGHTER   : **Nanay, paki-abot po ang binating itlog at kanin.** (Mother, please pass the scrambled eggs and rice.)
SON   : **Gusto ko rin po ng binating itlog.** (I also like scrambled eggs.)
MANG JOSE   : **Pakilagyan nga ng mainit na tubig ang tasa ko.** (Could you please pour hot water into my cup?)
ALING BETTY: **Mga bata, Inumin ninyo ang inyong tsokolate.** (Children, drink your chocolate.)
CHILDREN   : **Opo, inay.** (Yes, mother.)
ALING BETTY: **Kumain kayo nang mabuti para hindi magutom sa eskuwela.** (Eat well, so you won't get hungry in school.)

B. TANGHALIAN (Lunch)

LORENZO: **Ano ang pananghalian, Manang?** (What's for lunch, Manang?)
MAID   : **Nagluto ako ng paksiw na bangus at ginisang monggo.** (I cooked milkfish in vinegar and sauteed mung beans.)
LORENZO: **May kahalo bang bunga ng ampalaya?** (Does it have bittermelon fruit?)
MAID   : **Oo, isinama ko na pati dahon.** (Yes, I also included the leaves.)
LORENZO: **Naku, masarap ang kain ko ngayon.** (My, I shall have a good meal today.)
MAID   : **May minatamis din na saba.** (There is also sweetened saba.)

C. HAPUNAN (Supper)

Gabi na nang dumating si Mang Ignacio sa kanilang bahay. (It was already late in the evening when Mang Ignacio arrived home.)

MANG IGNACIO : **Masyado akong natrapik sa EDSA kaya ako ginabi.** (I was caught in a traffic along EDSA, that's why I'm late.)
ALING MAYA   : **Siya, kumain ka na. Baka gutom na gutom ka na. Iinit ko lang ang ulam. Kumain na ang mga bata. Nag-aaral sila sa kanilang kuwarto.** (Well, you better eat now. I will reheat your food. The children had already eaten. They are studying in their room.)
MANG IGNACIO : **Salamat. Masarap ang ulam. Gusto ko ng ginataang tilapia.** (Thank you. The viand is delicious. I like *tilapia* in coconut milk.)

Vocabulary List and Notes

almusal = breakfast, also **agahan**
siya = colloquial term for *all right* or *okay*, do not confuse with the pronoun **siya**
ulam = viand; dish of meat or vegetables that goes with rice in every meal
manang (for females) or **manong** (for males) = names used to address an older maid or any elderly person who serves in a household or sells commodities; **ate** (pronounced **a-te**) is frequently used to address a younger maid

Pagdalaw Sa Maysakit

Visiting an Ill Person

Dumalaw si Aling Lourdes sa kaibigang maysakit. May dala siyang isang dosenang dalandan. (Lourdes visited her sick friend. She brought a dozen oranges.)

LOURDES : **Tao po.**

PEDRO : **Aba! Si Aling Lourdes pala. Pasok kayo.** (Oh! It's Aling Lourdes. Please come in.)

LOURDES : **Kamusta ang asawa mo?** (How is your wife?)

PEDRO : **Mabuti-buti po ngayon. Pasok kayo. Narito siya.** (She's getting better now. Please come in. She is here.)

LOURDES : **Maria, kumusta ka na? Ano ba ang lagay mo ngayon?** (Maria, how are you? What is your condition now? How are you feeling now?)

MARIA : **Masakit ang aking dibdib at may lagnat ako sa hapon.** (My chest is painful and I have fever in the afternoon.)

LOURDES : **Maganda na ang kulay mo ngayon kaysa noong huli kitang dinalaw. May dala akong dalandan para sa iyo.** (Your color is better now than the last time I visited you. I brought some oranges for you.)

MARIA : **Naku, salamat, Lourdes. Nag-abala ka pa.** (Thank you, Lourdes. You shouldn't have bothered.)

LOURDES : **Mabuti'y patingin ka na sa doctor habang maaga nang gumaling ka.** (It's better for you to see a doctor this early so you can recover faster.)

MARIA : **Oo nga. Dadalhin ako ng aking anak sa PGH (or Philippine General Hospital) bukas. Wala raw bayad doon.** (Yes, that's true. My son will take me to PGH tomorrow. They say it's free there.)

LOURDES : **Siya, hindi na ako magtatagal para makapahinga ka na. At saka na ako paparito ulit.** (Well, I will not stay long so you can have some rest. I will visit you again.)

MARIA : **Maraming salamat sa pagdalaw mo.** (Thank you for visiting.)

LOURDES : **Adios.** (Goodbye.)

Notes

Tao po = a set expression used to announce the presence of a person outside of somebody's house, especially if there is no doorbell

aling or **mang** = names used to address unrelated older persons, **aling** (for females) or **mang** (for males) is placed before the names; even those of the same age, especially the older people themselves, call each other this way.

Sa Paaralan
At School

Tapos na ang bakasyon sa tag-araw ng mga estudiyante. Muling pumasok sa kanil-ang paaralan sina Antonio at Roberta. May nakilala silang bagong lipat mula sa ibang paaralan at nagpakilala sila. (The students' summer vacation had ended. Antonio and Roberta went back to school. They met a transferee from another school and they introduced themselves.)

ANTONIO : **Ang pangalan ko ay Antonio.** (My name is Antonio.)

ROBERTA : **Ang pangalan ko naman ay Robert.** (And my name is Roberta.)

RICKY : **Ako si Ricky. Galing ako sa Bulacan.** (I am Ricky. I came from Bulacan.)

ANTONIO : **Bakit ka lumipat dito sa Maynila?** (Why did you transfer to Manila?)

RICKY : **Mas malapit ang trabaho ng ama ko dito kaysa sa Bulacan kaya lumipat na rin ang buong pamilya namin dito.** (My father's work is nearer here than to Bulacan so the whole family decided to move here.)

ROBERTA : **Ano ba ang taon at seksiyon mo?** (What is your year and section?)

RICKY : **Pangalawang taon, seksiyon 2.** (Second year, section 2.)

ANTONIO : **Magkaseksiyon pala tayo sa pangalawang taon. Halika, sumama ka sa amin. Tumunog na ang kampana.** (It seems we belong to the same section in the second year. Come, join us. The bell has rung.)

RICKY : **Salamat.** (Thank you.)

ROBERTA : **Maraming nag-aaral dito. May pang-umaga at may panghapon na mga seksiyon. Mahusay rin ang mga guro rito.** (There are many students here. There are morning and afternoon sections. The teachers here are also good.)

RICKY : **Nasaan ang aklatan?** (Where is the library?)

ANTONIO : **Nasa ikatlong palapag. Ipapasyal ka namin mamaya sa buong eskuwela-han, sa aklatan, sa gym at palaruan sa likod ng gusali.** (On the third floor. We will tour you later around the school, to the library, gym and playground behind the building.)

ROBERTA : **May kantina rin banda roon. Doon tayo mananalhalian.** (There's a canteen over there. We will have lunch there.)

RICKY : **May dala akong baon.** (I brought my own lunch.)

ANTONIO : **Hindi bale. Dalhin mo, doon ka na kumain sa kantina.** (It doesn't matter. Bring your lunch with you and eat it in the canteen.)

RICKY : **Salamat. Maraming salamat. Sana maging magkakaibigan tayo.** (Thank you. Thank you very much. I hope we would be friends.)

ROBERTA : **Siyempre naman.** (Of course.)

Magbakasyon Tayo

Let's Go on a Vacation

Ang mag-anak na Santos ay pumunta sa isang bakasyunan sa Batangas. Malapit ang bakasyunan sa dagat at maraming mga punong niyog sa paligid. (The Santos family went to a resort in Batangas. The resort is near the sea and has many coconut trees all around.)

SON : **Lumangoy tayo sa dagat mamaya.** (Let's swim in the sea later.)

MOTHER : **Teka, hindi pa tayo nakakapag-ayos ng mga gamit natin. Pumunta muna tayo sa kubo na inilaan sa atin.** (Wait. We have not fixed our things yet. Let's go first to the nipa hut reserved for us.)

DAUGHTER : **Inay, tignan mo. May bangka sa aplaya. Puwede tayong mamangka.** (Mother, look. There's a boat on the beach. We can go boating.)

FATHER : **Makikipag-ayos tayo sa katiwala tungkol sa pamamangka. Kailangang mag-ingat tayo. Kung minsan lumalakas ang alon sa lugar na ito.** (We will make an arrangement with the caretaker regarding the use of the boat. We have to be careful. Sometimes the waves in this place can be very strong.)

MOTHER : **Ibaba na ninyo ang mga gamit mula sa kotse. Iyong mga kaldero, mga plato, kalan, ihawan, kubyertos at ang lalagyan ng yelo.** (Unload the things from the car. The pans, plates, stove, griller, the silverware and the ice container.)

FATHER : **Narito ang lahat. Ano ba ang iluluto natin ngayon?** (Everything is here. What are we going to cook now?)

MOTHER : **Ihawin mo na ang dalag na nabili natin sa daan. At ilaga mo na ang mga alimango. Nagluto na ako ng adobong manok at gulay sa bahay kaninang umaga.** (Grill the mudfish that we bought along the road. Boil the crabs, too. I already cooked chicken adobo and vegetables at home.)

FATHER : **Hoy, mga bata. Tulungan ninyo ako rito. Pagkapananghalian ay maglal-akad tayo sa aplaya. Makapamumulot kayo ng kabibe.** (Hey children. Give me a hand. After lunch, we'll walk along the beach. You can pick up shells.)

CHILDREN : **Tayo na, bilisan natin para makalangoy tayo kaagad.** (Come on, hurry so we can swim at once.)

Vocabulary Lists

ABBREVIATIONS

adj.	adjective	*conj.*	conjunction	*part.*	particle	*syn.*	synonym
adv.	adverb	*gr.*	greetings	*pr.*	pronoun	*v.*	verb
ant.	antonym	*interj.*	interjection	*pref.*	prefix	*vl.*	verbal
art.	article	*n.*	noun	*prep.*	preposition		

TAGALOG–ENGLISH

– A –

aba *interj.* exclamation of surprise, wonder, admiration

abala *adj.* busy, occupied

abo *n.* ashes

adiyos *interj.* Goodbye!

agad *adv.* at once, soon

ahas *n.* snake

aklatan *n.* library

alaala *n.* memory; gift

alaga *n.* someone under one's care

alahas *n.* jewelry

alam *vl.* to have knowledge of something

alat *n.* salty taste, **maalat** *adj.* salty

alikabok *n.* dust

alis *n.* depart

alisan *v.* to remove from

alisin *v.* to remove

aliwan *n.* entertainment, pastime

alon *n.* wave

ama *n.* father

amerikana *n.* a man's coat

amo *n.* master, boss, employer

amoy *n.* smell, odor

anak *n.* child; ~ **na lalaki** *n.* son; ~ **na babae** daughter

ani *n.* harvest

anino *n.* shadow

año *n.* year

anunsiyo *n.* advertisement, announcement

anyaya (*syn.* **paanyaya**) *n.* invitation

aplaya *n.* beach, seashore

aplikante *n.* applicant

aplikasyon *n.* application

apo *n.* grandchild

apoy *n.* flame

araro *n.* plow

araw *n.* sun; day

arte (*syn.* **sining**) *n.* art

artista *n.* performer; a person skilled in an art

asawa *n.* wife or husband

asim *n.* sour taste; **maasim,** *adj.* sour

asin *n.* salt

aso *n.* dog

aso *n.* smoke

aspile *n.* pin

asukal *n.* sugar

ate *n.* elder sister

awa *n.* pity; **kawawa,** *adj.* pitiful

away *n.* quarrel; a fight

ay! *interj.* exclamation of despair, sadness

ayaw *n.* dislike

ayos *n.* order, arrangement, appearance; *interj.* All right!

aywan idiomatic expression, to not know. **Aywan ko** I don't know.

– B –

baba *n.* chin

baba *n.* lowness; **mababa,** *adj.* low

babae *n.* woman, female

baboy *n.* pork; pig

baga *n.* live charcoal

baga *n.* lungs

bago *adv.* before

bagong pasok *n.* new entry, newcomer

bagsak-presyo *adj.* slashed or discounted price

baha *n.* flood

bahagi *n.* a part, portion

bahala na! common expression meaning "Come what may."

bahay *n.* house

bahay kubo *n.* nipa hut

baitang *n.* grade; steps (of stairs)

baka *part.* used to express doubt

bakal *n.* iron, steel

bakasyunan *n.* a resort

bakod *n.* fence; **bakuran** *n.* yard
bakya *n.* wooden shoes
balak *n.* plan, aim, purpose
balikbayan *n.* a person who returns to his/her homeland for a visit
balita *n.* news
balon *n.* water well
balot *n.* wrapping; **balutan** *n.* package
bandila *n.* flag, banner
bangka *n.* boat, banca
bangko *n.* bank
bangus *n.* milkfish
banig *n.* buri mat
bansa *n.* nation, country; **pambansa** *n.* national
bantay *n.* watchman, guard
baon *n.* food or money provision
bapor *n.* ship
barangay *n.* smallest political unit in Philippine government
barbero *n.* barber; **barberya** (*syn.* **pagupitan**) *n.* barbershop
barkada *n.* peer, a circle of friends
baro *n.* dress
basa *adj.* wet
basag *adj.* broken
basag-ulo *n.* (idiom) fight; **basagulero** *n.* troublemaker
baso *n.* drinking glass
bata *n.* child; ~**ng babae** girl; ~**ng lalaki** boy
batas *n.* law
bati *n.* greeting; *v.* to greet
bato *n.* stone; kidney
bawal *v/.* prohibited, not allowed
bawang *n.* garlic
bawa't *pron.* every, each
bayad *n.* payment
bayan *n.* town, country
bayani *n.* hero
bibig *n.* mouth
bigas *n.* rice
bigat *n.* weight, heaviness; **mabigat** *adj.* heavy
bigla *adj.* suddenly, at once
bilang *n.* number; *conj.* as
bili *v/.* amount paid for a thing
bilibid *n.* prison
bintana (*syn.* **durungawan**) *n.* window
binyag *n.* baptism
biro *n.* joke; **mapagbiro** *adj.* jester, full of jokes
bisig *n.* arms
bisita *n.* visitor/guest
biyahe *n.* trip, travel; **magbiyahe** *v.* to travel
bombilya *n.* electric bulb
boses (*syn.* **tinig**) *n.* voice
bote *n.* bottle
buhangin *n.* sand
buhay *n.* life
bukas *adv.* open; **buksan** *v.* to open

bukid *n.* field, farm
bukod sa *prep.* except, aside from, besides

– D –

daan (*syn.* **kalye, kalsada**) *n.* road, street; *adj.* hundred
dagat *n.* sea
dahon *n.* leaf
dakila *adj.* great; foremost
dalaw *n.* visit
dalawahan *n.* doubles
dalo *v.* to attend an event
daloy *n.* flow
damdamin *n.* emotion, feelings
damit *n.* cloth, dress
dangal (*syn.* **karangalan**) *n.* honor
dapat *pseudo v.* must, ought
dati *adj.* former; *adv.* formerly
daw *conj.* it is said
deposito *n.* money deposited in bank
dibdib *n.* breast, chest
dila *n.* tongue
dilaw *adj.* yellow
diligin *v.* to water, sprinkle water on
dilim (*syn.* **karimlan**) *n.* darkness
din *adv.* also, too
disgrasya (*syn.* **aksidente**) *n.* accident
dito *adv.* here (near the speaker)
diyan *adv.* there (near the person spoken to)
diyaryo (*syn.* **pahayagan**) *n.* newspaper
Diyos (*syn.* **Bathala, Maykapal**) *n.* God, supreme being
doktor (*syn.* **manggagamot**) *n.* doctor of medicine
doon *adv.* there (far from the person talking)
dugo *n.* blood
dulo *n.* end
dumating *v.* to arrive; **pagdating** *n.* **arrival**
dumi *n.* dirt, refuse
dunong (*syn.* **karunungan**) *n.* knowledge, ability
duwag *adj.* coward
duyan *n.* hammock, cradle

– E –

eksamen *n.* examination; *v.* to examine
electrika *n.* electric, electrical
elegante *adj.* elegant, classy
eskuwela *n.* school
espesyal *adj.* good; special, extraordinary
estasyon *n.* station, waiting shed
estudyante *n.* student

– G –

gabi *n.* night, evening
galing sa *vl*, come from
galit *n.* anger; galit *adj.* angry
gamit *n.* use, usefulness; gamitin *v.* to use
gamot *n.* medicine; gamutin *v.* to cure
ganda *n.* beauty
ganito *adv.* like this
ganyan *adv.* like that
gastos *n.* expenses
gatas *n.* milk
ginabi *v.* overtaken by nightfall
ginisa *n.* sauteed meat or vegetables
ginoo *n.* gentleman, mister
ginto *n.* gold
gising *adj.* awake; gisingin *v.* to wake up someone
gitna *n.* middle, center
goma *n.* rubber; rubber tire of cars
grado *n.* grade; class
gripo *n.* faucet
gugo *n.* refers to the bark from local gugo trees used as organic shampoo
guhit *n.* line
gulay *n.* vegetable
gulayan *n.* vegetable section in market; vegetable farm
gunting *n.* scissors
gupit *n.* haircut
gupitin *v.* to cut with a pair of scissors
guro *n.* teacher
gusali *n.* building
gusto *pseudo v.* like, desire
gutom *adj.* hungry; *n.* hunger

– H –

haba *adj.* elongated
haba *n.* length
habang *conj./adv.* while, so long as
hagdan *n.* ladder
halaga *n.* cost, importance
halalan *n.* election
halamang gamot *n.* herbal plant
halik *n.* kiss
halimbawa *n.* example
handaan *n.* celebration, party
hangal *adj.* ignorant, stupid
hanggang *conj.* until
hangin *n.* wind, air
hapon *n.* afternoon
hapunan *n.* supper
harap *n.* front; sa harap *prep.* in front
hardin (*syn.* halamanan) *n.* garden, lawn

hatinggabi *n.* midnight
hatol *n.* judgment, decision
hawak *n.* hold
hawakan *v.* to hold
hayop *n.* animal
heto *adv.* here, here it is
hilaga *n.* north
hilaw *n.* unripe (fruit), uncooked (food)
hindi *adv.* no, not
hininga *n.* breath
hinlalaki *n.* thumb
hinog *adj.* ripe
hintay *v.* to wait for
hintayan *n.* a waiting place
hipon *n.* shrimp
hiram *adj.* borrowed; hiramin *v.* to borrow
hiya *n.* shame; mahiya *v.* to be ashamed
hukbo *n.* army; ~ng-dagat *n.* navy
huli *adj.* late
humiga *v.* to lie down
huminga *v.* to breathe
humingi *v.* to ask for, to request
husto *adj.* exact, fit, enough
huwag *adv.* do not

– I –

iba *adj.* other, another, different
ibaba *n.* lower part; *v.* to lower the position; *prep.* under, below, down
ibabaw (*syn.* tuktok) *n.* above, on
ibig *v.* love; like; umibig *v.* to love
ibigay *v.* to give
ibon *n.* bird
ihawan *n.* griller, roaster
ilagay *v.* to put, to place
ilalim *adv.* beneath; sa ilalim *prep.* under
ilan *pron.* some; *adv.* how many
ilaw *n.* light, light fixtures
ilista *v.* to list down
ilog *n.* river
ilong *n.* nose
imbestigasyon (*syn.* pagsisiyasat) *n.* investigation
ina *n.* mother
ingay *n.* noise; maingay *adj.* noisy
inggit *n.* envy; mainggitin *adj.* envious
init *n.* heat, warmth, mainit *adj.* hot, warm
inumin *n.* a drink; inumin *v.* to drink
isahan *adj.* single, singular
isama *v.* to take along; include
isara *v.* to close something
isauli *v.* to return something
isda *n.* fish
isdaan *n.* place where fish is sold

isip *n.* mind, thought; **mag-isip** *v.* to think
isuot *v.* to wear, to put on
itaas *adv.* above; *v.* to put up
itapon *v.* to throw away
itim *adj.* black
itlog *n.* egg
ituro *v.* to teach something, to show or point
iwan *v.* to leave behind
iyak *n.* cry; **iyakin** *adj.* cry-baby

– **K** –

kaagad *adv.* immediately
kaarawan *n.* birthday
kababayan *n.* fellow citizen
kabayo *n.* horse
kabibi *n.* empty clam shell
kabihasnan *n.* civilization
kabisado *v.* memorized
kabuhayan *n.* livelihood
kabutihan *n.* goodness; virtue
kagabi *adv.* last night
kagalang-galang *adj.* honorable; respectable
kagalit *n.* enemy
kagatin *v.* to bite
kaginhawahan *n.* relief from pain, consolation; luxury
kahapon *n.* yesterday
kahon *n.* box
kahoy *n.* wood, lumber
kaibigan *n.* friend
kailangan *pseudo v.* to need something; *adv.* necessary
kainan *n.* eatery
kakanin *n.* rice delicacies
kakilala *n.* acquaintance
kalabaw *n.* carabao
kalahati *n., adj.* one half
kalakal *n.* merchandise, goods
kalakip *adj.* included, enclosed
kalan *n.* clay stove
kalawang *n.* rust
kalayaan *n.* independence, liberty; **malaya** *adj.* free
kaldero *n.* cauldron, pot
kalesa *n.* two-wheeled vehicle pulled by a horse
kaligayahan *n.* happiness, contentment
kalihim *n.* secretary
kaliwa *n.* left (direction)
kalusugan *n.* health, well-being
kamag-anak *n.* relative
kamatayan *n.* death
kamatis *n.* tomato
kamay *n.* hand

kambal *n.* twin
kamisadentro *n.* man's shirt
kamiseta *n.* undershirt
kampana *n.* church bell
kanan *n.* right (direction)
kandila *n.* candle
kanin *n.* cooked rice
kanina *adv.* a moment ago
kanluran *n.* west; **kanluranin** *adj.* western
kanta (*syn.* **awit**) *n.* song; **mang aawit** *n.* singer
kantina *n.* canteen
kapalaran *n.* fate
kapatid *n.* sibling, brother or sister
kape *n.* coffee
kapitbahay *n.* neighbor
karapatan *n.* right
karatula *n.* signboard
karayom *n.* needle
karne *n.* meat
karnihan *n.* place where meat is sold
kasama *n.* companion
kasapi *n.* member of an organization
kaserola *n.* caserole, cooking utensils
katas *n.* juice of fruits; **makatas** *adj.* juicy
katawan *n.* body
katulong *n.* helper, servant
kaunti *adj., adv.* few, little
kawad *n.* wire; –-**elektrika** *n.* electric wire
kawani *n.* employee
kawawa *adj.* pitiful
kawayan *n.* bamboo
kay to (name of person), **sa kay** for (name of person)
kaya *conj.* so, *v.* can, be able to
kaysa *conj.* than
kayumanggi *n.* color of race of Filipinos; *adj.* brown complexion
keso *n.* cheese
kinatawan *n.* representative
klase *n.* class in school; kinds
klub *n.* club
konsulta (*syn.* **magpatingin**) *n.* consult; **konsultasyon** *n.* consultation
kuko *n.* fingernail
kulambo *n.* mosquito net
kulay *n.* color
kulog *n.* thunder
kumain *v.* to eat
kumot *n.* blanket
kumpuni *v.* to repair
kumuha *v.* to get
kumusta *gr.* How are you?
kundiman *n.* native love song
kung *conj.* if, when, as to
kuru-kuro *n.* opinion
kurtina *n.* curtain

kusina *n.* kitchen
kusinera/o (*syn.* **tagapagluto**) *n.* cook
kutsara *n.* spoon
kutsero *n.* calesa driver
kutsilyo *n.* knife
kuwadro *n.* picture frame
kuwarto *n.* room
kuwenta *n.* bill, account
kuwento *n.* story, fiction
kuwero *n.* leather
kuwintas *n.* necklace

– L –

laban *n.* fight, contest
labanan *v.* to fight someone or something
labas *n.* outside; **sa labas** *adv.* outside; **palabas**
   n. presentation, show
labi *n.* lower lip
labing- *pref.* means more than 10 when placed
   before a cardinal number from one to
   nine, **labing-isa** 11; **labingwalo** 18
labis *n.* surplus; *adv.* more than enough
lagay (*syn.* **kalagayan**) *n.* condition, state
lagda (*syn.* **pirma**) *n.* signature
lagi *adv.* always
lagnat *n.* fever
lagyan *v.* to put
lahat *pron.* all, everybody
lahi *n.* race of people, nationality
lakad *n.* walk; **lumakad** *v.* to walk
lakas *n.* strength, force
laki *n.* size; **lumalaki** *present v.* growing,
   increasing in size
lalagyan *n.* container
lalaki *n.* man, male
lalamunan *n.* throat
lamang *adv.* only
lambat *n.* fishing net
lamig *n.* coldness; **malamig** *adj.* cold
lamok *n.* mosquito
langaw *n.* housefly
langgam *n.* ants
langis *n.* oil
langoy *n.* swim; **lumangoy** *v.* to swim
lansangan *n.* street
lapis *n.* pencil
laro *n.* play, game
laruan *n.* toy
lasa *n.* taste
lasing *n.* drunkard
lasingan *n.* a noisy drinking party
lason *n.* poison
lata *n.* tin can
laway *n.* saliva

laya *n.* freedom; **malaya** *adj.* free, independent
layo *n.* distance; **malayo** *adj.* far; distant
layon (*syn.* **layunin, pakay**) *n.* aim, purpose
libangan *n.* recreation, entertainment
libro (*syn.* **aklat**) book
ligaya *n.* happiness; *adj.* **maligaya**
ligo *n.* bath; **maligo** to take a bath
liham *n.* letter
lihim *n.* secret
likas *adj.* native of; *adj.* natural
likha *n.* creation; product
likod *n.* at the back, rear
lindol *n.* earthquake
linggo *n.* week; *n.* Sunday
linis *n.* cleanliness; **malinis** *adj.* clean; **linisin**
   v. to clean
lipon *n.* group
lipunan *n.* society
listahan (*syn.* **talaan**) *n.* list
litrato (*syn.* **larawan**) *n.* picture
litson *n.* roasted pig; **litsunin** *v.* to roast
longganisa *n.* native sausage
loob *n.* interior; **sa loob** *adv.* inside
luma *adj.* not new
lumapit *v.* to come near, to approach
lumipad *v.* to fly
lumipat *v.* to move to another place
lumubog *v.* to sink
lungsod *n.* city
luntian *adj.* green
lupa *n.* earth, ground, land
luto *n.* cuisine; *adj.* cooked food

– M –

maaari *v.* possible
maaga *adv.* early
mabaho *adj.* bad-smelling
mabait (*syn.* **mabuti**) *adj.* good (used with
   persons and animals)
mabangga *v.* to bump against, to collide with
mabango *adj.* fragrant
mabigat *adj.* heavy
mabuhay *interj.* Long live! *v.* to live
mabuti *adj.* good (character of an individual);
   well (mental and physical condition of an
   individual)
madalang *adv.* rare, infrequent
madalas *adv.* often, frequent
madali *adj.* easy; *adv.* fast
madilim *adj.* dark
magalang *adj.* courteous
magaling *adj.* good, excellent; free from
   sickness
mag-anak *n.* family

maganda *adj.* beautiful
mag-aral *v.* to study
mag-asawa *n.* husband and wife; *v.* to marry
magasin *n.* magazine
magdasal *v.* to pray
maghain *v.* to set the table
maghapon *adv.* all day long
maghugas *v.* to wash
magkano *adv.* how much?
magkapatid *adj.* a set of brothers or sisters
maglaba *v.* to wash clothes
maglaro *v.* to play; **manlalaro** *n.* player
magpaalam *v.* to bid goodbye
magpahinga *v.* to rest
magpalipas *v.* to while the hours away
magpareserba *v.* to have something reserved for someone
magpasyal *v.* to take a walk
magsasaka *n.* farmer
magsimba *v.* to hear mass, to go to church
magtanim *v.* to plant
magulat *v.* to be surprised
magutom *v.* to be hungry
mahaba *adj.* long
mahal *adj.* dear, precious, expensive
mahusay *adj.* efficient, exceptional
maingay *adj.* noisy
mainit *adj.* hot, warm
maitim *adj.* black
makabago *adj.* modern, up-to-date
makabayan *adj.* patriotic, nationalistic
makapal *adj.* thick
makina *n.* machine; sewing machine
makita *v.* to see
makiusap *v.* to plead, to make a request
makulit *adj.* annoying; wearisome
malamig (*ant.* **mainit**) *adj.* cold, cool
malapit (*ant.* **malayo**) *adj.* near
malayo *adj.* far
malinis (*ant.* **madumi**) *adj.* clean
maliwanag (*ant.* **madilim**) *adj.* clear, bright
malungkot (*ant.* **masaya**) *adj.* sad
malusog *adj.* healthy
mama *n.* a grown man, also a term used to address a man unknown to the speaker
mamamayan *n.* citizen
mamaya *adv.* by and by, later on (within the day)
mamulot *v.* to pick something
manalangin *v.* to pray
manang *n.* elder sister
manigo *adj.* prosperous
maniwala *v.* to believe
manok *n.* chicken
manong *n.* older person not related to speaker
mantika *n.* cooking oil

mantikilya *n.* butter
maputi *adj.* white
marami *adj.* much, many
marka *n.* grade; trade mark
marumi (*ant.* **malinis**) *adj.* dirty
marunong (*syn.* **matalino**) *adj.* intelligent, wise
masahe *n.* massage
masama *adj.* bad, wicked
masarap *adj.* delicious, tasty; pleasant
masaya *adj.* happy, cheerful
masipag *adj.* industrious
masunurin *adj.* obedient
masyado *adj.* excessive
mata *n.* eye
mataba (*syn.* **payat**) *adj.* fat
matamis *adj.* sweet
matamisin *v.* to make into dessert
matanda *n.* old person; *adj.* aged, elderly, old
matangkad (*syn.* **pandak**) *adj.* tall
matigas (*syn.* **malambot**) *adj.* hard
mayaman (*syn.* **mahirap**) *adj.* rich, wealthy
may-ari *n.* owner
maysakit *n.* patient, sick person
medyas *n.* socks, stockings
mesa *n.* table
minuto (*syn.* **sandali**) *n.* minute
misa *n.* religious mass
misang pasasalamant *n.* Thanksgiving Mass
miting *n.* pulong
mukha *n.* face
mula sa *prep.* from
mura *adj.* cheap

– N –

nakatira *v.* living in, a resident of
naku *interj.* an expression of surprise, shortened form of **Ina ko!**
naman *adv.* also, in like manner
namatay *v.* died
nang *conj.* when (for past actions); *adv.* any more, more
naparito *v.* came
naparoon *v.* went
narito *v.* here
naroon *v.* there
nasa *prep.* expresses position, location or direction
nasaan *adv.* where
negosyo *n.* business, industry
nerbiyos *n.* nervousness
nga *part.* please, really, truly
ngayon *adv.* now, today
ngipin *n.* teeth

ngiti *n.* smile
ngunit *conj.* but
nguso *n.* upper lip
ninang *n.* godmother
ningas *n.* flame
ninong *n.* godfather
ninuno *n.* ancestor
niyog *n.* coconut
noo *n.* forehead
noon *adv.* at that time
noong *conj.* when (for continuing actions)
nota *n.* musical note
nuno *n.* grandparent

– O –

o *conj.* or
oho (or opo) *interj.* yes sir/madam
oo *adj.* yes
oras *n.* hour, time
orasyon *n.* angelus
orihinal (*syn.* likas) *n.* original
ospital (*syn.* pagamutan) *n.* hospital
oyayi *n.* lullaby

– P –

paa *n.* foot
paalam *n.* farewell; *v.* goodbye
paano *adv.* how
paaralan (*syn.* eskuwela) *n.* school
pabuya *n.* tip, gratuity
pader *n.* wall
pag-asa *n.* hope
pagdadalmhati *n.* grief, extreme sorrow
pag-ibig *n.* love
pagkain *n.* food
pagkamatay *n.* death
pagkilos *v.* to act
pagod *adj.* tired, weary
pagod *n.* tiredness
pakinabang *n.* profit, gain
pako *n.* nail
pakpak *n.* wing
paksa *n.* subject, theme
palabas *n.* show
palad *n.* palm of hand; fate
palagay *n.* guess, personal opinion
palapag *n.* floor or story of a building
palaruan *n.* playground
palay *n.* rice plant
palayaw *n.* nickname
palayok *n.* clay pot
palengke *n.* market

paligid *n.* surroundings
palikuran *n.* toilet
pamahalaan *n.* government
pamantasan *n.* university
pamilya *n.* family
pampalamig *n.* refreshment
panahon *n.* time, season
pangalan *n.* name
pangalawang pangulo *n.* vice-president
panginoon *n.* master; Panginoon Lord
pangit *adj.* ugly
pangulo *n.* president
pantalon *n.* pants, trousers
papel *n.* paper
paraan, *n.* way
pareho *adj.* the same, similar
parusa *n.* punishment
pasaway *adj.* unconventional, stubborn
pasinaya *n.* inauguration
pasko *n.* Christmas
paso *n.* burn (injury from fire or heat)
paso *n.* flowerpot
paso (*syn.* lipas or pasado) *n.* lapsed
pasok *v.* to enter
patay *n.* dead; *adj.* lifeless; extinguished as in light
patingin *v.* to take a look
patnugot *n.* director, editor
patong (*syn.* suson) *n.* layer
pawis perspiration, anak-~ *n.* laborer
payak *adj.* simple
payat *adj.* thin
payong *n.* umbrella
pera *n.* money
pero (*syn.* nguni't) *conj.* but
pihado *adj./adv.* surely, certainly, certain, sure
pilak *n.* silver
pinggan *n.* plate
pinsan *n.* cousin
pinta *v.* to paint
pinto *n.* door
pintura *n.* paint
pipa *n.* pipe
piraso *n.* piece
pirma *n.* signature
pirmi *adv.* always; fixed
pisngi *n.* cheek
piso *n.* peso
pista *n.* feast; ~ngbayan town fiesta
plantsa *n.* flat iron
pluma *n.* fountain pen
posporo *n.* match
premyo (*syn.* gantimpala) *n.* prize, reward
probinsiya (*syn.* lalawigan) *n.* province
programa (*syn.* palatuntunan) *n.* program
proseso *n.* process

proyekto *n.* project
publiko *n.* public
pugon *n.* stove, oven
pula *adj.* red
pulbos *n.* powder
pulong *n.* meeting
pulubi *n.* beggar
puno *adj.* full
puno *n.* tree; leader, chief; source
punong-lungsod *n.* capital city
pusa *n.* cat
puso *n.* heart
putahe *n.* a dish or viand
putok *n.* blast
puwesto *n.* location; a stall or stand in a
  market

– R –

radyo *n.* radio
raw (or **daw**) *part.* it is said
regalo *n.* gift
rekado *n.* condiments for cooking
reklamo *n.* complaint
relihiyon *n.* religion
relo *n.* clock, watch
resibo *n.* receipt
residente *n.* resident
riles *n.* railroad, specifically for trains
rosas *n.* a kind of plant or its flower; pink color

– S –

saan *adv.* where
sabaw *n.* broth
sabay *adj.* at the same time
sabi *n.* what was said; *v.* to tell, to say
sabon *n.* soap
sagana *adj.* abundant, plenty
sagot *n.* answer
sahod *n.* salary, wage
sakay *n.* passenger; **sumakay** *v.* to ride in
sakim *adj.* selfish
sakit *n.* sickness; pain
saksi *n.* witness
sala *n.* sin; living room
salamat *n.* thanks
salamin *n.* mirror; eyeglasses
salapi *n.* money; a fifty centavo coin (not in
  circulation)
salawal *n.* trousers
saligang-batas *n.* constitution
salita *n.* word, language
salop (*syn.* **ganta**) *n.* a unit of measurement

particularly for rice approximately equivalent to two kilos
salu-salo *n.* party, banquet
samahan *n.* club, society
samahan *v.* to accompany
sama-sama *adv.* altogether
samba *n.* worship, **sumamba** *v.* to worship
sampaguita *n.* a shrub bearing fragrant
  white flowers, the national flower of the
  Philippines
sampu *adj. n.* ten
sandaan *adj. n.* one hundred
sandali *adv.* a moment
sanga *n.* branch
sapatos *n.* shoes
sarado *adj.* closed
sari-sari *adj.* of various kinds
sariwa *adj.* fresh
sarsa *n.* sauce
sasakyan *n.* vehicle
sayang *interj.* What a pity!
sayaw *n.* dance
seda *n.* silk
seksyon *n.* section (in class)
selyo *n.* stamp; dry seal
sepilyo *n.* toothbrush
serbidor *n.* server; waiter
serbisyo *n.* service
sero *n.* zero
sigarilyo *n.* cigarette
silangan *n.* east; the Orient
silid *n.* room; ~-**tulugan** bedroom; ~-**kainan**
  dining room
silya (*syn.* **upuan**) *n.* chair
simbahan *n.* church
simula *n.* beginning
sinangag *n.* fried rice
sinelas (*or* **tsinelas**) *n.* slippers
singil *n.* amount charged for services or sold
  goods
singsing *n.* ring
sinulid *n.* thread
sipon *n.* cold, runny nose
sira *n.* destruction, destroyed, torn, broken
siyudad (*syn.* **lungsod**) *n.* city
sobre *n.* envelope
sopas *n.* soup
subdibisyon *n.* subdivision
suka *n.* vinegar
sukat *n.* measurement
suki *n.* steady client
suklay *n.* comb
sulat *n.* letter; penmanship
sumama *v.* to go with
sumunod *v.* to follow
sundalo (*syn.* **kawal**) *n.* soldier

sunog *n.* fire
susi *n.* key
suskrisyon *n.* subscription

– T –

taas *n.* height; **mataas** *adj.* high
taba *n.* fat, **mataba**, *adj.* fat
tabak (*syn.* **bolo**) *n.* a native sword, shorter than a cutlass, that has everyday uses
tabako *n.* cigar; tobacco
tabing-dagat *n.* seashore
tabla *n.* wooden board, cut timber; **bahay na tabla** *n.* wooden house
tagapagsilbi *n.* server
tag-araw *n.* summer, dry season
taggutom *n.* famine
tag-ulan *n.* rainy season
tagumpay *n.* victory
tahanan *n.* home
tahi *v.* to sew; **pananahi** *n.* sewing; **mananahi** *n.* seamstress
tainga *n.* ears
takip *n.* cover
takot *n.* fear. **takot** *adj.* afraid; **matakot** *v.* to be afraid
taksi *n.* taxi
taksil *n.* traitor
talaan *n.* list, record
talambuhay *n.* biography
tali (*syn.* **panali**) *n.* string, anything used to tie
tamad (*ant.* **masipag**) *adj.* lazy
tanawin *n.* view, scenery
tanga *adj.* stupid, irresponsible
tanghali *adv.* late at noon; *n.* noon
tanim *n.* plant
tanong *n.* question
tanyag *adj.* well-known; popular
tao *n.* person, human being
taon *n.* year
tapat *adj.* faithful, honest
tasa *n.* cup
tauhan *n.* personnel
tawa *n.* laughter
tawad *n.* bargain, reduction in price; pardon, forgiveness
tawagan *v.* to call
tela *n.* cloth
tiisin *n.* sufferings; **tiisin** *v.* to endure
tiket *n.* ticket
tila *adv.* it seems
timbangan *n.* scale, balance
timog *n.* south
tinda *n.* goods; **tindahan** *n.* store
tingnan *v.* to look

tinidor *n.* table fork
tinta *n.* ink
tiya (*syn.* **tita**) *n.* aunt
tiyo (*syn.* **tito**) *n.* uncle
totoo *adj.* true
trabaho *n.* job, work, livelihood
transportasyon *n.* transportation
tren *n.* train
tubig *n.* water
tubo *n.* pipe
tuhod *n.* knee
tula *n.* poem
tulay *n.* bridge
tulong *n.* help
tuloy *interj.* come in; *v.* to go ahead
tungkol sa *prep.* about; referring to
tunog *n.* sound
tuntunin *n.* rule
tuwa *n.* gladness; **matuwa** *v.* to be glad
tuwalya *n.* towel
tuwid *adj.* straight
tuya *n.* sarcasm, irony
tuyo *adj.* dry; *n.* dried fish

– U –

ubo *n.* cough; **inuubo** *v.* coughing
ubod *n.* core; **~ ng sipag** *adj.* very industrious
ugali *n.* custom; habit
ugat *n.* human vein; root of a plant; **salitang-~** *n.* root word
uhaw *n.* thirst; **mauhaw** *v.* to be thirsty
ulam *n.* viand
ulan *n.* rain; **maulan** *adj.* rainy
ulap *n.* cloud
ulat *n.* report
uli *adv.* once again
uling *n.* charcoal
ulit *adv.* again; *n.* repetition, number of times; **sampung ~** ten times
ulo *n.* head
umaga *n.* morning
umako *v.* to assume responsibility
umalis *v.* to go away
umawit *v.* to sing
uminom *v.* to drink
umisip *v.* to think
umpisa (*syn.* **simula**) *n.* beginning, start
umupo *v.* to sit
umuwi *v.* to go home
una *adj.* first
unan *n.* pillow
uod *n.* worm
upa *n.* pay; rent
upang *conj.* so, so that

upuan *n.* chair
uri *n.* kind; quality
usapan *n.* conversation
utak *n.* brain; **mautak** *adj.* intelligent
utang *n.* debt
utos *n.* command, order
uwi (*syn.* **pasalubong**) *n.* anything brought
home by someone from a trip

– W –

wakas *n.* end; **at sa wakas** finally
wala *adj.* absent; *adv.* none
walang-hiya *adj.* shameless
walang-pagod *adj.* tireless

walis *n.* broom
wasto (*syn.* **tama**) *adj.* correct; appropriate
watawat *n.* flag, banner
welga *n.* labor strike
wika *n.* language

– Y –

yabag *n.* footstep
yakap *n.* embrace; **yakapin** *v.* to embrace
yaman *n.* wealth; **mayaman** *adj.* rich, wealthy
yari (*syn.* **gawa**) *adj.* style; finished product,
structure; ready made; *adj.* finished
yelo *n.* ice

ENGLISH–TAGALOG

– A –

a (or **an**) *indefinite art.* ang isa, isang, sa isa
about *prep.* tungkol sa
above *adv.* sa itaas; sa ibabaw
abstract *n.* buod
abundance *n.* kasaganaan
abundant *adj.* sagana
accept *v.* tanggapin
accompany *v.* samahan, saliwan (sa pagtugtog)
account *n.* kuwenta
aching *v.* sumasakit
act *n.* gawa
adaptability *n.* pagbabagay, pag-aayon
addition *n.* dagdag; **to add** *v.* dagdagan
adjustment *n.* pag-aayos
advertisement *n.* anunsiyo
advocate *n.* tagapagtanggol
after *adv.* pagkatapos
afternoon *n.* hapon
again *adv.* muli
against *prep.* laban sa
agreement *n.* kasunduan
air *n.* himpapawid; hangin
alive *adj.* buhay
all *pron.* lahat
almost *adv.* halos
alphabet *n.* alpabeto
already *adv.* na
also *adv.* din, rin
altar *n.* dambana
although *conj.* kahit
always *adv.* lagi, palagi
amount *n.* halaga; kabuuan

amusement *n.* libangan; aliwan
analysis *n.* pagsusuri
ancestor *n.* ninuno
and *conj.* at, at saka
angelus *n.* orasyon
anger *n.* galit; **angry** *adj.* galit
anniversary *n.* anibersaryo
answer *n.* sagot, tugon
ant *n.* langgam
appropriate *adj.* bagay, naaayon, angkop
arch *n.* arko
archipelago *n.* kapuluan
area *n.* lawak
argument *n.* pagtatalo
arm *n.* braso, bisig
army *n.* hukbo
art *n.* sining
as *adv.* katulad, kaparis, kagaya
ash *n.* abo
ask *v.* itanong
asleep *adj.* tulog
assimilate *v.* isama
assist *n.* tumulong
assistant *n.* katulong
at *prep.* sa
ate *v.* kumain
attack *n.* sumpong (in relation to sickness);
paglusob (in relation to war)
attend *v.* dumalo
aunt *n.* sister of either parent, addressed as
Tita
authority *n.* kapangyarihan
avoid *v.* iwasan
award *n.* gantimpala, pabuya

– B –

baby *n.* sanggol; also a term of endearment
bachelor *n.* binata
back *n.* likod; **at the back** *prep.* sa likuran
bad *adj.* masama
balance *n.* timbangan (or **weighing scales**); panimbang (or **steadiness**)
ball *n.* bola; sayawan
ballot *n.* balota
bamboo *n.* kawayan
banana *n.* saging
band *n.* banda ng musiko
baptism *n.* binyag
barber *n.* barbero
bargain *n.* baratilyo, pagkasunduan; *v.* tumawad sa halaga
basin *n.* palanggana
basis *n.* batayan
basket *n.* buslo
bath *n.* paligo
bathe *v.* maligo
bathroom *n.* paliguan; banyo
beautiful *adj.* maganda
beauty *n.* kagandahan
become *v.* maging
bed *n.* kama
bedroom *n.* silid-tulugan
before *adv.* bago, dati, noong una
beggar *n.* pulubi
behavior *n.* ugali, gawi
belief *n.* paniwala
bell *n.* kampana, kampanilya
below *adv.* sa ibaba
belt *n.* sinturon
beset *v.* paligiran, lusubin
between *prep.* sa gitna, sa pagitan
big *adj.* malaki
bird *n.* ibon
birthday *n.* kaarawan
bite *v.* kagatin
bitter *adj.* mapait
black *adj.* itim, maitim
blanket *n.* kumot
blessed *adj.* pinagpala, masuwerte
blood *n.* dugo
blow *v.* hipan
blue *adj.* asul, bughaw
boat *n.* bangka
body *n.* katawan
boiling *v.* kumukulo
bolo *n.* itak, tabak
bone *n.* buto
book *n.* aklat, libro
boost *v.* itaas, tulak
borrow *v.* humiram

boss *n.* pinuno, hepe, tagapamahala
bottle *n.* bote
bottom *n.* ilalim
box *n.* kahon
boy *n.* batang lalaki; **house ~** *n.* utusang lalaki
brain *n.* utak
branch *n.* sanga ng tanim; sangay isang opisina
bread *n.* tinapay
breath *n.* hininga
breathe *v.* huminga
bridge *n.* tulay
brief *n.* maikli; magtagubilin
bright *adj.* maliwanag (in relation to light); marunong
bring *v.* dalhin
broadcast *n.* pagbabalita; *v.* ibalita
broadsheet *n.* malaking pahayagan
broken *v.* sira, basag
broth *n.* sabaw
brother *n.* kapatid na lalaki; **~-in-law** *n.* bayaw
brown *adj.* kayumanggi (in relation to color of race); kulay tsokolate, kulay kape
brush *n.* (**tooth~**) sepilyo; (**hair~**) brush sa buhok
building *n.* gusali
bulb *n.* bombilya
bullet *n.* bala
burn *v.* masunog. *n.* paso
burst *n.* putok
business *n.* negosyo
but *conj.* pero, nguni't
butter *n.* mantekilya
butterfly *n.* paruparo
button *n.* butones
buy *v.* bumili
by means of *prep.* sa pamamagitan ng

– C –

cake *n.* keyk
call *n.* tawag; *v.* tawagin
care *n.* alaga; *v.* alagaan
careful *adj.* maingat
carpenter *n.* karpintero, anluwagi
carry *v.* dalhin
cat *n.* pusa
Catholic *n.* katoliko
cause *n.* dahilan
ceiling *n.* kisame
celebrate *v.* magdiwang
celebration *n.* pagdiriwang, pista
center *n.* gitna
century *n.* isandaang taon
certificate *n.* katibayan

chair *n.* silya, upuan
challenge *n.* hamon
chance *n.* pagkakataon
change *n.* sukli; pampalit
change *v.* suklian; palitan
character *n.* pagkatao, katangian
cheap *adj.* mura
cheerful *adj.* masaya, masigla
cheese *n.* keso
chest *n.* dibdib
chicken *n.* manok
chief *n.* puno
child *n.* bata, anak
chin *n.* baba
Christmas *n.* Pasko
chronicler *n.* taga-ulat, tagapagsalaysay
church *n.* simbahan
citizen *n.* mamamayan
city *n.* lungsod
civilization *n.* kabihasnan
class *n.* klase, uri
classroom *n.* silid-aralan
clean *adj.* malinis
clear *adj.* malinaw, maliwanag
climb *v.* umakyat
clock *n.* relo, orasan
close *v.* isara
cloth *n.* damit; tela
cloud *n.* ulap
coal *n.* uling; karbon
coat *n.* amerikana
coconut *n.* niyog; coconut milk *n.* gata
cold *adj.* malamig
collar *n.* kuwelyo
color *n.* kulay
comb *n.* suklay
come *v.* pumarito
comfort *n.* aliw; *v.* aliwin
committee *n.* lupon
communication *n.* pakikipag-usap
companion *n.* kasama
condition *n.* kalagayan, ayos
confidence *n.* tiwala
constitution *n.* saligang-batas
contemporary *n.* kapanahon; *adj.* magkap-anabay
cook *n.* tagapagluto, kusinero/a
cook *v.* magluto
copy *n.* sipi, kopya; *v.* kopyahin
cork *n.* tapon
cotton bulak
cough *n.* ubo
courage *n.* tapang
courgeous *adj.* matapang
courteous *adj.* magalang
courtesy *n.* paggalang

cousin *n.* pinsan
cover *n.* takip; *v.* takpan
cow *n.* baka
coward *adj.* duwag
creative *adj.* malikhain
credit *n.* utang
cross *n.* krus
cruel *adj.* malupit
cry *v.* umiyak; *n.* iyak
cuisine *n.* luto
culinary *adj.* tungkol sa pagluluto
culture *n.* kultura, kalinangan
cup *n.* tasa, kopa
curtain *n.* kurtina
custom *n.* ugali
customer *n.* mamimili; regular ~ or regular
   seller *n.* suki
cut *n.* hiwa; *v.* hiwain; putulin

– D –

damage *n.* sira; *v.* sirain
danger *n.* panganib
dangerous *adj.* mapanganib
dark *adj.* madilim
darkness *n.* karimlan
daughter *n.* anak na babae
day *n.* araw
dead *n.* patay
dear *adj.* mahal
death *n.* kamatayan
debt *n.* utang
deep *adj.* malalim
delicacies *n.* (refer to) minatamis, kakanin
   and other special or unusual foods
delicate *adj.* maselan
derive *v.* kunin, manggaling
describe *v.* ilarawan
description *n.* pagkakalarawan
develop *v.* painamin, paunlarin
dialect *n.* salita, diyalekto
diaper *n.* lampin
different *adj.* iba, magkaiba
digestion *n.* pagtunaw
diligent *adj.* masipag
diploma *n.* sertipiko ng pagtatapos
direction *n.* gawi, dako, banda
director *n.* patnugot
dirty *adj.* marumi
disaster *n.* sakuna
discipline *n.* disiplina
discussion *n.* pagtatalo, pag-uusap
disease *n.* sakit
distance *n.* layo, agwat
distant *adj.* malayo

divide *v.* hatiin
dizzy *n.* hilo; *v.* mahilo
do *v.* gawin
dog *n.* aso
doll *n.* manika
door *n.* pinto
doubt *n.* alinlangan
down *adv.* sa ibaba
drama *n.* dula
dress *n.* baro, damit (generic term)
drink *v.* uminom; *n.* inumin
driver *n.* (of car) tsuper; (of rig) kutsero
drop *v.* mahulog
drown *v.* malunod
drunk *adj.* lasing, lango
dry *adj.* tuyo
dub *v.* lagyan
dumb *adj.* pipi; hangal
dust *n.* alikabok

– E –

ear *n.* tainga
early *adv.* maaga
earning *n.* kita, suweldo
earth *n.* lupa, mundo
east *n.* silangan
eastern *adj.* silanganan
easy *adj.* madali
education *n.* pag-aaral
egg *n.* itlog
elbow *n.* siko
election *n.* halalan
electric *adj.* elektrika
embarrass *v.* hiyain
embarrassed *adj.* napahiya
employee *n.* kawani
end *n.* katapusan, wakas
enough *adv.* sapat; husto
enrich *v.* painamin, palaguin
equal *adj.* magkapantay; magkatumbas
eraser *n.* pambura
error *n.* mali, kamalian
even *adv.* pantay; kahi't; **even if** *adv.* kahi't na
evening *n.* gabi
event *n.* pangyayari
every *adv.* bawa't, bawa't isa; **everyone** *adv.* lahat
exact *adj.* husto, tama
example *n.* halimbawa
exchange *n.* palitan; *v.* magpalit; ipagpalit
expat (or **foreigner**) *n.* dayuhan, banyaga
expenses *n.* gastos
experience *n.* karanasan
eye *n.* mata

eyebrow *n.* kilay
eyeglasses *n.* (spectacles) salamin sa mata
eyelash *n.* pilikmata

– F –

face *n.* mukha; *v.* harapin
faith *n.* pananampalataya
fall *v.* mahulog
false *adj.* hindi totoo; hindi tapat
familiar *adj.* kilala
family *n.* mag-anak, pamilya
far *adj.* malayo
farm *n.* bukid; kabukiran
farmer *n.* magsasaka
fast *adj.* mabilis, matulin
fat *adj.* mataba
fate *n.* kapalaran
father *n.* ama
father-in-law *n.* biyenang lalaki
faucet *n.* gripo
fault *n.* kasalanan, mali
favorite *n.* paborito
fear *n.* takot, pangamba
feather *n.* balahibo
feeble *adj.* mahina
feeling *n.* damdamin
female *n./adj.* babae
fence *n.* bakod; *v.* bakuran
festivity *n.* kasayahan, pista
fever *n.* lagnat
few *adv.* kaunti, iilan
fight *n.* away; *v.* awayin
finger *n.* daliri
fire *n.* sunog
first *adj.* una
fish *n.* isda
fix *v.* ayusin
flag *n.* bandila, watawat
flame *n.* ningas, apoy
flower *n.* bulaklak
fly *n.* langaw
fly *v.* lumipad; sumakay sa eroplano
follow *v.* sumunod
food *n.* pagkain
foot *n.* paa
for *prep.* para sa, para kay
force *n.* lakas
forehead *n.* noo
fork *n.* tinidor
formidable *adj.* mahirap talunin; mabigat na kalaban
fragrance *n.* bango
fragrant *adj.* mabango
free *adj.* malaya

freedom *n.* kalayaan
frequent *adj.* madalas
fresh *adj.* sariwa
friend *n.* kaibigan
from *prep.* sa, buhat sa, mula sa
front *adv.* harapan
fruit *n.* bungang-kahoy, prutas
fry *v.* prituhin
full *adj.* puno
furniture (or **appliances**) *n.* kasangkapan
future *n.* hinaharap; *adv.* sa darating na panahon

– G –

gain *n.* tubo, pakinabang
game *n.* laro
garage *n.* garahe
garbage *n.* basura, dumi
garden *n.* halamanan, hardin
general *n.* heneral; *adj.* lahat
genesis *n.* simula
get *v.* kunin
girl *n.* batang babae
give *v.* magbigay
glass *n.* (**drinking ~**) baso; *n., adj.* kristal
go *v.* umalis, lumakad, pumaroon, pumunta
goat *n.* kambing
godfather *n.* ninong
godmother *n.* ninang
gold *n.* ginto
good *adj.* mahusay, magaling, mabuti
government *n.* pamahalaan
grace *n.* grasya, biyaya
grain *n.* butil
grass *n.* damo
grave *n.* libingan
gray *adj.* kulay-abo
great *adj.* dakila
green *adj.* luntian, berde
ground meat *n.* giniling na karne
group *n.* pangkat, lupon; *v.* magtipon
guard *n.* bantay; *v.* bantayan
guide *v.* akayin, ituro
gun *n.* baril

– H –

hair *n.* buhok; balahibo
half *adj.* kalahati
hammer *n.* martilyo
hand *n.* kamay
happy *adj.* masaya, maligaya
hard *adj.* matigas; mahirap (similar to **difficult**)

harvest *n.* ani
hat *n.* sumbrero
hate *n.* matinding galit
have (or **has**) *v.* mayroon
head *n.* ulo, puno
headache *n.* sakit ng ulo
health *n.* kalusugan
healthy *adj.* malusog
heart *n.* puso
heat *n.* init
help *n.* tulong; **helper** *n.* katulong
here *adv.* dito
hero *n.* bayani
hesitant *adj.* nagaalanganin
high *adj.* mataas
history *n.* kasaysayan
hole *n.* butas
hope *n.* pag-asa
horse *n.* kabayo
hospital *n.* ospital, pagamutan
hospitality *n.* magiliw na pagtanggap sa panauhin
hot *adj.* mainit
hour *n.* oras
house *n.* bahay, tahanan
how *adv.* paano
humble *adj.* mababang-loob; *n.* kababaang-loob
humor *n.* katatawanan, pagpapatawa
husband *n.* asawang lalaki

– I –

ice *n.* yelo
ice cream *n.* sorbetes
idea *n.* palagay; kuru-kuro
if *conj.* kung
important *adj.* mahalaga
in *prep.* sa, sa loob
indigenous *n.* katutubo
industrious *adj.* masipag
initial *adj.* pauna
ink *n.* tinta
insect *n.* kulisap
inside *prep.* sa loob
instruction *n.* turo
instrument *n.* kagamitan
insurance *n.* seguro
intention *n.* balak, hangarin
introduce *v.* ipakilala
invite *v.* anyayahan
iron *n.* bakal
island *n.* pulo, isla
itchy *adj.* makati

– J –

jail *n.* bilangguan, piitan
jaw *n.* panga
jealousy *n.* panibugho
jewel *n.* alahas
join *v.* pagsamahin, pagdugtungin
joke *n.* biro; *v.* biruin
journey *n.* paglalakbay
judge *n.* hukom; huwes
juice *n.* katas
jump *v.* tumalon, lumukso

– K –

keep *v.* itago
key *n.* susi
kick *v.* sipain
kind *n.* uri; *adj.* maawain; mabait
kiss *v.* halik
knee *n.* tuhod
kneel *v.* lumuhod
knife *n.* kutsilyo, lanseta
knot *n.* buhol; pusod (of hair); *v.* itali
know *v.* malaman
knowledge *n.* karunungan, kaalaman

– L –

laborer *n.* manggagawa
land *n.* lupa
language *n.* wika
last *adj.*, huli sa lahat
late *adj.*, huli
laugh *n.* tawa; *v.* tumawa
law *n.* batas
lawyer *n.* abugado; manananggol
lazy *adj.* tamad
lead *n.* tingga
leader *n.* pinuno, puno
leaf *n.* dahon
learn *v.* matuto, mag-aral
leather *n.* balat ng hayop
left *adj.* kaliwa (opposite of **right**)
leg *n.* binti
lesson *n.* aralin
letter *n.* sulat, liham; titik
level *adj.* patag, pantay
liar *adj.* sinungaling
library *n.* aklatan
lift *v.* buhatin
light *n.* ilaw, liwanag
light *adj.* magaan
like *adj.* katulad

like *v.* ibig, gusto
line *n.* guhit
linguist *n.* dalubhasa sa wika
lip *n.* labi
list *n.* listahan, talaan
listen *v.* makinig
literature *n.* panitikan, literatura
live *v.* mabuhay; nakatira (**to dwell**); *n.* buhay
lock *n.* kandado; ~ed nakakandado
long *adj.* mahaba
look *v.* tingnan
loose *adj.* maluwag
loss *n.* pagkawala
loud *adj.* malakas
love *n.* pag-ibig
low *adj.* mababa
lumber *n.* tabla, kahoy
lung *n.* baga

– M –

machine *n.* makina
mad *adj.* baliw
make *v.* gawin
male *n./adj.* lalaki
man *n.* lalaki
manager *n.* tagapamahala
map *n.* mapa
market *n.* palengke
marriage *n.* kasal
mat *n.* banig
match *n.* posporo
material, *n.* gamit
mature *adj.* (for fruits) hinog; (for man and animals) nasa hustong gulang
meaningful *adj.* makahulugan
measure *n.* sukat
meat *n.* karne, laman
medicine *n.* gamot
medium *n.* paraan
meeting *n.* pulong, miting
memorize *v.* isaulo; kabisahin
middle *n.* gitna
milk *n.* gatas
mind *n.* isip
mine *pron.* akin; minahan
minute *n.* minuto, sandali
mirror *n.* salamin
mixed *adj.* halu-halo
money *n.* salapi
monkey *n.* unggoy
month *n.* buwan
monument *n.* bantayog
morning *n.* umaga
mosquito *n.* lamok

mother *n.* ina, nanay
mother-in-law *n.* biyenang babae
mountain *n.* bundok
mouth *n.* bibig
move *v.* kumilos, gumalaw
movement *n.* kilusan
much *adv.* marami
music *n.* tugtugin, musika

– N –

nail *n.* pako; (**finger–** or **toe–**) kuko
naked *adj.* hubad
name *n.* pangalan, ngalan
narrow *adj.* makitid
nation *n.* bansa, bayan
native *n.* taal
nature *n.* kalikasan
near *adj.* malapit
necessary *adj.* kailangan
neck *n.* leeg
needle *n.* karayom
negotiate *v.* pakikipag-ayos; pakikipagkasun-
   duan
neighbor *n.* kapitbahay
new *adj.* bago
news *n.* balita
nickname *n.* palayaw
night *n.* gabi
no *adv.* hindi
noise *n.* ingay
none *adj.* wala
noon *n.* tanghali
north *n.* hilaga
nose *n.* ilong
note *n.* (of music) nota
now *adv.* ngayon
number *n.* bilang

– O –

obedient *adj.* masunurin
offer *v.* alukin
oil *n.* langis
old *adj.* matanda (referring to a person); luma
   (for things)
only *adv.* lamang
open *adj.* bukas; *v.* buksan
opinion *n.* palagay
opposite *adj.* kasalungat
orange *n.* dalandan
order *n.* utos, ayos
organization *n.* samahan, kapisanan
ornament *n.* gayak, palamuti, dekorasyon

other *adj.*, iba
out *adv.* sa labas
oven *n.* pugon
over *prep.* sa ibabaw
overeating *n.* sobrang pagkain
overtake *v.* lampasan
owner *n.* may-ari

– P –

page *n.* pahina
pain *n.* sakit
paint *n.* pintura
paper *n.* papel
parcel *n.* balutan
pardon *n.* patawad
parent *n.* magulang
past *adj.* nakaraan
paste *n.* pandikit; *v.* idikit
payment *n.* bayad, kabayaran
peace *n.* katahimikan
pen *n.* pluma
pencil *n.* lapis
people *n.* taong-bayan
perhaps *adv.* marahil
person *n.* tao
pet *n.* alagang hayop
picture *n.* larawan, litrato
pig *n.* baboy
pin *n.* aspile
pitiful *adj.* kaawa-awa
pity *n.* awa
plant *n.* tanim
plate *n.* pinggan
play *n.* laro; *v.* maglalaro
pleasure *n.* kasiyahan
plow *n.* araro
pocket *n.* bulsa
poison *n.* lason
poor *adj.* mahirap
popular *adj.* bantog, kilala
populated *v.* pinamamayanan
positive *adj.* tiyak
post *n.* haligi, poste ng bahay
pot *n.* paso (for plant); palayok (for cooking)
potato *n.* patatas
powder *n.* pulbos
power *n.* kapangyarihan
precision *n.* kawastuhan
present *adv.* ngayon, kasalukuyan
present *n.* regalo, handog
price *n.* halaga
prison *n.* see **jail**
process *n.* paraan
proclaim *v.* ihayag

proof *n.* katibayan
property *n.* ariarian
protest *v.* lumaban; sumalungat; *n.* paglaban
public *adj.* pangmadla; *n.* madla bayan
publish *v.* ilathala
pull *v.* hilahin; batakin
punctuality *n.* pagdating sa oras
punishment *n.* parusa
purpose *n.* balak; layon
push *v.* itulak
put *v.* ilagay
puzzle *n.* palaisipan; *v.* tarantahin

– Q –

quality *n.* uri, klase
quantity *n.* dami
quarrel *n.* away; *v.* awayin
queen *n.* reyna
question *n.* tanong; *v.* magtanong
quick *adj.* madali
quiet *adj.* tahimik, walang kibo
quite *adv.* halos, tila
quiz *n.* pagsusulit

– R –

railroad *n.* riles
rain *n.* ulan
rat *n.* daga
rattan *n.* yantok
razor *n.* labaha
read *v.* bumasa
ready *adj.* handa
reason *n.* dahilan, katwiran
receipt *n.* resibo
receive *v.* tanggapin
recipe *n.* paraan ng pagluluto
record *n.* talaan
red *adj.* pula
reflection *n.* pagdidili-dili
regional *adj.* panrehiyon
religion *n.* relihiyon
remember *v.* alalahanin
remove *v.* alisin
request *n.* kahilingan
respect *n.* paggalang; *v.* igalang
rest *n.* pahinga; *v.* magpahinga
revision *n.* pagbabago
revolution *n.* paghihimagsik
reward *n.* gantimpala
rhythm *n.* kumpas
rice *n.* bigas; **cooked ~** *n.* kanin
rich *adj.* mayaman

right *adj.* tama, wasto; kanan; karapatan
ring *n.* singsing
river *n.* ilog
road *n.* daan, kalye
roadside *n.* tabi ng daan
roasted *adj.* inihaw
roof *n.* bubong
root *n.* ugat (of plants)
rope *n.* lubid
rough *adj.* magaspang
round *adj.* bilog
run *v.* tumakbo
rust *n.* kalawang

– S –

sad *adj.* malungkot
safe *adj.* ligtas
salad *n.* ensalada
salt *n.* asin
salty *adj.* maalat
same *adj.* pareho, tulad
sand *n.* buhangin
scale *n.* timbangan
school *n.* paaralan
science *n.* agham, siyensiya
script *n.* iskrip, manuskrito
sea *n.* dagat
seal *n.* tatak
seat *n.* upuan, silya
second *adj.* ikalawa
secret *n.* lihim
secretary *n.* kalihim
see *v.* makita, tingnan
seed *n.* buto, binhi
send *v.* ipadala
sentence *n.* pangungusap
separate *adj.* hiwalay; *v.* maghiwalay
shallow *adj.* mababaw
shame *n.* hiya, kahihiyan
shameless *adj.* walang-hiya
sharp *adj.* matalas, matulis
sheep *n.* tupa
ship *n.* bapor
shirt *n.* kamisadentro
shoe *n.* sapatos
short *adj.* maikli
side *n.* tagiliran, tabi
signage *n.* tanda, marka
signature *n.* lagda, pirma
silk *n.* seda
silver *n.* pilak
sin *n.* kasalanan
sister *n.* kapatid na babae
size *n.* laki

skin *n.* balat
skirt *n.* palda
sky *n.* langit
sleep *b.* matulog
slow *adj.* mabagal, mahina
slowly *adv.* dahan-dahan
small *adj.* maliit
smile *n.* ngiti
smoke *n.* usok
smooth *adj.* makinis
snake *n.* ahas
sneeze *v.* magbahing
snore *n.* hilik; *v.* maghilik
soap *n.* sabon
society *n.* lipunan
socks *n.* medyas
soft *adj.* malambot
some *adj.* ilan
son *n.* anak na lalaki
song *n.* awit, kanta
soul *n.* kaluluwa
sound *n.* ingay, tunog
soup *n.* sopas, sabaw
sour *adj.* maasim
south *n.* timog
special *adj.* katangi-tangi; di-pangkaraniwan
spoon *n.* kutsara
square *n.* parisukat
staff *n.* tauhan
stage *n.* entablado
staircase *n.* hagdanan
stamp *n.* selyo sa sulat
star *n.* bituin, tala
starch *n.* gawgaw
station *n.* himpilan
steam *n.* singaw
step *n.* hakbang
sticky *adj.* malagkit
stiff *adj.* matigas
stingy *adj.* maramot
stomach *n.* tiyan
stone *n.* bato
story *n.* kuwento
stove *n.* kalan, pugon
street *n.* daan, kalye
strength *n.* lakas
strong *adj.* malakas
stubborn *adj.* matigas ang ulo, makulit
study *v.* mag-aral
succulent *adj.* makatas
sudden *adj.* bigla, kaagad
sugar *n.* asukal
summer *n.* tag-araw
sun *n.* araw
supper *n.* hapunan
surname *n.* apelyido

sweet *adj.* matamis
swim *v.* lumangoy
synonym *n.* magkasingkahulugan
system *n.* paraan, sistema

– T –

table *n.* mesa
tail *n.* buntot
tailor *n.* sastre, mananahi
take *v.* kunin
talented *adj.* matalino
talk *v.* magsalita
tall *adj.* matangkad (person); mataas
taste *n.* lasa; *v.* tikman
tax *n.* buwis
teach *v.* magturo
teacher *n.* guro, maestro/a
tear *n.* luha; *v.* punit
tell *v.* sabihin
than *conj.* kaysa
that *pron.* iyan, iyon
there *adv.* doon, diyan
thick *adj.* makapal
thief *n.* magnanakaw
thin *adj.* payat, manipis
thing *n.* bagay
this *pron.* ito; **these** ang mga ito (plural)
though *conj.* kahit na
thought *n.* akala, isip
thread *n.* sinulid
throat *n.* lalamunan
thumb *n.* hinlalaki
thunder *n.* kulog
ticket *n.* tiket
tight *adj.* masikip
time *n.* panahon, oras, sandali
tin *n.* lata
tired *adj.* pagod
today *adv.* ngayon
toe *n.* hinlalaki ng paa
together *adv.* magkasama
toilet *n.* palikuran, banyo
tomorrow *adv.* bukas
tongue *n.* dila
tooth *n.* ngipin
top *adv.* sa ibabaw
touch *n.* hipo; *v.* hipuin
town *n.* bayan
trade *n.* kalakalan
tradition *n.* kaugalian
train *n.* tren
trait *n.* katangian
translate *v.* salin
travel *n.* paglalakbay; *v.* maglakbay

tray *n.* bandehado
treasurer *n.* ingat-yaman
tree *n.* punong-kahoy; puno
trial *n.* pagsubok
trouble *n.* ligalig; basag-ulo
trousers *n.* salawal
true *adj.* totoo
twice *adv.* makalawa
twin *n.* kambal
typhoon *n.* bagyo

– U –

ugly *adj.* pangit
umbrella *n.* payong
under *prep.* sa ilalim
understand *v.* intindihin, unawain
until *adv.* hanggang
up *prep.* sa itaas
upright *adj.* tuwid
us *pron.* sa atin, tayo
use *v.* gamitin
useful *adj.* mahalaga

– V –

vacation *n.* bakasyon
value *n.* halaga
variety *n.* pagkaiba-iba
vegetable *n.* gulay
vehicle *n.* sasakyan
verdant *adj.* luntian
verse *n.* tula
very *affix; adj.* napaka-
victory *n.* tagumpay
view *n.* tanawin
vinegar *n.* suka
visit *n.* dalaw; *v.* dumalaw
voice *n.* boses, tinig
vote *n.* boto; *v.* iboto
voyage *n.* paglalakbay

– W –

wage *n.* sahod
wait *v.* maghintay
walk *v.* lumakad
wall *n.* dingding; tabike
wallet *n.* pitaka
war *n.* digmaan, giyera

warm *adj.* mainit
wash *v.* maghugas; hugasan (except clothes)
waste *n.* dumi, basura
watch *n.* relo; *v.* bantayan
water *n.* tubig
wave *n.* alon
weak *adj.* mahina
weather *n.* panahon
week *n.* linggo
weight *n.* bigat
well *n.* balon; *adj.* mabuti, walang sakit
west *n.* kanluran
wheel *n.* gulong
when *adv.* kailan. *conj.* kung
where *adv.* saan
while *conj.* samantala
whip *n.* pamalo
whisper *n.* bulong
whistle *n.* sutsot; pito
white *adj.* puti
who *pron.* sino
why *adv.* bakit
wife *n.* maybahay, asawang babae
wind *n.* hangin
window *n.* bintana
wine *n.* alak
wing *n.* pakpak
wire *n.* kawad, alambre
wise *adj.* matalino; marunong; **wisdom** *n.* katalinuhan; karunungan
woman *n.* babae
wood *n.* kahoy
word *n.* salita
work *n.* gawain; hanapbuhay
worm *n.* bulate, uod
wound *n.* sugat
write *v.* sumulat
writer *n.* manunulat
wrong *adj.* mali

– Y –

yard *n.* bakuran; yarda
year *n.* taon
yellow *n.* dilaw
yes *adv.* oo, opo/oho
yesterday *adv.* kahapon
young *adj.* bata
youth *n.* kabataan

Review Exercises

PART I

A. Use the following words in sentences.

Words that name	Words that describe	Action Words (in any tense)
tao	**maganda**	**umalis**
bahay	**lalong malaki**	**lumakad**
katulong	**mayaman**	**bumasa**
ikaw	**maingay**	**kumain**
iyan	**palatawa**	**maglaro**
Maynila	**pinakamabait**	**pumunta**
pagkain	**mabuti**	**maglinis**
kayo	**napakainit**	**basahin**
bibliya	**malinis na malinis**	**dalawin**
bulaklak	**masarap**	**kanin**

B. Write a paragraph of about 100 words describing anybody or anything.

C. Translate the following active sentences into passive.

1. **Kumakain ang bata ng tinapay.**

   _____

2. **Bumili ako ng sapatos sa Makati.**

   _____

3. **Ang katulong namin ay nagluto ng gulay.**

   _____

4. **Tumawag ng doktor ang maysakit.**

   _____

5. **Kumuha ng lapis ang bata sa bahay.**

   _____

D. Translate the following paragraph into Tagalog.

The Lord Jesus and His friends were in a small boat (**bangka**) on the sea. A storm (**bagyo**) came up quickly. The waves were big. The wind was strong. The water was filling the boat. The men called to the Lord Jesus. They said, "Do you not care if we drown?" The Lord Jesus stood up in the boat. He spoke to the wind and the sea, saying "Quiet, be still!" It was calm (**tahimik**) at once.

PART II

A. Write five words to describe each of the following:

pagkain	bulaklak	simbahan	bata
1.	1.	1.	1.
2.	2.	2.	2.
3.	3.	3.	3.
4.	4.	4.	4.
5.	5.	5.	5.

B. Translate the following words and phrases into Tagalog.

1. my mother
2. our church (including speaker and listener)
3. his love
4. their study
5. your hope (singular)
6. her cooking
7. our planting
8. his poverty
9. my happiness
10. your work (plural)
11. John's plan
12. baby's laugh
13. man's anger
14. Mary's name
15. March wind
16. father's letter
17. cat's eye
18. priest's sermon
19. child's food
20. animal's feet

C. Answer the following questions.

1. **Kanino bang aklat ito?**
2. **Ilan buwan na kayo sa Pilipinas?**
3. **Anu-ano ang inyong ginagawa ngayon?**
4. **Bakit kayo nag-aaral ng Tagalog?**
5. **Anong mga wika ang inyong alam?**

D. Fill in the blanks with the correct answer.

Synonym	Antonym
maganda	_____
masipag	_____
madilim	_____
banal	_____
malinis	_____

E. Tick (√) the letters of the appropriate answer to the sentence on the left.

1. **Ako ay naiinitang mabuti.**
   a. **Ako ay magluluto**
   b. **Ako ay maliligo.**
   c. **Ako ay mag-aaral.**

2. **Payat na payat ang anak nila.**
   a. **Dapat siyang uminom ng gamut sa ubo.**
   b. **Dapat siyang malungkot.**
   c. **Dapat siyang kumain nang marami.**

3. **Maingay ang klase.**
   a. **Paalisin ang mga bata.**
   b. **Pagalitan ang mga bata.**
   c. **Bigyan ng maraming gawain.**

4. **Marunong at mabait ang guro.**   a. **Siya'y kinayayamutan.**
                                              b. **Siya'y kinatutuwaan.**
                                              c. **Siya'y dapat tulungan.**

5. **Nasa Pilipinas ako.**   a. **Dapat akong magsalita ng Ingles.**
                                              b. **Dapat kong matulog sa hapon.**
                                              c. **Dapat akong mag-aral ng Tagalog.**

PART III

A. Fill in the blanks with the correct pronouns. Then, change # 1–17 into the inverse or conversational sentence order

1. **Ang kapatid ko ay marunong. _____ ay nag-aaral na mabuti.**
2. **Ang mga bata ay kumakain. _____ ay nagugutom.**
3. **Maraming pera si Ramon. Iyon ay ibinigay ng _____ ama.**
4. **Halika, Helen. Sumama _____ sa amin.**
5. **Kunin _____ ang aklat sa mesa.**
6. **_____ lahat ay inaanyayahan niya.**
7. **Mayroon ba kayong pagkain para sa _____?**
8. **Hindi isinama si Peter sa sine. Umiiyak _____.**
9. **Isang araw, _____ ay nagpasyal sa Luneta.**
10. **Nakita _____ ang maraming bapor sa dagat.**
11. **Kunin _____ ang inyong aklat.**
12. **Isama ninyo ako kung pupunta _____ sa Baguio.**
13. **Ang bahay _____ ay nasa Pandacan.**
14. **Nakita _____ na ba ang Tagaytay?**
15. **_____ ay mga tunay na kaibigan.**
16. **Sila ay magbabakasyon sa _____ bahay.**
17. **Gabi na nang _____ ay umalis.**
18. **Huwag _____ magagalit sa akin.**
19. **Nalulungkot ba _____?**
20. **Marami _____ bang kaibigan sa Maynila?**
21. **Magsalita _____ ng Tagalog sa ating klase.**

B. What are the missing words in the following sentences?

1. **Ang papel at pluma ay gamit sa _____.**
2. **Sina Tom at Mary ay _____.**
3. **Ang _____ ay para sa mga nagugutom.**
4. **Ang _____ ay mabango at maganda.**
5. **Si Mang Tomas ay nagtatanim. Siya ay _____.**
6. **Si Gng. Cruz ay nagtuturo. Siya ay _____.**
7. **Tayo ay umiinom ng _____ kapag nauuhaw.**
8. **Maraming nababasa sa mga _____.**
9. **Ang batang _____ ay nakatutuwa.**
10. **Ang batang _____ ay nakagagalit.**

C. Fill in with the appropriate adjective.

1. **Si John ay basa nang basa. Siya ay maraming nalalaman. Nasasagot niya ang lahat ng tinatanong ng guro. Si John ay _____.**

2. **Ang dalaga ay laging naglilinis ng kanilang bahay. Siya ang nagluluto ng pagkain. Siya ang naglalaba ng mga damit. Ang dalaga ay _____.**

3. **Ayaw niyang magtrabaho. Gusto niya ay matulog lamang. Siya ay hindi tumutulong sa kanyang ina. Kung may gagawin sa bahay siya ay umaalis. Bumabalik lamang siya kung kakain. Siya ay _____.**

4. **Hindi niya makita ang kanyang kausap. Ang lahat ay madilim. Ang mga bulaklak ay walang kulay para sa kanya. Siya ay _____.**

5. **Mahirap si Peter. Wala siyang pagkain. Wala siyang damit. Wala siyang mga magulang. Si Peter ay _____ .**

D. Write five examples for each of the following categories.

mga hayop	mga pagkain	mga gawain	mga hanapbuhay
1.	1.	1.	1.
2.	2.	2.	2.
3.	3.	3.	3.
4.	4.	4.	4.
5.	5.	5.	5.

PART IV

A. Answer the following questions in complete sentences.

1. **Pumunta ba kayo sa palengke kahapon?**
2. **Nagsasalita na ba kayo ng Tagalog?**
3. **Umiinom ka ba ng kape sa umaga? (in the morning)**
4. **Aalis na ba kayo? Hindi pa ako aalis.**
5. **Sumulat ba kayo sa inyong kaibigan sa Amerika?**

B. Translate the following sentences into Tagalog.

1. I bought a big house in Quezon City.
2. We read (or are reading) in the class.
3. We shall go to your house tomorrow.
4. Peter's clothes are clean.
5. My dress is not clean.

C. Fill in the blanks with **ang**, **ng**, **sa** or their plural forms.

1. _____ bisita _____ bagong kasal ay mga kaibigan at kamag-anak _____ kanilang bayan.
2. **Kami ang sumakay _____ kotse, kasama _____ katulong at _____ anak ko.**
3. **_____ bahay _____ aming kaibigan ay nasa Nueva Ecija.**
4. **Umalis kami _____ Maynila nang ika – 10:00 _____ umaga.**

5. Maraming pagkain _____ mahabang mesa.
6. Maganda _____ asawa _____ aking kaibigan.

PART V

A. -UM- AND MAG- VERBS

1. Fill in the blanks with the -um- and mag- derivatives of the following words.

	takbo (-um-)	alis (-um-)	salita (mag-)	alaga (mag-)
Infinitive	_____	_____	_____	_____
Imperative	_____	_____	_____	_____
Past	_____	_____	_____	_____
Present	_____	_____	_____	_____
Future	_____	_____	_____	_____

2. Translate the following sentences into Tagalog.

a. Mary wrote a book.

_____

b. He walked to school.

_____

c. Peter and his friends left early.

_____

d. Mary cannot cook rice.

_____

e. Why didn't you clean your hands?

_____

f. Do you sell mangoes?

_____

g. I want to buy two mangoes.

_____

h. He reads well.

_____

i. You should write to your mother every week.

_____

j. He who studies well will speak Tagalog.

_____

k. Did you eat your breakfast?

_____

l. Did Peter leave this morning?

_____

m. Don't you like to swim?

_____

3. Create sentences using the tenses and forms of the following verbs.

umawit _____

dumating _____

magbihis _____

gumawa _____

pumasok _____

bumalik _____

lumakad _____

B. **-IN** VERBS

1. Form the **-in** derivatives of the following words.

sabihin	awitin	dalhin (to call)	sirain	tawagin
_____	_____	_____	_____	_____
_____	_____	_____	_____	_____
_____	_____	_____	_____	_____
_____	_____	_____	_____	_____
_____	_____	_____	_____	_____

2. Change the following sentences from active into passive by using **-in** verbs.

a. **Kumain sila ng isda.**

_____

b. **Sumulat siya sa akin ng liham.**

_____

c. **Bumabasa si Juan ng pahayagan.**

_____

d. **Ang aking katulong ay nagluluto ng pagkain.**

_____

e. **Si Jesus ang nagsabi nito.**

_____

f. **Bumati kayo kay Juan para sa akin.**

_____

g. **Nagmamahal ka ba sa Diyos?**

_____

3. Give the future tense of the following active verbs and place the appropriate stress marks.

a. to read _____
b. to bring _____
c. to wake _____
d. to change _____
e. to play _____
f. to wet _____
g. to say _____
h. to cure _____
i. to leave _____
j. to remove _____

C. **Saan** and **Nasaan**

1. When do you use **saan**?
   _____

2. When do you use **nasaan**?
   _____

3. Translate the following questions and sentences into Tagalog.

   a. Where is your home?
      _____

   b. Where is your friend?
      _____

   c. Where is your friend going?
      _____

   d. Where is your church?
      _____

   e. Where did you eat?
      _____

   f. John is in the city.
      _____

D. Look for the wrong words in the following questions and sentence. If there are any, give the correct ones.

1. **Dito siya nakatira.**
   _____

2. **Saan ang iyong nanay?**
   _____

3. **Nasaan ang kaibigan niya?**

_____

4. **Sa bahay ba si Maria?**

_____

5. **Nasaan sila pumaroon?**

_____

Part VI

A. Translate the following time, words and phrases.

	Tagalog			English
1. today	_____	7.	**kanina**	_____
2. tomorrow	_____	8.	**mamaya**	_____
3. last week	_____	9.	**noong Enero**	_____
4. day before	_____	10.	**bukas ng hapon**	_____
5. yesterday	_____	11.	**sa Linggo**	_____
6. next year	_____	12.	**sa isang taon**	_____

	Tagalog		Spanish
13. 5:00 p.m.	_____	18.	_____
14. 2:00 p.m.	_____	19.	_____
15. 8:15 a.m.	_____	20.	_____
16. 10:30 a.m.	_____	21.	_____
17. 12:00 nn.	_____	22.	_____

B. Give the derivatives of the following words using the **ma-** and **maka-** affixes.

	makaalis	**makalakad**	**matulog**
Infinitive	_____	_____	_____
Imperative	_____	_____	_____
Past	_____	_____	_____
Present	_____	_____	_____
Future	_____	_____	_____

C. Translate the following sentences into Tagalog

1. What did you see yesterday?

_____

2. He was able to buy shoes.

_____

3. He slept on the floor.

_____

4. Don't be angry with him.

_____

5. He was not able to pay.

_____

6. He woke the baby unintentionally.

_____

Part VII

A. Arrange the words and particles in the following sentences, and replace with correct ones.

1. **marumi ang bata ang raw ba**

_____

2. **siya ay bata ba pa**

_____

3. **siya ay kumain rin ay ba po**

_____

4. **nakaalis nab a siya**

_____

5. **nakapag-aral hindi siya pa**

_____

6. **bakit siya hindi makatatakbo nang mabilis**

_____

7. **ba ito ang aklat mo**

_____

B. Give the Tagalog equivalent of the following words and phrases.

1. good   _____
2. very good   _____
3. how good   _____
4. industrious   _____
5. very industrious _____
6. most industrious _____

C. Translate these sentences into Tagalog.

1. Peter is brighter than John.

_____

2. John is taller than his brother.

_____

3. My house is as beautiful as his.

_____

4. His child is small.

_____

5. His child is smaller than my child.

_____

6. His child is of the same height as mine.

_____

7. His dog is not as bad as his neighbor's.

_____

8. John and Peter are brothers.

_____

9. Jack and his friend are of the same color.

_____

10. My sister is more beautiful than I.

_____

D. Create sentences using the following words.

1. **maganda** _____

2. **kay ganda** _____

3. **magandang-maganda** _____

4. **napakaganda** _____

5. **pinakamaganda** _____

6. **magkasintaas** _____

7. **hindi kasinggulang** _____

8. **hindi kasimbait** _____

E. Translate the following into Tagalog.

1. Don't eat now.

   _____

2. He cannot ride a horse.

   _____

3. Can you swim?

   _____

4. Yes, I can swim.

   _____

5. You should study Tagalog everyday.

   _____

6. Why don't you eat your supper?

   _____

7. Do you know his name?

   _____

8. What do you need?

   _____

PART VIII

A. Create sentences from the following root words using the prefixes on the left. Afterwards, give the English translation of your sentences.

1. **lambot** using **pa-in**   3. **upo** using **pa_in**

2. **kain** using **magpa-**   4. **inom** using **magpa-**

B. Translate the following sentences into English.

1. **Huwag mong sirain ang papel.**

   _____

2. **Pinasulat ko siya ng liham.**

   _____

3. **Siya'y pinaalis ng kanyang ama.**

   _____

4. **Ang kanyang takot ay nagpatakbo kay Juan.**

   _____

5. **Pinabasa niya ako ng pahayagan.**

   _____

C. Give the plural form of the following adjectives in two ways.

maganda _____ _____
mabuti _____ _____

D. Translate the following phrases into English.

1. **ang mabait** _____
2. **ang mabait na tao** _____
3. **and bumabasa** _____
4. **ang binabasa** _____
5. **ang patakbo** _____
6. **ang maglaba** _____

E. Translate the following sentences into English using the passive voice of verbs.

1. **Kanyang iniligtas ako.**

   _____

2. **Siya'y pinalo ng kaibigan niya.**

   _____

3. **Hindi niya ako sinulatan.**

   _____

4. **Ako'y kanyang binigyan ng aklat niya.**

   _____

5. **Ang iyong ibinigay ay akin na.**

   _____

6. **Ang sa kanya ay hindi magagamit ng iba.**

   _____

Answers to Review Exercises

PART I

C. 1. Ang tinapay ay kinakain ng bata.
   2. Binili ko ang sapatos sa Makati.
   3. Nagluto ng gulay ang katulong namin.
   4. Tinawag ng maysakit ang doktor.
   5. Kinuha ng bata ang lapis sa bahay.

D. Ang Panginoong Hesus at ang Kanyang mga kaibigan ay nasa isang maliit na bangka sa dagat. Isang bagyo ang dumating nang bigla... Ang mga alon ay malalaki. Malakas ang hangin. Napupuno ng tubig ang bangka. Tinawag ng mga lalaki ang Panginoong Hesus. Ang sabi nila, "Wala bang halaga sa inyo na kami'y malunod?" Tumayo ang Panginoong Hesus sa bangka. Nagsalita Siya sa hangin at sa dagat at sinabi Niya, "Tahimik!" Naging tahimik kaagad.

PART II

B. 1. ang aking ina
   2. ang ating simbahan
   3. ang kaniyang pag-ibig
   4. ang kanilang pag-aaral
   5. ang kaniyang pag-asa
   6. ang kaniyang pagluluto
   7. ang ating pagtatanim
   8. ang kaniyang kahirapan
   9. ang aking kaligayahan
   10. ang inyong trabaho
   11. ang balak ni John
   12. ang tawa ng sanggol
   13. ang galit ng lalaki
   14. ang ngalan ni Mary
   15. ang hangin ng Marso
   16. ang sulat ng ama
   17. ang mata ng pusa
   18. ang sermon ng pari
   19. ang pagkain ng bata
   20. ang paa ng hayop

E. 1. b   2. c   3. c   4. b   5. c

PART III

A. 1. siya
   2. sila
   3. kanyang
   4. ka
   5. mo
   6. kaming
   7. amin; akin; kanila
   8. siya
   9. kami; sila
   10. namin; nila
   11. mo; ninyo
   12. kayo
   13. ko; namin
   14. mo
   15. sila; kayo; kami
   16. aming; ating; inyong
   17. (any nominative pronoun)
   18. kang; kayong
   19. kayo; sila
   20. ka
   21. ka; kayo

B. 1. pagsulat
   2. magkaibigan; magkapatid; etc.
   3. pagkain
   4. bulaklak
   5. magsasaka
   6. guro
   7. tubig
   8. pahayagan; aklat; magasin
   9. mabait; maganda
   10. masam

C. 1. marunong
   2. masipag
   3. tamad
   4. bulag
   5. kaawa-awa

PART IV

B. 1. **Bumili ako ng isang malaking bahay sa Quezon City.**
   2. **Bumabasa kami sa klase.**
   3. **Pupunta kami sa inyong bahay bukas.**
   4. **Malinis ang mga damit ni Peter.**
   5. **Hindi malinis ang aking baro.**

C. 1. <u>Ang mga</u> **bisita** <u>ng</u> **bagong kasal ay mga kaibigan at kamag-anak** <u>sa</u> **kanilang bayan.**
   2. **Kami ay sumakay** <u>sa</u> **kotse, kasama** <u>ang</u> **katulong at** <u>ang</u> **anak ko.**
   3. <u>Ang</u> **bahay** <u>ng</u> **aming kaibigan ay nasa Nueva Ecija.**
   4. **Umalis kami** <u>sa</u> **Maynila nang ika-10:00 ng umaga.**
   5. **Maraming pagkain** <u>sa</u> **mahabang mesa.**
   6. **Maganda** <u>ang</u> **asawa** <u>ng</u> **aking kaibigan.**

PART V

A. 1.

Infinitive	tumakbo	umalis	magsalita	mag-alaga
Imperative	tumakbo	umalis	magsalita	mag-alaga
Past	tumakbo	umalis	nagsalita	nag-alaga
Present	tumatakbo	umaalis	nagsasalita	nag-aalaga
Future	tatakbo	aalis	magsasalita	mag-aalaga

   2. a. **Sumulat ng aklat si Mary.**
      b. **Lumakad siya papunta sa paaralan.**
      c. **Umalis nang maaga si Peter at ang kanyang mga kaibigan.**
      d. **Hindi makapagluto si Mary ng kanin.**
      e. **Bakit hindi ka naglinis ng mga kamay?**
      f. **Nagbebenta ba kayo ng mga mangga?**
      g. **Gusto kong bumili ng dalawang mangga.**
      h. **Mahusay siyang bumasa.**
      i. **Dapat kang sumulat sa iyong ina linggu-linggo (or minsan sa isang linggo)**
      j. **Kung sino ang nag-aaral nang mabuti ay magsasalita ng Tagalog.**
      k. **Kumain ka ba ng almusal?**
      l. **Umalis ba si Peter ngayong umaga?**
      m. **Ayaw mo bang lumangoy?**

B. 1.

Infinitive	sabihin	dalhin	sirain	tawagin
Imperative	sabihin	dalhin	sirain	tawagin
Past	sinabi	dinala	sinira	tinawag
Present	sinasabi	dinadala	sinisira	tinatawag
Future	sasabihin	dadalhin	sisirain	tatawagin

   2. a. **Kinain nila ang isda.**
      b. **Sinulat niya ang liham sa akin.**
      c. **Binabasa ni Juan ang pahayagan.**
      d. **Niluluto ng aking katulong ang pagkain.**
      e. **Sinabi ni Hesus ito.**
      f. **Batiin ninyo si Juan para sa akin.**
      g. **Minamahal mo ba ang Diyos?**

3. a. **babasa**
   b. **magdadala**
   c. **gigising**
   d. **magbabago**
   e. **maglalaro**
   f. **magbabasa**
   g. **magsasabi**
   h. **gagamot**
   i. **aalis**
   j. **mag-aalis**

C. 1. **Saan** is used with an action word.
   2. **Nasaan** is used without. Both ask for location.
   3. a. **Nasaan ang iyong bahay?**
      b. **Nasaan ang iyong kaibigan?**
      c. **Saan pupunta ang iyong kaibigan?**
      d. **Nasaan ang iyong simbahan?**
      e. **Saan ka kumain?**
      f. **Si John ay nasa lungsod.**

D. 1. (no error)
   2. **Nasaan**
   3. (no error)
   4. **Nasa**
   5. **Saan**

PART VI

A. 1. **ngayon**
   2. **bukas**
   3. **noong isang linggo**
   4. **kamakalawa**
   5. **kahapon**
   6. **sa isang taon**
   7. a while ago or earlier in the day
   8. later
   9. last January
   10. tomorrow afternoon
   11. on Sunday or next Sunday
   12. next year

13. ikalima ng hapon
14. ikadalawa ng hapon
15. ikawalo at labinlima ng umaga
16. ikasampu at kalahati ng umaga
17. ikalabindalawa at kalahati ng tanghali
18. **alas sinko ng hapon**
19. **alas dos ng hapon**
20. **alas otso kinse ng umaga**
21. **alas diyes y medya ng umaga**
22. **alas dose y medya ng tanghali**

B.

Infinitive	**makaalis**	**makalakad**	**matulog**
Imperative	(none)	(none)	**matulog**
Past	**nakaalis**	**nakalakad**	**natulog**
Present	**nakaaalis**	**nakalalakad**	**natutulog**
Future	**makaaalis**	**makalalakad**	**matutulog**

C. 1. **Ano ang nakita mo kahapon?**
   2. **Nakabili siya ng sapatos.**
   3. **Natulog siya sa sahig.**
   4. **Huwag kang magalit sa kanya.**
   5. **Hindi siya nakabayad.**
   6. **Nagising niya ang bata.**

PART VII

A. 1. **Marumi raw ba ang bata?**
   2. **Siya ba ay bata pa?**
   3. **Siya rin po ba ay kumain?**
   4. **Nakaalis na ba siya?**
   5. **Hindi pa siya nakapag-aral.**
   6. **Bakit hindi siya makatakbo ng mabilis?**
   7. **Ito ba ang aklat mo?**

B. 1. good – **mabuti**
   2. very good – **napakabuti**
   3. how good – **kay buti** or **mabuting-mabuti**
   4. industrious – **masipag**
   5. very industrious – **napakasipag** or **masipag na masipag**
   6. most industrious – **pinakamasipag.**

C. 1. **Lalong marunong si Peter kaysa kay John.**
   2. **Lalong mataas si John kaysa sa kanyang kapatid na lalaki.**
   3. **Ang aking bahay ay kasingganda ng kaniyang bahay.**
   4. **Maliit ang kanyang anak.**
   5. **Lalong maliit ang kanyang anak kaysa sa anak ko.**
   6. **Magkasintaas ang anak niya at ang anak ko.**
   7. **Ang kanyang aso ay hindi kasinsama ng aso ng kapitbahay niya.**
   8. **Magkapatid sina John at Peter.**
   9. **Si Jack at ang kanyang kaibigan ay magkasingkulay.**
   10. **Lalong maganda ang aking kapatid kaysa sa akin.**

E. 1. **Huwag kang kumain ngayon.**
   2. **Hindi siya marunong sumakay sa kabayo.**
   3. **Marunong ka bang lumangoy?**
   4. **Oo, marunong akong lumangoy.**
   5. **Kailangan mong mag-aral ng Tagalog araw-araw.**
   6. **Bakit hindi ka kumain ng iyong hapunan?**
   7. **Alam mo ba ang kanyang pangalan?**
   8. **Ano ang kailangan mo?**

PART VIII

B. 1. Don't tear the paper.
   2. I made him/her write a letter.
   3. His father made him/her leave.
   4. His fear made Juan run.
   5. He/She made me read the newspaper.

C. 1. **magaganda; mga maganda**
   2. **mabubuti; mga mabuti**

D. 1. the good one
   2. the good man
   3. the one reading
   4. the thing being read
   5. the manner of running or the running of (something such as a contest)
   6. the washing of clothes

E. 1. I was saved by him.
   2. He was hit by his friend.
   3. He had not written to me.
   4. His/her book was given to me by him.
   5. What you have given me is mine already.
   6. What is his/hers cannot be used by another.

Reading Materials

Note on this section: Students should not be discouraged at the complexity and difficulty of these texts, especially the essays. These are advanced and native level texts meant to be studied with a teacher. This revised edition has a few additional short texts that are more suited for a beginning student: some tongue-twisters in Tagalog, plus a Tagalog folk song and a children's song. The English translations are included to facilitate comprehension.

TAGALOG TONGUE TWISTERS are a fun way to practice your pronunciation, as well as learn new vocabulary and reinforce grammar. Try to recite and repeat the following phrases as fast as you can!

Bumili ako ng bituka ng butiki sa butika.
I bought a gut of a lizard at a pharmacy.

Minikaniko ni Monico ang makina ng Minica ni Monica.
Monico fixed the engine of Monica's Minica.

Pitumput-pitong puting pating
Seventy seven white sharks.

BAHAY KUBO
A Tagalog folk song

Bahay-kubo, kahit munti
Ang halaman doon ay sari-sari
Singkamas at talong
Sigarilyas at mani
Sitaw, bataw, patani

Kundol, patola, upo't kalabasa
At tsaka meron pang
Labanos, mustasa
Sibuyas, kamatis, bawang at luya
Sa paligid-ligid ay puno ng linga

NIPA HUT
A Tagalog folk song

Nipa hut, even though it's small,
has all kinds of plants:
Turnip and eggplant
Winged bean and peanut,
String bean, hyacinth bean, lima bean.

Gourds, white squash & pumpkin,
And there are also
Radish, mustard,
Onion, tomato, garlic and ginger
And all around it are sesame seeds.

AKO AY MAY LOBO
A Tagalog children's song

Ako ay may lobo
Lumipad sa langit
'Di ko na nakita
Pumutok na pala

Sayang ang pera ko
Pinambili ng lobo
Kung pagkain sana
Nabusog pa ako

I HAD A BALLOON
A Tagalog children's song

I had a balloon
It flew to the sky
I didn't see it anymore
Apparently it popped

It was a waste of money
Using it to buy the balloon
If I used it on food
I would have been full

ANG PAGPAPANTAY-PANTAY SA LIPUNAN

Manuel A. Quezon (1878–1944)

President of the Commonwealth of the Philippines, 1935 to 1944

Talagang totoong ang Pilipinas ay may malaking pagsulong sa mga bagay tungkol sa bayan at sa kabuhayan sa loob ng huling 30 taon. Sa pagkamakabayan at puno ng pamahalaan, dumating tayo sa panahong nasa ating lahat ang mga karapatan ng isang pamahalaang malasarili at dahil dito'y masisiguro natin ang pagdating ng talagang kalayaan.

Sa kabuhayan, isang bansa tayong malakas sa kalakal ng Amerika; ang ating kalakal sa labas at loob ay dumarami at ang yaman ng bansa natin ay lumalaking mabuti. Gumagawa tayo ng pagsulong sa kalinisan, pagtuturo, at paggawa ng mga daan at lahat ng pahatiran.

Nguni't ang maraming may pakinabang dito ay ang mayayaman lamang. Ang mayaman ay maaaring mabuhay sa bigay ng salapi nila at pati mga anak nila ay lumalaki na palaging mayroon. Ang kanilang ibig ay mga ugaling mahalaga lamang ang lipunan at saya at iba pang ibig ng katawan nila. Talagang ugali nila ang sumunod sa kabuhayang masaya nang walang gawa at damdaming makatao.

Ang mga taong hindi naman mayaman at hindi naman mahirap ay mayroon ngayong mabubuting kabuhayan kaysa noong panahon ng Kastila. Ang mga kailangan para sa kabihasnan ngayon ay kanila nang kaya. Ang anak nilang lalaki at babae ay kumakain na ng mabuti, nagsusuot ng mabuting damit at nag-aaral ng mataas na karunungan.

Nakalulungkot sabihin, ngunit siyang totoo na ang kabuhayang iyan ay walang-wala sa bayang manggagawa. Lahat na ng mga gumagawa sa lupa, at pumapasok sa mga trabaho ay kaunti lamang ang ibinubuti ng lagay kaysa noong panahon ng Kastila. Totoo nga na ang sahod ngayon ay lumaki kaysa noong nasa kapangyarihan tayo ng Espanya at ang sahurin dito ay mataas kaysa alin mang bansa dito sa Silangan, bukod sa Hapon. Ngunit dapat nating isipin na ang pera noon ay maraming bagay at kailangan ang nabibili kaysa pera ngayon; at saka, sa samahan ng may patrabaho at manggagawa ay may palagayang hindi mababayaran ng salapi. Noon ang may paggawa at manggagawa ay malapit sa bawa't isa at ang ayos nila ay parang totoong magkapatid at mag-anak, kaya ang pagsasama nila at pagmamahalan ay malakas kaysa salapi. Ngayon ang samahan ay parang mag-ibang tao at lahat ay gumagawa para sa kanyang sarili, gaya rin sa ibang lupa na mayroong malalaking kalakal. Ang ating mga tao na man ay walang reklamo sa buhay na iyan mangyari'y ang palagay nila ay dapat tiisin ang lahat ng bigay ng Diyos para dumating sa atin ang awa ng langit.

Ngayon ang manggagawang Pilipino, hindi man nag-aral ay ayaw nang maniwala na ibig ng Diyos na ang iba ay mabuhay na mayaman at ang iba'y mabuhay sa hirap at pagtitiis. Ang manggagawang Pilipino ngayo'y naniniwala na siya rin ay mahal ng Ama sa Langit gaya rin ng ibang taong Kanyang ginawa; at dahil dito ang daigdig ay hindi ginawa ng Diyos para sa ilan lamang kundi para sa lahat.

Ang pagsulong ng Bansa sa pagpantay-pantay ng buhay sa lipunan ay talagang iniuutos ng Saligang Batas (Constitution) natin. Ang ating palatuntunan na tinanggap ng bayan sa paglagay sa inyo at sa akin man sa tungkulin natin, ay nagbibigay sa atin ng mabigat na tungkuling magkaroon at mag-alaga sa mga manggagawa. Dapat tayong maging masipag na sa alinmang batas ay huwag nating payagan na ang manggagawa ay gawan ng masama ng may paggawa, at huwag payagan ang anumang bagay na makasisira sa layon ng pagkakapantay-pantay. Sa pagharap sa kinabukasan ng bagong bansa nating ito ay hindi dapat na tayo'y manghawak sa lakas ng batas kundi sa lakas ng tapat na pagsasama ng tao at ng pamahalaan ng naririto para sa layong sila'y alagaan para sa kanilang sariling buhay at kaligayahan.

Maging ang Kagawaran ng Katarungan (Department of Justice) o Kawanihan ng Paggawa (Bureau of Labor) ay parehong handang tumulong sa inyo sa paggawa ng mga kailangang batas para maitakip sa mga kulang ng mga batas na sinusunod ngayon at sa ganito ay maayos at magamot ang mga masamang nangyayari sa bayan at para magawa rin ang palatuntunang ipinasusunod ng ating Saligang Batas at gayon din ang mga inaantay nila sa atin na nasasabi sa palatuntunan nating panghalalan.

PAG-IBIG SA TINUBUANG LUPA (Excerpt)
Written in Barcelona, Spain, 1882
by **Dr. Jose P. Rizal** (1861–1896)
National hero, Philippines

Narito ang isang magandang paksa; at dahil din sa kanyang kagandahan ay napakadalas nang talakayin. Ang pantas, makata, makasining, manggagawa, mangangalakal, o mandirigma, matanda o bata, hari o alipin—ang lahat ay nakapag-isip na tungkol sa kanya, at nakapaghandog ng pinakamahalagang bunga ng kanilang isip o ng kanilang puso. Buhat sa taga Europang mulat, malaya't mapagmalaki sa kanyang maluwalhating kasaysayan, hanggang sa negro sa Aprika, na hinango sa kanyang mga kagubatan at ipinagbili sa hamak na halaga; buhat sa matatandang bayang ang mga anino'y aali-aligid pa sa kanilang mga mapapanglaw ng guho, libingan ng kanilang mga kaluwalhata't pagdurusa, hanggang sa mga bansang makabago't lagi ng kumikilos at puno ng buhay, ay mayroong isang pinakamamahal na dilag, maningning, dakila, nguni't walang habag at malupit, na tinatawag na Inang Bayan. Libu-libong dila ang sa kanya'y umawit, libu-libong kudyapi ang naghandog sa kanya ng kanilang mga makatang lalong matataas ang pangarap, ang naghain sa kanyang harap o sa kanyang alaala ng kanilang pinakamaningning na katha. Siya ang naging sigaw ng kapayapaan ng pag-ibig at ng kaluwalhatian, palibhasa'y siya ang laman ng lahat ng pag-iisip, at katulad ng liwanag na nakukulong sa isang malinis na bubog, siya'y tumatagos hanggang sa labas, na parang mga sinag na buhay na buhay.

At ito ba'y magiging sagwil upang siya'y pag-ukulan natin ng panahon? At tayo ba'y hindi maaaring mag-ukol sa kanya ng anumang bagay, tayong walang ibang kasalanan kundi ang pagkakahuli ng pagsilang sa maliwanag? Nagbibigay ba ang dantaong ika-labinsiyam ng karapatang huwag kumilala ng utang na loob? Hindi. Hindi pa nasasaid ang mayamang mina ng puso; sagana pa tuwina ang kanyang alaala, at bahagya man ang pagkakapukaw ng kanyang alaala, at bahagya man ang pagkapukaw ng ating kalooban, ay makasusumpong tayo sa kaibuturan ng ating kaluluwa na kung di man isang masaganang kayamanan, ay abuloy na bagaman dahop ay puspos naman ng kasiglahan. Katulad ng mga matatandang ebreong nangag-alay sa templo ng mga kauna-unahang bunga ng kanilang pag-ibig, tayong mangingibang lupain ay nag-uukol ng mga kauna-unahang tinig sa ating Inang Bayang nababalot ng mga panginorin at mga ulap ng umaga, lagi nang maganda at matulain, at sa tuwi-tuwina'y lalong sinasamba habang sa kanya'y nawawalay at nalalayo.

At ito'y hindi nararapat pagtakhan sa dahilang ang pag-ibig sa Inang Baya'y isang damdaming tunay na katutubo; sapagka't naroroon ang mga kauna-unahang alaala ng kamusmusan, isang masamang tulang awitin na ang kabataan lamang ang nakakikilala at sa mga bakas nito'y sumisibol ang bulaklak ng kawalang-malay at ng kaligayahan;

sapagka't doo'y nahihimbing ang buong nakaraan at nababanaagan ang isang hina-harap; sapagka't sa kanyang mga kagubatan at sa kanyang mga kaparangan, sa bawa't punungkahoy, sa bawa't halaman, sa bawa't bulaklak, ay nakikita ninyong nakaukit ang gunita ng isang nilikhang minamahal ninyo, gaya ng hininga niya sa mahalimuyak na simoy ng hangin, ng kanyang awit sa mga bulong ng bukal ng ngiti niya sa bahaghari ng langit, o ng mga buntung-hininga niya sa magulong halinghing ng hangin sa gabi. Ang sanhi nito'y sapagka't doo'y nakakikita kayo, sa pamamagitan ng mga mata ng inyong gunita, sa ilalim ng tahimik na bubong ng matandang tahanan, ng isang angkang nag-aalaala at naghihintay sa inyo, nag-uukol sa inyo ng mga isipan at mga pagkabalisa nila; sa wakas, sapagka't sa kanyang langit, sa kanyang araw, sa kanyang mga karagatan at sa kanyang mga kagubatan ay nakakatagpo kayo ng tulain, ng paggiliw at ng pag-ibig, at hanggang sa libingan na ring pinaghihintayan sa inyo ng isang abang puntod upang kayo'y isauli sa sinapupunan ng lupa. Mayroon kayang isang kadiyusang nagtatali ng ating mga puso sa lupa ng ating inang-bayan, na nagpapaganda't nagpaparilag sa lahat, naghahandog sa atin ng lahat ng bagay sa ilalim ng isang anyong matulain at malamb-ing, at nakararahuyo sa ating mga puso? Saapagka't sa papaano mang anyo humarap siya, maging nararamtan ng matingkad na pula, napuputungan ng mga bulaklak at laurel, makapangyarihan at mayaman; maging malungkot at nag-iisa, nababalot ng basahan, at alipin, nagmamakaawa sa kanyang mga anak na alipin din; maging anaki'y diwata sa isang halamang maalindog, naliligid ng mga bughaw na alon ng karagatan, nakahahalina at marikit, gaya ng pangarap ng napaglalalangang kabataan; maging natatakpan ng isang lambong ng yelo, nakaupong malungkot sa mga dulo ng daigdig, sa silong ng isang langit na walang araw at walang tala; maging anuman ang kanyang ngalan, ang kanyang gulang o ang kanyang kapalaran, siya'y lagi na nating minamahal, gaya ng pagmamahal ng anak sa kanyang ina sa gitna ng gutom at ng karalitaan.

TAPOK AT BANLIK (Excerpt)
First Prize, Essay in Filipino, 2005 Palanca Awards
Dr. Luis P. Gatmaitan
Physician and Writer of Children's Stories

"Putik pong malinis ang karaniwang putik. Pero ang banlik po ay putik na ubod ng dumi kasi'y galing sa bundok," gayon ang paliwanag sa akin ng isang nanay sa Infanta nang bisitahin namin ang lugar nila upang magsagawa ng art therapy sa mga batang nakaligtas sa landslide. Paulit-ulit kasing nababanggit ng mga bata ang salitang banlik kapag sila'y nagbabahagi ng kanilang kuwento. Akala ko, nakasanayan lamang nilang tawaging banlik ang putik. Gaya ng may iba-iba tayong katawagan sa isang bagay sa isang partikular na lugar.

May pagkakaiba pala ang putik at banlik. Akala ko, kasukdulan na ng dumi kapag sinabing putik. Naiisip ko ang kalabaw ng aking Tatang na nakaugaliang maglublob sa putikan kapag tapos na ang maghapong pag-aararo. Hirap na kinukuskos ni Tatang ang katawan ng kalabaw upang matungkab ang natuyong putik na nakakulapol dito. Pero may antas pa pala ng pagiging marumi. Mas marumi ang gumuhong lupa mula sa kabundukan sapagkat dala-dala nito ang mga ugat ng puno, damo, kulisap, itlog ng ahas, at kung anu-ano pang alamat at elementong matatagpuan doon.

Mula sa mga guho ng Real, Infanta, at Nakar (na mas kilala sa katawagang REINA) sa Quezon, di na mabilang ang mga kuwentong narinig ko. Mga salaysay ito ng pagka-lubog at pagbangon mula sa banlik. Mga kuwentong marahil ay paulit-ulit na ikuku-wento ng mga batang nakaligtas para di nila malimutan ang mga ama, ina, lolo, lola, amain, tiyahin, pamangkin, apo, kapatid, kaibigan, at kalaro na inangkin ng rumara-gasang agos mula sa kabundukan isang gabing walang tigil ang pagbuhos ng ulan.

Aaminin ko, may daga sa aking dibdib nang una kong makaharap ang mga batang nakaligtas sa trahedya. Nandu'n ang pangamba ko na baka naiisip nilang 'kay lakas naman ng loob ng mamang ito na tumayo sa aming harapan gayong hindi naman niya talagang gagap ang tindi ng aming dinaanang tahedya.' O baka naman ganito ang nasa isip nila: 'hay naku, heto ulit ang isa pang grupo na pakukuwentuhin na naman kami nang nangyari sa amin hanggang sa kami'y maiyak!' Ewan ko ba pero noong una, parang nahihiya akong tumayo sa harap nila. Pakiramdam ko ba'y napapalibutan ako ng mga taong higit pa ang kakayahan kaysa sa 'kin. Ang mga batang kaharap ko ay mga batang nakayang lampasan ang kahindik-hindik na delubyong dumating sa Quezon! Hindi sila mga ordinaryong bata.

Sino nga ba kami para makialam sa kanilang buhay? Dumating na lang kami sa kanilang lugar nang walang kaabog-abog. Pero inari nila kaming mabuting kaibigan, waring mga piling panauhin sa isang magarang piging. Kapag ibinabahagi na sa amin ng mga bata ang kanilang naranasang sakit o takot, ramdam kong 'yun ang kanilang paraan ng pagsasabi ng 'mahalaga po sa amin na nandito kayo.' Sa pagbubukas nila ng loob sa amin, nasaksihan ko ang dakilang himala ng pakikipagkapwa-damdamin.

Sabi ng isang kaibigan ko, "ang mga bata raw ang nagsisilbing barometrong panukat ng isang komunidad. Kaya makabubuting pagmasdan ang kanilang hitsura't galaw, at mapakinggan ang kanilang sinasabi o di sinasabi."

Totoo 'yun. Dahil paano nga ba maitatago ang nararanasang paghihikahos ng pamilya kung ang kilik na bata ay maputla ang balat, malaki ang tiyan, litaw ang butuhing dibdib, at walang kislap ang mga mata? Paano nga ba maililihim ang bunga ng nagdaang sakuna sa mga bata samantalang may mga gabing dinadalaw sila ng ban-gungot, pag-ihi sa banig, at pangangatal sa pagkaalala ng sakuna? Mahirap lurukin ang kalagayan ng isang komunidad kung ang pagbabatayan ay ang sinasabi ng kanilang tatay, nanay, at iba pang matatanda sa pamilya. Kayang-kayang kasing itago ng mga magulang ang lahat ng kanilang nararamdaman. Kaya nila kaming papaniwalain na ayos lang ang lahat kahit hindi. Iba ang mga bata.

Sa Real ko nakita ang batang kamukha ni Frankenstein. Nang makilala ko si Bunso, si Frankenstein ang unang pumasok sa aking isip. Paano kasi, punong-puno ng tahi ang kanyang ulo, batok, at leeg (para talagang 'yung karakter na si Frankenstein sa pelikula). Nangawit kaya ang kamay ng mga siruhano nang inoperahan nila ang batang ito? Sangkaterbang pilat ang iniwang alaala ng sakuna sa mukha at katawan ni Bunso.

"Nadaganan po siya nang gumuho ang Repador Building," paliwanag agad ng isang guro nang makita niyang waring nagtatanong ang aking mga mata sa hitsura ng batang kaharap ko. "Hindi po siya nakita agad. Akala nga po nila ay patay na si Bunso. Mabuti't nadala sa Maynila para maoperahan ang nabasag niyang bungo."

Mula noon, tuwing titingnan ko si Bunso, nahahabag ako. Kung ako kaya ang nasa katayuan niya, makakaya ko kaya ang sinuong niya? Walang sinabi sa mga tahing nasa mukha at ulo ni Bunso ang aking nag-iisang keloid bunga ng inoperahang seba-ceous cyst sa aking likod. E, paano pa kaya ang mga pilat ni Bunso na di ko nakikita? Pihadong nag-iwan ng malalalim na pilat sa kanyang murang puso ang sakuna.

Kung nasa ibang lugar lamang si Bunso, pihadong panay tukso ang matatanggap niya mula sa ilang pilyong bata dahil sa kanyang kakaibang hitsura. Pero dito sa Real, walang nangahas bumiro kay Bunso. Siguro kasi'y ang karanasan ni Bunso ay karana-san din ng buong bayan. Ang bawat isang tahi sa mukha at ulo ni Bunso ay nagpapalu-tang lamang sa kanyang katapangan.

Hindi sinasadya'y naalala ko ang mga batang may kanser sa aming pagamutan. Sila man ay parang si Bunso rin sa maraming pagkakataon. Nasa isang sitwasyon sila na kahit tayong matatanda na ay mahihirapan din. Hindi biro-biro ang diagnosis na kanser para sa sinumang kaanak. Ang aming mga anghel, di pa man nakababasa ng alpabeto, ay hindi rin ipinuwera ng sakit na ito. Sinong magulang ang hindi madudurog ang puso kapag nakita niyang tinitiis ng minumutyang anak ang hapdi ng turok ng karayom sa kemoterapi?

Pero kagaya ng mga batang nakaligtas sa trahedya ng Quezon, ang mga bata ring ito ay di nawawalan ng pag-asa na gagaling sila. Kapag nasimulan na ang kanilang kemoterapi, nagsisimulang malagas ang kanilang buhok kasabay ng pagpatay ng gamot sa mababagsik na cancer cells. Pagkatapos, mistulang isang komunidad na na-wash out ang hitsura ng ulo ng aming mga paslit. Pero nandun ang pag-asa na maaaring malampasan nila ang sakit na kanser.

Hitik sa kuwento, games, at activity ang tatlong araw na kasama namin sila. Nakatulong din na palagi kong bitbit ang aking digital camera. Manipis kasi ito at maliit lang kaya madaling ilagay sa bulsa. Sa tuwing pipindutin ko ito, una-unahang nagpo-pose ang mga bata para sa kodakan. Pagkatapos ay titingnan din kaagad ang picture nila, magtatawanan o magtutuksuhan ayon sa nakitang hitsura sa kamera. Minsan nga ay sila pa ang nagpipriprisintang magpakuha ng litrato. Agad kong nakuha ang loob nila. Laking pasasalamat ko sa aking digital camera. Nakapasok ako sa mundo ng mga bata nang di sinasadya. Sa bawat klik ng kamera, palapit nang palapit ang loob namin sa isa't isa.

Noong unang araw, sinadya naming huwag munang sumalat sa trahedyang sinapit nila. Gusto lang naming magbukas sila ng kanilang mga sarili. At dahil mga lupa at banlik ang tumabon sa kanilang mga bahay at buhay, ninais namin na sa pagpapakilala nila sa kanilang sarili ay dumampot sila ng isang bagay mula sa paligid na kumakatawan sa kanila. Gusto naming bumalik ang tiwala nila sa bundok, lupa, puno, at bato.

"Kagaya po ako ng batong ito," pakilala ni Cynthia. "Ang ibig ko pong sabihin, matibay po ako, hindi kaagad madudurog. At saka, noong tumatakas po kami, mga matitigas na batong kagaya nito ang hinahanap naming tuntungan para hindi kami malubog sa banlik."

May mga dala rin kaming librong pambata para ikuwento. Subalit sa bawat kuwentong isinasalaysay ko, humuhugot sila sa nagdaang sakuna upang idugtong sa aming kuwento. Kung tutuusin, walang kinalaman sa bagyo o baha ang isang kuwentong isinalaysay ko. Tungkol ito sa pagmamahal ng isang sapaterong ama sa isang anak na ipinanganak na putol ang dalawang paa. Sa naturang kuwento, palihim palang gumagawa ng sapatos ang ama upang ialay sa anak niya. Kapag nalalapit na ang kaarawan ng bata, pilit na iniimadyin ng ama ang lumalaking sukat ng paa ng anak niya. Ngunit lingid sa kaalaman ng ama, napapanaginipan pala ng anak na walang paa ang mga sapatos na nililikha para sa kanya sa tuwing bisperas ng kaarawan niya.

Matapos ang pagkukuwento, hiniling ko sa mga bata na lumikha ng isang pares ng sapatos para sa bidang batang babae sa kuwento, at kailangang kumbinsihin nila ako na ang kanilang sapatos ang dapat kong piliin. Nagulat ako nang makitang karamihan ay bota ang iginuhit. Yung isang grupo ay nagdrowing ng botang may mataas na takong. Yung isang grupo pa ay gumuhit ng sapatos na convertible sa bota at ipinagdiinan pang ang sapatos nila ay water-resistant. Kasi raw, nang mga sumunod na araw matapos ang sakuna, mga bota na ang kanilang sapin sa paa. Natuwa ako na iginawa nila ng pambihirang bota ang batang bida sa libro. Ayaw raw nilang marumhan ng banlik ang bago nilang kaibigan.

Iniiwasan ko pa sanang banggitin ang nagdaang sakuna. Sa isip-isip ko, tatalakayin namin ito sa mga susunod pang araw. Pero ipinahiwatig na nilang handa na silang harapin ang kani-kanilang kuwento, katunayan ang mga iginuhit nilang sapatos na pambaha.

Tinanong namin ng kasama kong facilitator kung ano ang limang mahahalagang bagay na ililigtas nila sakaling may mangyaring sakuna. Maraming sumagot na ang ililigtas nila ay ang kanilang uniporme at gamit sa eskuwelahan (na para bang magka-kalakas-loob pa ang mga prinsipal ng mga eskuwelahan na ideklarang may pasok kina-bukasan). 'Yung iba, TV at pridyider ang gustong iligtas, na siyempre pa'y sinundan ng tawanan. Kahit yata sanrekwang adrenaline ang ipundar ng katawan, hindi kakayanin ng mga paslit na ito na buhatin ang kanilang pridyider!

Pero sa ilan, mga tao ang kanilang binanggit na ililigtas. Sa kanila, hindi mahalaga na "ano" ang tanong namin, kundi "sino" ang ililigtas nila. Mula sa mga sagot na damit, pagkain, notebook, telebisyon, at pridyider, lumabas ang pangalan ng kanilang lolo't lola, tatay, nanay, kapatid, at pamangkin.

Hanggang ngayon, hindi mawala sa isip ni May kung paanong nakabitaw ang lola niya sa kanyang kamay noong tinatangay sila ng rumaragasang agos. Hindi na nakita pa ang lola niya, nalibing sa natuyong banlik sa kung saan. At si May, hindi niya mapa-tawad ang sarili na hindi niya nailigtas ang lola niya. Di lang si May ang nagbahagi nito kundi ilan pang batang pipituhin o wawaluhing gulang na pawang nakangabitaw sa mahigpit na pagkakakapit sa mga kaanak nila. Nandu'n ang masidhing pagnanais na mailigtas ang kapamilyang minamahal. Kung tutuusin, kasama sa mga karapatan ng mga batang kagaya nina May ang unang mailigtas sa panahon ng trahedya. Pero para sa mga batang kagaya nila, higit na mahalagang nailigtas nila ang mahihina na nilang lolo't lola o ang mga nakababatang kapatid na karga-karga nila. Napag-isip-isip ko, sa panahon pala ng sakuna, nagbabagong-anyo ang mga bata. Gusto nilang maging tagapagligtas. Gaya ng napapanuod nilang cartoons sa TV na inililigtas ng superhero ang mga biktima.

Nang inaakala naming palagay na ang loob nila sa amin, hiniling namin sa kanila na isulat o idrowing ang naganap noong gabi ng Nobyembre 29, 2004. Naupod ang mga krayolang kulay-brown sa kanilang mga iginuhit. Nagkulay-tsokolate ang kanilang mga papel. Nagmistulang dagat iyon ng tsokolate, parang mga kumunoy na walang katapusan, inaangkin ang bawat batang nahuhulog doon.

Sabi ni Raymond, nagulat na lang sila sa napakabilis na pagtaas ang tubig. Wala na silang panahon pang maka-tapok (lengguwaheng Quezon para sa 'paglikas sa matataas na lugar'). Ang tanging nakita ng Nanay niya na mataas ay ang magkatabing puno ng abokado sa kanilang bakuran. Agad nila itong inakyat. Mahigpit na kumapit doon habang ginaw na ginaw, kasama ang isa pa niyang pamangkin. Sa kabilang puno, doon naman umakyat ang Nanay niya, ang ate niya, at isa pang pamangkin. Ngunit hindi naging mabait sa kanila ang mga punong ito. Nabali ito at sapilitang tinangay ang Nanay niya at dalawang pamangkin. Sila na lamang ng kanyang ate ang natira.

Nanlambot ako nang marinig ang kuwento ni Raymond. Hindi sila nailigtas ng matatayog na puno sa kanilang bakuran. Nag-uunahang pumatak ang luha sa mga mata ni Raymond sa pagkaalala sa ina at mga kalarong pamangkin. Paano pa ako kakain ng abokado gayong sa bawat pagbanggit ng prutas na ito ay ibinabalik sa aking gunita ang alaala ng pamilya ni Raymond?

Iisa ang hitsura ng kanilang drowing: mga bahay na nakalubog sa banlik at bubong lang ang makikita, mga taong nakatalungko sa bubungan, mga taong nakakapit sa mga sanga ng puno, mga bahay na inaanod ng rumaragasang banlik, mga nabunot na puno at troso, nalulunod na kalabaw, baboy, at aso. Nagulat pa ako dahil kahit stick figure lamang ang iginuhit ng karamihan, malinaw pa ring nakasaad doon kung ano ang kasarian o kung bata o matanda ang nakita nilang nalunod!

"Matandang babae po itong nalunod na ito," sabay turo sa drowing. "Ito naman po ay batang lalaki."

Sa narinig ay pilit gumagawa ng koneksyon ang aking naririnding utak. Magkaano-ano kaya ang matandang babae at batang lalaki? Maglola kaya ang dalawa? O baka wala naman talaga silang kaugnayan sa isa't isa. Sabay lamang silang nalunod.

Hindi rin nakaligtas sa drowing ng mga bata ang buwan, ulan, at kidlat. Napansin ko agad ang kakaibang hitsura ng buwan. Nilagyan nila ito ng mukha. Nakalabi ang buwan!

"Kasi po, sobrang lungkot noong gabing 'yon. Pulos hiyawan at iyakan ang maririnig. Maraming namatay. Maraming nawalan ng bahay. Nakakatakot ang mga troso at banlik. Parang umiiyak ang langit sa nangyari. Kaya naglagay po ako ng umiiyak na buwan."

Kakaiba rin ang sinulat na kuwento ni Jenny. Kapansin-pansin na magaling siyang humagod ng mga salita. Nang gabing 'yon, maaga raw siyang nahiga sa kama. Masarap daw matulog dahil malakas ang ulan. Makapal na kumot ang gamit niya. Akala niya'y panaginip ngunit nagising na lang siyang mistulang dagat na ang kanyang silid.

Nagkakagulo na ang kanyang buong pamilya. Nag-aapurang lumikas silang lahat patungo sa kanugnog na bundok, ingat na ingat na huwag madapa o malubog sa rumaragasang banlik. Tinapos niya ang maigsing sanaysay sa pagbanggit ng mga kaanak na nakaligtas.

"Mabuti naman at nakaligtas ang buong pamilya mo sa sakuna," sabi ko kay Jenny.

Hindi ko inaasahan ang tugon ni Jenny. "H-Hindi po."

Dito na unti-unting nanginig ang tinig ni Jenny. Sa paputol-putol na kuwento ay nalaman kong kasama palang inanod ang kanyang ina, at di na rin natagpuan pa. Pinalaya na niya ang luha na kanina pa pilit pinipigil.

Maingat ang pagkukuwento ni Jenny. Hindi niya binanggit ang kinahinatnan ng kanyang magulang. Kung ang pagbabatayan ko lamang ay ang sinulat na sanaysay ni Jenny, hindi ko iisiping may matinding nangyari sa pamilya ni Jenny. Sinadya niyang iwasan sa kanyang kuwento ang sinapit ng kanyang ina.

Sabi ng nanay ko, kapag sobrang masakit na raw ang nangyayari sa atin, di man sinasadya ay pilit tumatakas ang gunita. Gumagawa ito ng sariling paniniwalaan para malampasan niya ang personal na trahedya. Ayaw na ni Jenny na isiping may nawala sa kanya kaya hindi na niya ito ikinuwento pa. Pero nasukol si Jenny ng aking tanong kaya napilitan siyang magtapat. Noon lamang niya inamin ang pagkamatay ng nanay niya. Nang mga sandaling 'yun, pakiramdam ko, napakapakialamero ko. Nabulabog ko nang di sinasadya ang kanyang pananahimik.

Iyon din siguro ang dahilan kung bakit ang batang Frankenstein na si Bunso ay ayaw magbigay ng salaysay. Ayaw nitong magsulat ng kahit ano. "Baka puwedeng magdrowing na lamang," payo ko pa. Pero iniwasan din nito ang mga krayolang ibinigay namin. Hinayaan na lamang namin si Bunso na sumali sa lahat ng aktibidad namin: kasali sa larong "Open the basket", kasama ring umaawit sa kanilang "group cheer", kasabay na kumakain ng iba pang bata, nagtataas ng kamay para sa libreng kopya ng libro matapos ang aking pagkukuwento. Kapag makakasalubong ko siya, matipid siyang ngingiti kapag binabati. Pero ang kapansin-pansin sa kanya, kung ako'y nagpapahinga sa isang sulok, basta na lamang siyang tatabi sa aking kinauupuan, hahaplusin ang aking braso, o hahawakan ang aking palad. Minsan naman, napapansin kong nakakapit siya sa kamay ng iba pang nakatatanda sa kanya.

Iginalang ko ang pananahimik ni Bunso. Walang kaso kung wala siyang maalala sa nangyari. May kapangyarihan naman talaga ang ating isip na limutin ang mga pang-yayari na hindi nakalulugod sa atin. Hanggang sa nakita niyang nagtapat ang lahat ng kanyang kasama sa nangyari sa kanilang buhay. Nakita niya kung paanong umiyak at humagulgol ang mga kapwa bata matapos ibahagi sa grupo ang kanilang isinulat o iginuhit. Noon nagkalakas-loob si Bunso na basagin ang pananahimik.

Siya ang pinakahuling batang pumunta sa harap at nagkuwento ng buhay. Wala siyang artwork o sinulat na sanaysay. Pero naikuwento niya, sa pagitan ng hikbi, ang nangyari. Nagpunta sila sa Repador building sa pag-aakalang ligtas dito kasama ang kanyang tatay, isang kapatid, at lola. Bigla na lamang daw may gumuho sa loob ng building, at basta na lamang siyang tumalsik. Naiwan sa guho ng Repador ang kanyang magulang at kapatid. Hindi na niya nalaman kung ano ang nangyari sa kanila.

Dinugtungan na lamang ng mga guro ang nangyari ky Bunso. Kung paanong ito'y natagpuang nakaipit sa mga guho. Kung paanong inilipad ito ng helikopter patungong Maynila para operahan ang bungong nabasag. Hindi na nahukay pa sa guho ang mga mahal ni Bunso, sama-sama nang nalibing doon. Masisisi ko ba si Bunso kung waring nabura na sa kanyang gunita ang sinapit ng mga kaanak?

PAMBANSANG AWIT NG PILIPINAS
Composed by Julian Felipe, Original Spanish lyrics by **Jose Palma**
Filipino lyrics by the Institute of National Language

Bayang magiliw
Perlas ng Silanganan
Alab ng puso
Sa dibdib mo'y buhay

Lupang hinirang
Duyan ka ng magiting
Sa manlulupig
Di ka pasisiil

Sa dagat at bundok
Sa simoy at sa langit mong bughaw
May dilag ang tula at awit
Sa paglayang minamahal

Ang kislap ng watawat mo'y
Tagumpay na nagniningning
Ang bituin at araw niya'y
Kailan pa ma'y di magdidilim

Lupa ng araw ng luwalhati't pagsinta
Buhay ay langit sa piling mo
Aming ligaya na pag may mang-aapi
Ang mamatay nang dahil sa iyo!

SA AKING KABABATA
Dr. Jose P. Rizal (1861–1896)
National hero, Philippines
(written when Rizal was eight years old)

Kapagka ang baya'y sadyang umiibig
Sa kanyang salitang kaloob ng langit,
Sanglang kalayaan nasa ring masapit
Katulad ng ibong nasa himpapawid.

Pagka't ang salita'y isang kahatulan
Sa bayan, sa nayo't mga kaharian,
At ang isang tao'y katulad, kabagay
Ng alin mang likha noong kalayaan.

Ang hindi magmahal sa kanyang salita
Mahigit sa hayop at malansang isda,
Kaya ang marapat pagyamaning kusa
Na tulad sa inang tunay na nagpala.

Ang wikang Tagalog tulad din sa Latin
Sa Ingles, Kastila at salitang anghel,
Sapagka't ang Poong maalam tumingin
Ang siyang naggawad, nagbigay sa atin.

Ang salita nati'y huwad din sa iba
Na may alfabeto at sariling letra,
Na kaya nawala'y dinatnan ng sigwa
Ang lunday sa lawa noong dakong una.

PAG-IBIG SA TINUBUANG LUPA
Andres C. Bonifacio (1863–1897)
Philippine hero and Father of the Philippine revolution

Aling pag-ibig pa ang hihigit kaya
sa pagkadalisay at magkadakila
Gaya ng pag-ibig sa sariling lupa?
Aling pag-ibig pa? Wala na nga, wala.

Pagpupuring lubos ang palaging hangad
Sa bayan ng taong may dangal na ingat,
Umawit, tumula, kumata't at sumulat,
Kalakhan din niya'y isinisiwalat.

Walang mahalagang hindi inihandog
Ng may pusong wagas sa Bayang nagkupkop,

Dugo, yaman, dunong, katiisa't pagod,
Buhay ma'y abuting magkalagut-lagot.

Bakit? Alin ito na sakdal ng laki,
Na hinahandugan ng busong pagkasi,
Na sa lalong mahal nakapangyayari,
At ginugulan ng buhay na iwi?

Ay! Ito'y ang inang bayang tinubuan:
Siya'y una't tangi sa kinamulatan
Ng kawili-wiling liwanang ng araw
Na nagbigay-init sa buong katawan.

Kalakip din nito'y pag-ibig sa bayan,
Ang lahat ng lalong sa gunita'y mahal,
Mula sa masaya'y gasong kasanggulan
Hanggang sa katawa'y mapasa-libingan.

Sa aba ng abang mawalay sa bayan!
Gunita ma'y laging sakbibi ng lumbay,
Walang alaala't inaasam-asam
Kundi ang makita'y lupang tinubuan.

Pati ng magdusa'y sampung kamatayan
Wari ay masarap kung dahil sa bayan
At lalong mahirap. Oh, himalang bagay!
Lalong pag-irog pa ang sa kanya'y alay.

Kung ang bayang ito'y masasa-panganib
At siya ay dapat na ipagtangkilik,
Ang anak, asawa, magulang, kapatid;
Isang tawag niya'y tatalikdang pilit.

Hayo na nga, hayo, kayong nangabuhay
Sa pag-asang lubos ng kaginhawahan
At walang tinamo kundi kapaitan,
Hayo na't ibangon ang naabang bayan!

Kayong nalagasan ng bunga't bulaklak
Kahoy niyaring buhay na nilanta't sukat,
Ng bala-balaki't makapal na hirap,
Muling manariwa't sa baya'y lumiyag.

Ipahandug-handog ang buong pag-ibig
At hanggang may dugo'y ubusing itigis;
Kung sa pagtatanggol, buhay ay mapatid,
Ito'y kapalaran at tunay na langit!

ANO ANG PAGKAIBA NG FILIPINO SA TAGALOG? (Excerpt)
Isagani R. Cruz
Educator and Writer

Ngayon nama'y singkronik ang gagamitin kong pamaraan para pag-ibahin ang Filipino at Tagalog. Gagamitin kong texto ang orihinal sa Filipino at ang salin sa Tagalog ng unang pangungusap sa Seksyon 2.2.2 ng *Palisi sa Wika ng Unibersidad ng Pilipinas* (1992).

FILIPINO: Magiging boluntaryo ang pagturo sa Filipino.
TAGALOG: Ang pagtuturo sa Filipino ay kusangloob.

Pansinin ang balangkas ng pangungusap. Sa Filipino'y una ang panaguri, tulad ng napansin nina [Fe] Otanes. Sa Tagalog ay ginagamit ang panandang *ay*. Sa pormal na gamit ng Tagalog ay talagang ginagamit ang *ay*. Pormal ang gamit ng Filipino, dahil ito nga ang opisyal na palisi ng Unibersidad ng Pilipinas, pero hindi ginagamit ang ay. Ito ang unang pagkaiba ng Filipino sa Tagalog. Pormal o lebel-panulat ang karaniwang ayos ng pangungusap na walang ay. Pansinin ang pagkawala ng pag-ulit ng unang pantig ng salitang-ugat na turo. Ang salitang pagtuturo ay Tagalog; ang salitang pagturo ay Filipino. Ayon kay Teresita Maceda na naging Direktor ng Sentro ng Wikang Filipino sa Unibersidad ng Pilipinas, ang dahilan sa pag-alis ng pag-ulit ng unang pantig ng salitang-ugat ay ang impluwensiya ng mga wikang bernakular na tulad ng Cebuano. Nahihirapan daw ang mga Bisaya na mag-ulit ng pantig, kung kayat nagiging katawatawa o hindi istandard ang pagsalita ng Bisaya ng Tagalog. Pero sa wikang Filipino'y iba na. Hindi na kailangang mahiya ang Bisaya dahil tama na ang ugaling Bisaya sa paggamit ng panlapi at salitang-ugat. Ito ang ikalawang pagkaiba ng Filipino sa Tagalog. Inuulit ang pantig ng salitang-ugat o ang pantig ng panlapi sa Tagalog; hindi na kailangang ulitin ang mga pantig sa Filipino.

Pansinin ang paggamit ng hiram na salita mula sa Ingles sa pangungusap na Filipino. Sa halip ng kusangloob na taal na Tagalog ay boluntaryo mula sa voluntary ang ginagamit sa Filipino. (Sa totoo lang ay dapat na boluntari ang halaw sa voluntary, pero naging siokoy na boluntaryo, na hango naman sa voluntario, pero hindi sa Kastila kundi sa Ingles nanggaling ang pagkasiokoy ng salita.) Mas laganap kasi sa kamaynilaan ang salitang voluntary kaysa kusangloob. Madalas nating marinig ang salitang voluntary kung may humihingi ng kontribusyon o kung may naghahakot para dumami ang dadalo sa isang lektyur o kung may nagsisimula ng organisasyon. Bihira natin marinig ang kusangloob. Sa Filipino ay karaniwang ginagamit ang mas madalas gamitin. Ito ang ikatlong pagkaiba ng Filipino sa Tagalog. Mas hawak sa leeg ang Tagalog ng panulatan o matandang gamit ng salita; mas nakikinig sa talagang ginagamit o sinasalita ang Filipino.

Pansinin na hindi sa Kastila humiram ng salita kundi sa Ingles. Sa Tagalog, kahit na sa makabagong Tagalog, kapag humihiram ng salita'y unang naghahanap sa wikang Kastila, bago maghanap sa wikang Ingles. Ganyan ang mungkahi ni [Virgilio] Almario at ng maraming nauna sa kanya. Ito ang ikapat na pagkaiba ng Filipino sa Tagalog. Kahit na sa makabagong Tagalog ay Kastila pa rin ang wikang karaniwang hinihiraman; sa Filipino'y Ingles ang karaniwang hinihiraman, dahil nga Taglish ang ugat ng Filipino.

Samakatwid ay apat ang pagkaiba ng Filipino sa Tagalog batay lamang sa iisang pangungusap na hango sa palisi ng Unibersidad ng Pilipinas. Kung pag-aaralan natin ang buong palisi na nakasulat sa Filipino at ang buong salin nito sa wikang Tagalog ay sigurado akong mas marami tayong makikitang pagkaiba ng Filipino sa Tagalog. Iyon lamang pangailangan na isalin ang textong Filipino sa Tagalog ay patunay na na magkaiba ang dalawang wika.

Ngayon nama'y magbibigay ako ng ilang feature na sa palagay ko'y nagdidiferensyeyt sa Filipino at Tagalog. Dahil hindi naman ako linggwista'y hindi ko mapapatunayan na palatandaan nga ang mga ito ng pagkaiba, pero ibibigay ko ang mga ito para mairiserts ng ibang iskolar. Ipapaubaya ko na sa mga nag-aral ng lingguwistika ang pagpatunay o pagwalang-saysay sa mga natuklasan kong ibang feature ng Filipino sa Tagalog.

Una, sa Tagalog ay hindi ginagamit ang panghalip na **siya** para tukuyin ang hindi tao, pero sa Filipino ay karaniwan nang ginagamit ang **siya** para sa mga bagay. Halimbawa'y "Maganda siya." Maaaring hindi tao at hindi man lamang buhay ang tinutukoy ng **siya**; maaaring kotse o damit o kulay.

Ikalawa, sa Tagalog ay hindi karaniwang dinaragdagan ng **-s** ang isang pangngalang isahan para gawing maramihan ito. Sa halip ay gumagamit ng pantukoy, pamilang, o pang-uri na tulad ng napansin ni Santos. Pero sa Filipino ay madalas gamitin ang **-s** para gawing maramihan ang isang pangngalan. Ang una kong narinig na gumamit ng feature na ito ay ang mga taga-Davao noon pa mang 1969. Doon, ang dalawa o higit pang softdrink na coke ay cokes. Sa kamaynilaan ngayon, hindi ginagamit ang Tagalog na mga parent ko kundi ang Filipinong parents ko; halimbawa'y sa "strict ang parents ko."

Dapat kong banggitin dito ang pananaw ni Matute. Ang sabi niya tungkol sa salitang **barongs** ay ito:

Bakit **barongs** ang tawag namin, ang itinatanong mo, Kabataan? Hindi ba iyan ang dating tinaguriang barong Tagalog? Oo. Ngunit dumami na nang dumami ang allergic, pinamamantalan ng punong taynga sa salitang Tagalog. Gaya na nga ang Wikang Tagalog, hindi Wikang Filipino. Kaya, inalis na ang salitang Tagalog sa salitang barong Tagalog. Ginawang barong na lamang, ngunit sapagkat sa Ingles, kapag marami'y dinaragdagan ng titik **s**, kaya't ang barong ay naging barongs. Bakit bumilis ang bigkas? A, iyan ay sapagkat ang Pasay man ay naging Pasay (mabilis) na at ang Davao ay naging Davao (mabilis) na. Kaya bakit ang barongs ay hindi magiging barongs (mabilis)?

Mapapansin na pati si [Genoveva Edroza] Matute ay naniniwalang iba ang wikang Tagalog sa wikang Filipino. Hindi nga lamang siya kumikiling sa wikang Filipino, pero inaamin niya na iba ang wikang ito sa wikang kinagisnan niya bilang manunulat sa Tagalog. Siya na nga mismo, sa aking pagkaalam, ang unang nakapansin sa paggamit ng **-s** bilang palatandaan ng pagkamaramihan.

Ikatlo, sa Davao ko pa rin unang narinig ang paggamit ng **mag-** sa halip ng **-um-** sa mga pandiwa. Hindi karaniwang umaakyat ng bahay ang Davaoeños, kundi nag-aakyat o nag-akyat. Kung sabagay ay sa timog-katagalugan ay talaga namang napapalitan ang **-um-**ng **mag-**; sa Parañaque lamang, na napakalapit na sa Maynila, ay nakain sila sa halip ng kumain. Sa madaling salita, hindi nakakapagtaka na sa Filipino ay mas madalas gamitin ang **mag-** kaysa sa **-um-**. Gaya nga ng sinabi ni Ma. Lourdes Bautista sa isang papel na binasa niya noong 1989 sa kumperensya ng Language Education Council of the Philippines: "It is clear that the affix used for English verbs in actor focus is **mag-** and never **-um-** (perhaps because it is easier to use a prefix than an infix), and therefore this reinforces the predominance of **mag-** over **-um-**."

Ikaapat, at ito'y suhestyon ni Barry Miller. Sa Tagalog ay **i-** ang ginagamit sa tinatawag nina Otanes na benefactive-focus na pandiwa. Ang **-an** ay karaniwang directional focus. Ito ang dahilan kung bakit, sa libro nina Teresita Ramos at Bautista tungkol sa mga pandiwa ay ibili ang benefactive-focus at bilhan ang directional focus. Sa Tagalog, ang karaniwan nating sinasabi kung nakikibili tayo sa McDonald's ay "Ibili mo nga ako ng hamburger." Sa Filipino, ang karaniwan nating sinasabi ay "Bilhan mo nga ako ng hamburger." (Natural, kung dalawang sandwich ang ipinabibili natin, sa Tagalog ay sasabihin nating "Ibili mo nga ako ng dalawang hamburger." Sa Filipino ay sinasabi nating "Bilhan mo nga ako ng dalawang hamburgers.")

Ikalima, sa Tagalog ay laging inaalis ang sobra sa isang katinig sa isang klaster ng katinig kung inuulit ang isang pantig. Halimbawa'y nagpiprisinta ang sinasabi sa Tagalog dahil ginagawang **p** na lang ang klaster na **pr** sa inuulit na pantig na **pri**. Sa Filipino ay ginagamit ang buong klaster; samakatwid, nagpriprisinta o magprapraktis. Hindi na takot sa klaster ang Filipino, di tulad ng Tagalog na hangga't maaari'y umii-was sa nagkukumpul-kumpulang katinig.

Ikaanim, dahil laganap na ang Filipino sa kabisayaan ay hindi na maaaring ibatay lamang ito sa Tagalog na tulad ng nais mangyari ng mga Tagalista. Napakarami ng mga Bisaya at hindi makatarungan na sila ang babagay sa mga Tagalog gayung napakaunlad na ng lunsod ng Cebu at lingua franca ng Bisayas at Mindanaw ang wikang Cebuano. Isang pagkaiba ng Cebuano sa Tagalog ay ang kawalan ng mga salitang panggalang na **po** at **ho**. Kung pag-iisahin tayo ng wikang Filipino at hindi paghihiwahiwalayin ay dapat huwag ipagpilitan ng mga Tagalog na gumamit ng **po** at **ho** ang mga Bisaya. Hindi naman nangangahulugan ito na walang galang sa matanda o sa kapwa ang mga Bisaya; sa katunayan ay kasinggalang ang mga Bisaya ng mga Tagalog sa kanilang mga magulang at iba pang karaniwang pinag-uukulan ng galang. Pero wala sa wika ng mga Bisaya ang mga salitang panggalang na **po** at **ho**. Hindi tao ang pinag-uusapan dito kundi wika. Sa wikang Cebuano ay hindi tanda ng paggalang ang paglagay ng **po** at **ho**. Samakatwid, sa wikang Filipino ay hindi dapat siguro isama ang **po** at **ho**. Gamitin na lamang ito sa Tagalog o sa diyalekto ng Filipino na ginagamit sa katagalugan.

Anim na pagkaibang estruktural ang naibigay ko para namnamin ng ating mga ling-gwista. Maliliit na bagay ang mga ito, pero makabuluhan kung mapatunayan. Ngayon nama'y babalikan ko ang malaking isyu tungkol sa relasyon ng Filipino sa Tagalog.

Diyalekto lamang ba ng Tagalog ang Filipino? Ito ang palagay ni Ma. Lourdes Bautista. Maaari, at ito'y hindi dapat problemahin dahil sa kasaysayan ng wikang Ingles ay diyalekto lamang ng Englisc ang East Midland nang ito'y ginamit ni Chaucer sa London. Pero ang diyalektong ito sa London ang naging kasalukuyang tinatawag nating Ingles. Kung diyalekto man ng Tagalog ang Filipino ng kamaynilaan ay pansamantala lamang naman ito. Sa susunod na mga dantaon ay tatawagin na itong Filipino at kaka-limutan na ang Tagalog kung saan ito nagmula, gaya ng pagtalikod ng kasaysayan sa iba pang diyalekto ng Englisc. Samakatwid ay hindi ako sang-ayon kay Otanes na ang Filipino at ang Tagalog ay parehong wika kung estruktura at balarila ang pinag-uusa-pan at nagkakaiba lamang sila sa larangan ng sosyolinggwistika. Sa palagay ko'y iba ang Filipino sa Tagalog kahit na estruktura at balarila ang pag-uusapan. Ang kanyang diniscrayb sa kanyang libro'y Filipino at hindi Tagalog. Aksidente lamang ng kasaysay-an na hindi pa naiimbento ang salitang Filipino noong panahong sinusulat ni Otanes ang kanyang gramatika, pero siya ang kaunaunahang nakapansin na may Educated Manila Tagalog na dapat seryosohin. Kaya nga, kapag isinalin ang Reference Grammar sa Filipino ay dapat tawagin itong Gramatika ng Filipino sa halip ng Gramatika ng Tagalog. Sa ganitong paraan ay lilinaw ang kasaysayan ng ating wikang pambansa. Kung si Lope K. Santos ang gumawa ng balarila ng Tagalog, si Fe T. Otanes naman ang gumawa ng gramatika ng Filipino.

May kongklusyon ba ako? Mayroon. Nagsimula ako sa pamagitan ng pagbanggit ng mga teoretikal na prinsipyong aking pinaniniwalaan, isa na nga ang ginawa ni Gonzalez sa Philippine English. Pagkatapos ay nagbigay ako ng ilang halimbawa ng totoong gamit ng wika ng ating mga tinitingalang manunulat, upang patunayan na hindi tama ang karaniwan nating akala ukol sa balarila. Pagkatapos kong magbigay ng kasaysayan ng Filipino na batay sa kasaysayan ng wikang Ingles ay pinuna ko ang ilang katangian ng wikang Filipino na iba sa wikang Tagalog. Ano ang patutunguhan ng lahat ng ito?

Sa aking palagay, ang perents sa larangan ng wika ay ang mga sikat na writer na tulad nina [Fren] Abueg, Almario, Lualhati Bautista at [B.S.] Medina [Jr.]. Kung totoo nga na ang ginagawa ng perents ay inaakalang tama ng kabataan, masasabi nating inaakala at nagiging tama ang talagang ginagawa ng ating mga batikang manunulat. Hindi ko ipinakita na ito rin ang ginagawa ng nakararaming Filipino sa kasalukuyan. Pero nai-pakita ko, sa palagay ko, na kung ang pinakamagandang gamit ang pagbatayan, ang wikang umiiral ngayon sa paligid natin, lalo na sa labas ng katagalugan, ay Filipino at hindi Tagalog. Naipakita ko na rin sana na may pagkaiba, maliit man o malaki, ang Filipino sa Tagalog.

(With permission from the author. Material is accessible at http://isaganircruz.blog-spot.com/2006/10/ano-ang-pagkaiba-ng-filipino-sa.html.)

LIST OF ONLINE AUDIO RECORDINGS

Lesson 01
Lesson 02
Lesson 03
Lesson 04
Lesson 05
Lesson 06
Lesson 07
Lesson 08
Lesson 09
Lesson 10
Lesson 11
Lesson 12
Lesson 13
Lesson 14
Lesson 15

Lesson 16
Lesson 17
Lesson 18
Lesson 19
Lesson 20
Lesson 21
Lesson 22
Lesson 23
Lesson 24
Lesson 25
Lesson 26
Lesson 27
Lesson 28
Lesson 29
Lesson 30

Lesson 31
Lesson 32
Lesson 33
Lesson 34
Lesson 35
Lesson 36
Lesson 37
Lesson 38
Lesson 39
Lesson 40
Lesson 41
Lesson 42
Lesson 43
Lesson 44

Subfolder (Dialogues/Vocabulary)

Lesson 03 Dialogue
Lesson 03 Vocabulary
Lesson 04 Dialogue
Lesson 04 Vocabulary
Lesson 05 Dialogue
Lesson 05 Vocabulary
Lesson 06 Dialogue
Lesson 06 Vocabulary
Lesson 07 Dialogue
Lesson 07 Vocabulary
Lesson 08 Dialoguc
Lesson 08 Vocabulary
Lesson 09 Dialogue
Lesson 09 Vocabulary
Lesson 10 Dialogue
Lesson 10 Vocabulary
Lesson 11 Dialogue
Lesson 11 Vocabulary
Lesson 12 Dialogue
Lesson 12 Vocabulary
Lesson 13 Dialogue
Lesson 13 Vocabulary
Lesson 14 Dialogue
Lesson 14 Vocabulary
Lesson 15 Dialogue
Lesson 15 Vocabulary

Lesson 16 Dialogue
Lesson 16 Vocabulary
Lesson 17 Dialogue
Lesson 17 Vocabulary
Lesson 18 Dialogue
Lesson 18 Vocabulary
Lesson 19 Dialogue
Lesson 19 Vocabulary
Lesson 20 Dialogue
Lesson 20 Vocabulary
Lesson 21 Dialogue
Lesson 21 Vocabulary
Lesson 22 Dialogue
Lesson 22 Vocabulary
Lesson 23 Dialogue
Lesson 23 Vocabulary
Lesson 24 Dialogue
Lesson 24 Vocabulary
Lesson 25 Dialogue
Lesson 25 Vocabulary
Lesson 27 Dialogue
Lesson 27 Vocabulary
Lesson 28 Dialogue
Lesson 28 Vocabulary
Lesson 29 Dialogue
Lesson 29 Vocabulary

Lesson 30 Dialogue
Lesson 30 Vocabulary
Lesson 32 Dialogue
Lesson 32 Vocabulary
Lesson 33 Dialogue
Lesson 33 Vocabulary
Lesson 34 Dialogue
Lesson 34 Vocabulary
Lesson 36 Dialogue
Lesson 36 Vocabulary
Lesson 37 Dialogue
Lesson 37 Vocabulary
Lesson 38 Dialogue
Lesson 38 Vocabulary
Lesson 40 Dialogue
Lesson 40 Vocabulary
Lesson 41 Dialogue
Lesson 41 Vocabulary
Lesson 42 Dialogue
Lesson 42 Vocabulary
Lesson 43 Dialogue
Lesson 43 Vocabulary
Lesson 44 Dialogue
Lesson 44 Vocabulary